T0305259

The State, Markets and Development

The State, Markets and Development

Beyond the Neoclassical Dichotomy

Edited by

Amitava Krishna Dutt
Kwan S. Kim

Department of Economics
University of Notre Dame
Notre Dame, Indiana, USA

and

Ajit Singh

Faculty of Economics
Cambridge University, UK

Edward Elgar

Published by
Edward Elgar Publishing Limited
Gower House
Croft Road
Aldershot
Hants GU11 3HR
England

Edward Elgar Publishing Company
Old Post Road
Brookfield
Vermont 05036
USA

British Library Cataloguing in Publication Data
State, Markets and Development: Beyond the
Neoclassical Dichotomy
  I. Dutt, Amitava Krishna
  338.9

Library of Congress Cataloguing in Publication Data
State, markets, and development: beyond the neoclassical dichotomy/
  edited by Amitava Krishna Dutt, Kwan S. Kim, and Ajit Singh.
      p.   cm.
  Papers presented at a conference held at Notre Dame University in
April, 1992.
    Includes index.
    1. Industry and state—Developing countries—Congresses.
2. Privatization—Developing countries—Congresses.   3. Developing
countries—Economic policy—Congresses.   I. Dutt, Amitava Krishna.
II. Kim, Kwan S.   III. Singh, Ajit, 1940– .
9616.D452S73 1994
8.9'009172'4—dc20   94–321
                                                                 CIP

ISBN 1 85278 929 8

Printed on FSC approved paper
Printed and bound in Great Britain by Marston Book Services Ltd, Oxfordshire

Contents

Figures

Tables

Contributors

Amitava Krishna Dutt, Professor and Chairperson, Department of Economics, and Departmental Fellow, Kellogg Institute of International Studies, University of Notre Dame.

David Felix, Professor, Department of Economics, Washington University, St Louis.

Irfan ul Haque, Principal Economist, National Economic Management Division, Economic Development Institute, The World Bank.

Kwan S. Kim, Professor, Department of Economics, and Departmental Fellow, Kellogg Institute of International Studies, University of Notre Dame.

Juan Carlos Moreno, Regional Adviser, United National Economic Commission for Latin America, Mexico Office, Mexico, and Visiting Fellow, Kellogg Institute of International Studies, University of Notre Dame (Spring 1992).

Jaime Ros, Associate Professor, Department of Economics, and Departmental Fellow, Kellogg Institute of International Studies, University of Notre Dame.

Helen Shapiro, Associate Professor, Harvard Business School, Harvard University.

Ajit Singh, Reader, Faculty of Economics, Cambridge University, and Visiting Professor, Department of Economics, University of Notre Dame.

Lance Taylor, Professor, Department of Economics, New School of Social Research, New York.

Preface

This volume of essays grew out of a conference organized at the University of Notre Dame on 'State, Markets and Development' in April 1992. It was sponsored by the Kellogg Institute for International Studies and the Department of Economics at the University of Notre Dame. We are grateful to the Institute and the Department for financial and organizational support, and to the participants of the conference – especially those who commented on the papers contained in this volume – for creating a stimulating atmosphere in which the papers were presented and discussed. We are also grateful to Carole Martin for her assistance in preparing the index, and to Edward Elgar and his production staff, especially Julie Leppard, for efficiently and expeditiously publishing this book.

The book is divided into two parts. The first part, on general perspectives, contains four chapters which critically analyse mainstream neoclassical views on states and markets, and provide alternative perspectives on state–market interaction.

The first chapter, written by the editors, provides a background for the rest of the papers in the book. It examines the nature of the state–markets dichotomy of neoclassical economics, an approach which is argued to have encouraged unnecessary pendulum swings between the two institutions, the latest phase of which is the acceptance of privatization and liberalization as passwords to development. It then turns to alternative economic theories, perspectives from outside economics, and the actual experience of developing countries to argue that it is misleading to view states and markets as alternatives, and that it is preferable to examine the strengths and weaknesses of each institution to see how they can both foster development.

Ul Haque views the market–state debate from a modified neoclassical perspective. While arguing that the market should play a critical role in resource allocation, he emphasizes the complementary nature of the relationship between the state and the market. In particular, he argues that state support for business is essential if the economy is to secure international competitiveness. Thus, the proper role of the state is seen to be determined not so much by the extent of government intervention, as by an effective collaboration between government and business.

Singh starts with a critical assessment of the World Bank's view concerning the role of the state, as stated in the *World Development Report* for 1991.

Questioning the validity of the *Report's* 'market-friendly' characterization of East Asian states, the chapter outlines an alternative perspective and argues for a forceful and aggressive 'industrial policy'. Citing evidence from Japanese and other experiences, Singh defends the logic of such state actions as targeting strategic industries for development; carefully managing both market collusion and competition, and managing foreign trade and investment. The state and markets must be viewed as playing a role, each an irreplaceable partner to the other in development.

Taylor examines the interaction between state and private sectors with a focus on understanding growth in post-socialist economies. He focuses on the nature and role of state-owned and privately-owned enterprises and their interactions, drawing on both mainstream and structuralist theoretical models. He argues that the closure of state-owned enterprises may well reduce private sector growth. He also discusses the possibility of financial instability arising from the ownership structures of private firms, highlighting problems that will arise from the use of stock transfers as a mode of privatization. Finally, he comments on the broader issue of the institutional prerequisites for the successful development of capitalism in post-socialist economies.

The second part of the book, entitled 'Empirical Studies', also contains four chapters, dealing with state–market interactions in Latin America as a whole, in Mexico, Brazil, and in South Korea and India.

Felix considers the implications of the rolling back of the state in Latin America. He argues that the ongoing efforts for privatization in the region are bound to fail. This is because its macroeconomic benefits are likely to be disappointing in the absence of quick, positive and sustainable results, which are unlikely because of such factors as the foreign debt overhang, prolonged underinvestment in the stocks of physical and human capital, and the bleak prospects for massive foreign direct investment. Furthermore, political support for the neoliberal policies is fragile: the unions and bureaucrats are generally hostile to it, and the business élites and intelligentsia are split on the issues. Finally, contradictions in the neoliberal adjustment strategy also work against the success of the privatization scheme.

Moreno and Ros put the issues of market reform and the role of the state in Mexico in historical perspective. They begin with the origins of backwardness in the 18th and 19th centuries (when the economy was state-centred but the state was weak) and discuss the liberal misperceptions which led to the support of privatization and liberalization policies. They then discuss the important developmental – especially through public investment and import-substitution policies – role played by the state in Mexico's modern economic growth until 1980, particularly during the 1940–80 period. Finally, they consider the period after 1980, during which policies resulted in greater market orientation and integration with the world economy, and suggest that the retreat of the state has resulted from misperceptions similar to those of the mid-19th century.

Shapiro discusses the relationship between the state and the private sector in Brazil's development experience between 1950 and 1990, with special emphasis on fiscal and regulatory regimes, industrial policies and business–government relations. Shapiro argues that the state's highly interventionist and expansionary role explains in large part the high rates of growth in the economy up to the late 1970s. However, such policies and the institutions (such as indexation) created during this high-growth phase also made it difficult for the Brazilian economy to adjust to the development problems of the 1980s and beyond, characterized by high rates of inflation and stagnation in growth. She concludes that economic restructuring is not simply reducing trade barriers, but should involve institutional change and creating new forms of public–private interaction.

Dutt and Kim provide a comparative, political economy analysis of the role of the state in economic development in India and South Korea, stressing the roles of history, culture and social values. Going beyond the boundaries of economics narrowly defined, they argue that while the South Korean state has assumed a dominant role in a corporatist system with relative autonomy from civil society, the state in India has been severely constrained by pressures from dominant classes and other interested parties, and has been relatively incapable of implementing programmes for development. They conclude that differences in the nature of the state and in the relationship of the state to civil society, rather than different roles of the market and the state, best explain the strikingly different development performances of the two Asian countries.

The Editors

PART I

General Perspectives

1. The State, Markets and Development

Amitava Krishna Dutt, Kwan S. Kim and Ajit Singh

INTRODUCTION

What role should the state and markets play in economic development? What role have they played in developing economies? In the work of economists, especially neoclassical economists, the answers to these questions take the form of extolling the virtues of one and denouncing the other, and which of the two finds favour depends on when the question is answered. Very soon after the growth of the subdiscipline of development economists in the post-World War II era, the consensus was that development could not be left to markets: planned state intervention was a *sine qua non* for development in less developed economies. By the 1970s, however, the pendulum had swung the other way: the state was seen as the problem, not the solution, and free markets were increasingly being seen as the panacea.[1] At present, privatization and liberalization seem to be the passwords to development, with mainstream academic economists, the World Bank, the International Monetary Fund and policymakers in most countries chanting this tune.

The purpose of this chapter is to attempt to go beyond this state–markets dichotomy and the related pendulum swings by arguing that both the state and markets can help and hinder development, and that it is quite misleading to view the market and state always as alternatives.[2] To this end it will critically examine neoclassical views on the state and markets, explore ideas from alternative economic theories of development and from beyond the boundaries of economics narrowly defined, and examine actual development experience to examine and explain the role that the state and markets have played in developing countries.

The remainder of this chapter is divided into three sections. The first will briefly summarize neoclassical views on the state and markets. The subsequent section will discuss the role of the state and markets from alternative approaches both within and outside economics. The final section will comment on the actual experience of developing countries.

NEOCLASSICAL VIEWS ON THE STATE AND MARKETS

We take the neoclassical approach as our point of entry both because it is the dominant approach to development economics and economics more generally, and because it has played a powerful intellectual role in treating the market and the state as rival forms of organization, a view from which we wish to dissent.[3]

The neoclassical approach to the treatment of the state and markets – in its most basic form – starts from a general equilibrium system satisfying a number of assumptions which ensure that its equilibrium is a Pareto-optimal allocation. It then shows that if these assumptions are not satisfied the market will fail in the sense that the equilibrium will not be Pareto-optimal, so that there is a case for state intervention. The presence of externalities, public goods, increasing returns to scale, imperfect information, 'few' buyers or sellers, for instance, can lead to market failures, causing both allocative inefficiencies and unemployment; the state can thus have allocative (usually with Pigovian taxes and subsidies) and stabilization roles to play. Moreover, even if the general equilibrium is Pareto-optimal, if the income distribution is undesirable, the state will have a redistributive role.

The conceptions of markets and the state and their roles implicit in this approach are as follows. Markets are collections of optimizing, self-seeking buyers and sellers who interact with each other in trading goods, services and factors production at prices 'determined' by impersonal market conditions. These markets (given some assumptions regarding the preferences of consumers and the technology of firms, and some properties of markets which make them 'perfect'), lead to Pareto-optimum outcomes as the unintended consequence of individual attempts to maximize profits or utility. Questions relating to the properties of markets and their equilibrium have received a great deal of attention in neoclassical economics. The state, on the other hand, is exogenous to the economic process; it is simply that undefined organization that solves problems arising in markets.

Some remarks on this neoclassical conception of markets and the state are in order. First, by itself the neoclassical approach does not take a side on the market versus state debate: which one is favoured depends on the empirical importance of market failures (or distributional problems). The early espousal of state intervention in development economics was in large part based on the belief that in less developed economies the conditions which lead to perfect markets are not satisfied: externalities are pervasive, as are information problems, monopolies and economies of scale (see, for instance, Rosenstein-Rodan, 1943; Scitovsky, 1954). The later pro-market wave was not based on the view that such market failures are unimportant. On the contrary, examples of market failure abound in recent neoclassical literature on growth and development (see, for instance, Romer, 1986; Lucas, 1988; Murphy, Shleifer and Vishny, 1989; Stokey, 1991). Within the economics profession, the shift in opinion is based rather on the disillusionment with the actual record of the state in bringing about development, and related theoretical arguments suggesting that the state cannot solve the problems of market failures. While the actual performance of less developed economies will be discussed in a later section, the theoretical developments will be mentioned in some of the following discussion.

Secondly, the division between the roles of market and state is not as precise as the theory seems to imply. For instance, even in the absence of state 'intervention' to cure market problems, the state must do a variety of things not explicitly mentioned, but implicitly assumed, in this approach. It must, for instance, maintain law and order to protect private property and ensure that contracts are honoured; such activities require the use of force which can only be legitimately wielded by the state. Even Nozick (1974) recognizes that the libertarian state must provide 'protection against force, theft, fraud and the enforcement of contracts'. We will return to some implications of this observation below.

Thirdly, the basic neoclassical approach does not go far enough in exploring whether the alleged distortions which take the economy away from a Pareto-optimal state cannot be removed by markets, thereby making state action unnecessary. Coase (1960), and a large literature following him, has argued that inefficiencies resulting from market imperfections can be resolved by collective actions of individuals with a suitable mechanism worked out by them; the argument for markets and against the state is thereby strengthened. The actual relevance of this argument is not, however, obvious: transactions costs have to be small, as Stiglitz (1989) points out, and problems of free-riders and revealed preferences of individuals prevent a private optimal solution from emerging.

Fourthly, the approach takes state intervention to be exogenous in the sense that there is no theory of why governments actually intervene. The subsequent literature on rent-seeking and public choice theory have changed this. Rent-seeking – activities of private agents to expend resources to obtain state protection in the form of import quotas to increase their rents (see Krueger, 1974) – has been generalized (see Bhagwati, 1982) to cover any form of activity by economic agents which utilizes resources to increase profits, but which does not produce goods or services directly increasing consumer satisfaction. This has been called 'directly unproductive profit-seeking' (DUP). The argument is that state provision of subsidies or other kinds of protection would give rise to DUP activity which would divert resources away from productive activity. The analysis of DUP activity does not in itself require any assumption regarding the nature of the state or of politicians and bureaucrats – all that it implies is that private agents can get protection by incurring costs (perhaps by making state officials aware of their legitimate problems). The public choice-theoretic framework with self-seeking, utility-maximizing politicians and bureaucrats extends this analysis with a model of political behaviour (see Buchanan and Tullock, 1962; Buchanan, Tollison and Tullock, 1980). In some versions of this argument (see Stigler, 1975), the state is seen as an unnecessary entity whose function is to serve as a 'regulator' which acts in its own self-interest, identified as the self-seeking enrichment of public officials. Policymakers bargain for political support from interest groups by transferring income and other resources; everything that a government does is considered to result in a transfer of income. Not only does all this lead to economic inefficiency, but it results in worsened income distribution when public sector leaders are the owners of wealth. These contributions thus strengthen the pro-market view.

Fifthly, the approach appears to ignore the question of the nature and effectiveness of state intervention: it seems to assume that if markets fail, states must improve the situation, rather than discussing the relative merits of state intervention versus markets. Subsequent developments within neoclassical theory have rectified this position, and the result is greater scepticism regarding state intervention. For instance, it is argued that practically it is difficult, if not impossible, for state intervention to be beneficial, on account of the difficulties of obtaining precise information regarding the nature of market failures and their causes. Although such things as externalities may be present, it is impossible in practice to know what the level of optimum taxes/ subsidies is. The state will not have all the information to solve all the problems. In the presence of some distortions, attempts at tinkering with some may well make things worse according to the theory of the second best (Lal, 1985). Stiglitz (1992) emphasizes the information-related problems that can handicap the state more than markets in which decentralized decision-making units can have access to information on matters directly concerning them. Furthermore, the state and its constituent elements may lack the incentives of profit-seeking market participants to cut costs, promote efficiency and to innovate. Wolf (1990) proposes a generalized theory of non-market failures and argues that government failures can arise from: disjunction between costs and revenues (because those who use the markets are not the same as those who pay for them) and redundant and rising costs (due to such factors as the absence of market-imposed discipline), internalities and organizational goals (that is, internal goals which organizations have to pursue in the absence of market-imposed goals), derived externalities (relating to unanticipated side effects of non-market activities), and distributional inequities (due to the fact that the more powerful can design policies to favour them disproportionately). These non-market failures must be weighed against market failures when choosing between what Wolf calls the 'two imperfect alternatives of the state and markets'.[4] While these contributions do not necessarily lead to a pro-market view (it clearly does in the hands of Lal and Wolf, but Stiglitz recognizes areas of comparative advantage for the state), they tend to view the state and the market as alternatives.

ALTERNATIVE PERSPECTIVES INSIDE AND OUTSIDE ECONOMICS

The neoclassical approach, of course, is not the only approach to development economics. Two important alternative approaches to the subject are the Marxist and structuralist approaches (see Chenery, 1975; Bardhan, 1988; Dutt, 1992).

The structuralist approach is sometimes characterized as emphasizing rigidities such as the absence of substitution possibilities in economies (see Chenery, 1975), but it is perhaps preferable to distinguish it in terms of its methodology. This may be described as starting with aggregative accounting relations involving different relevant and important factors, and then using 'stylized facts' regarding these factors to develop complete models which can determine the variables of interest in terms of accounting identities, behavioural and other relations and some given of the analysis (see Dutt, 1992).[5]

Several features of this approach are worth noting for present purposes. First, unlike the neoclassical approach, there is no attempt in this approach to construct a theoretical benchmark case of 'no government intervention' (aside from distributional considerations), so that it is not theoretically possible to disentangle the roles of the state and market forces. Secondly, even with smoothly functioning markets (however they are defined) there is no guarantee that the economy will achieve some desirable outcome (such as Pareto-optimality). There are various types of equilibria in models using this approach, allowing for unemployed workers and even excess capacity, due to such problems as the lack of effective demand, the shortage of foreign exchange or insufficient savings; greater price flexibility can in fact lead to worse results. Thirdly, the structuralist models and theories contain various parameters which are treated as exogenous in simpler models, and these may be affected by state action; for instance, the mark-up rate of firms can depend on state policies regarding industrial concentration and in the mediation of wage bargaining. Finally, in the structuralist literature there is little analysis of the state and markets *per se*, merely an analysis of their effects. These comments imply that structuralist theories can be thought of as providing one part of a more general political economy analysis in which the state and social aspects of markets can be brought in more appropriately at a later stage. The last comment leaves this option open, the third suggests ways of linking the structuralist economic analysis to the broader analysis, and the first two show that there is no artificial distinction between markets and states and no presumption that markets achieve desirable outcomes by themselves.

The Marxist approach, in its narrowly-economic form, starts from the basis that class struggle determines the distribution of income in capitalist economies. Capitalists who receive the surplus in the form of profits are driven by competition to accumulate and change technology, and this results in capitalist growth. The interaction between the growth process and the distribution of income, which affects the rates of profits, determines the characteristics of capitalist growth and crisis. In this analysis the state can affect the distribution of income and its movement over time, and hence the course of growth. It may be noted that the comments we have made on the structuralist approach apply to this type of Marxist approach as well.

The Marxist approach is, however, much broader than this narrow economic analysis would suggest, and it must be credited with its greater appreciation of the role of the state in the development process.[6] In the classical Marxist view, the state is the instrument of the ruling class, not the defender of the general interest. One stream in Marxist writing emphasizes ideological and political factors which explain how the ruling class captures – by coercion or consent – the state to serve its own interests. Another stream emphasizes the structural constraints in which the state finds itself in capitalist society, that lead it to pursue policies which ensure the reproduction of capital.

Both these views, however, can be called reductionist in the sense that they explain the activities of the state in terms of social and economic forces. To be sure, in the writings of Marx and Engels, the state does sometimes exhibit 'relative autonomy', but this is the result of special 'Bonapartist' conditions which make it impossible for the establishment of a clear class hegemony. While such a state must have its own interests and purposes, this conception does not really jettison the reductionist view of the state as serving the interests of the dominant class or classes; since the bourgeoisie need not have common interests, the state may act as regulator of the interests of different dominant classes to ensure the stability of the social order. Despite recent Marxist attempts to stress the relative autonomy of the state in the more recent Marxist literature, Skocpol (1985, p. 5) argues that, 'at the theoretical level, virtually all neo-Marxist writers on the state have retained deeply embedded society-centred assumptions, not allowing themselves to doubt that, at base, states are inherently shaped by classes or class struggles and function to preserve the expanding modes of production'.

This consideration of Marxist approaches to the state obviously takes us beyond the boundaries of economics narrowly defined. In areas beyond these boundaries we find, in fact, other ways of looking at states and markets, but these, too, have been accused of reducing the state to society.[7] Durkheim, in his analysis of the breakdown of social order due to the increased division of labour, shared Marx's idea that the state's action and the society's politics are mainly reflections of the more fundamental forces of socio-economic change. Even Weber's analysis of the role of the state and efficient bureaucracies was a part of his analysis of the broader tendency of the spread of rationality in society. The diverse literature on modernization and development, as exemplified in the work of Parsons, Smelser, Huntington and others, despite its considerable contributions to the analysis of political instability in developing countries, also reduces politics to socio-economic variables. The pluralist and structure-functionalist perspectives dominant in political science and sociology in the US viewed the state mainly as an arena in which economic interest groups or normative social movements competed or co-operated with one another in shaping public policy decisions, again reducing the state to socio-economic factors.[8]

In opposition to these reductionist views, there has emerged a new movement which attempts to bring political factors back in by stressing the autonomy of the state and recognizing the autonomy of political forces in the analysis of development issues (see Skocpol, 1985; Kohli, 1986). Such autonomy is argued to exist both because those in political power can – and do – make choices which reflect their own ideologies and interests, and because political traditions have a continuity of their own and are not transformed readily by socio-economic changes. This project of bringing the state back in, however, is not seen by its supporters as implying the neglect of socio-economic forces which shape and limit the state's behaviour. The autonomy, clearly, is a relative one and the relationship between the state and civil society remains an important object of analysis.

Discussion of the relative autonomy of the state leads us to ask questions regarding the nature of states and regimes, and the implications for development (see Rueschemeyer and Evans, 1985; Kohli, 1987; Rueschemeyer and Putterman, 1992). What are the objectives of the state and its ideology? When are these objectives more likely to further the needs of development rather than the material well-being and power of its constituents or its political allies? It is obvious that the 'public choice' conception of states is too narrow. Given its objectives, what types of organizational resource make it more likely to implement its objectives? Of obvious importance are Weberian ideas of the nature of bureaucracy. Since the objectives and the effectiveness of the state depend on the relationship between the state and civil society, especially the dominant classes of society, questions arise as to the degree of state autonomy from societal pressures, as well as the extent of channels of co-operation and information flows between the state and these classes. This requires a consideration of the characteristics of dominant and other classes, and their relationship to each other and to the state, as well as the type of regime – authoritarian or democratic.

Turning from the state to markets, it may appear that though social sciences outside economics may tell economists much about the state, regarding markets, it is economics that must export to the others. While this is the viewpoint of imperialistic economists such as Becker, as well as rational choice sociologists such as Coleman,[9] it seems to us that even regarding markets, economists can learn much from other social sciences since the conception of markets in economics is extremely narrow. As we saw earlier, neoclassical economics starts by treating markets as perfect, and then identifies what conditions must be met for markets to become perfect to analyse the effects of not meeting these conditions. But by the very nature of the project, lists of conditions tend to overlook some relevant factors.

One set of issues usually omitted is the institutional arrangements which sustain the norms which set the boundaries within which buyers and sellers compete in markets. These norms could relate to such things as the agreement to forego violence and fraud in competition. Research in economic sociology has reminded us that market interaction is embedded in social relationships (see Granovetter, 1985). It has been argued that 'every market is an institutionalized system for the mediation of competition and that the structure of these systems varies by their historical and cultural context' (Abolafia and Biggart, 1991). These issues have, of course, not escaped the attention of economists. Commons (1959, p. 713), writes that competition 'is an artificial arrangement supported by the moral, economic and physical sanctions of collective action'.[10] Even Adam Smith, that supposed champion of free markets, can be interpreted as emphasizing the role of both self-interest and sympathy and social norms for the smooth functioning of markets (see Wilson, 1979; Sen, 1986); but these have not been emphasized in mainstream economics.

Where do these norms come from? Are they voluntarily adopted by self-seeking traders, do they permeate into the 'economic' sphere from other social spheres such as family or 'community', or are they the result of chance and evolutionary mechanisms? Whatever the role of these different mechanisms, it is clear that the norms can be – and frequently are – broken by individuals seeking to achieve their immediate selfish interests; to deny this would be to replace the neoclassical undersocialized view of human action by an oversocialized view (Granovetter, 1985). While groups can evolve means for punishing such behaviour, one does not need to adopt an extreme Hobbesian position to see that the success of such means requires the backing in force of state power. Commons in fact emphasizes the role of courts in mediating competition. Trade associations need to seek the authority of the state to govern the market in order to reduce breaches of rules of competition and manipulation of the markets (see Abolafia and Biggart, 1991). Moreover, the state can play a powerful role in promoting such norms, norms which arguably can become eroded in a Durkheimian manner as the division of labour spreads in the course of economic development. The neoclassical approach to markets, by ignoring these problems and taking an undersocialized conception of human action, does not allow a proper appreciation of this important role of the state.

Further corollaries follow from the recognition of this market-building role of the state. DUP activities need not be confined to the types of intervention-induced or intervention-seeking behaviour with which neoclassical economics is concerned: they may be directed at inducing state officials to bend the market-governing rules in their favour. It is not clear that removing neoclassical-type interventions will actually reduce DUP activity, as private agents and state officials seek private gains from DUP activities involving these market-governing roles of the state.

THE ACTUAL EXPERIENCE OF DEVELOPING COUNTRIES[11]

Turning to empirical and policy issues, the economic crisis of the developing countries in the last decade has raised in an acute form the question of the appropriate spheres of the state and the market in economic development.

The Bretton Woods institutions and most mainstream economists ascribe the economic failings of the Third World countries in the last decade to too large a role of the government in these economies, and to inappropriate government policies such as import substitution and large grandiose investment projects with long gestation lags. By the same token, the successes of the countries which have escaped the crises of the 1980s and continued to grow are attributed in these theses to a more limited and balanced role of the state, as well as to the more apt 'market-conforming' economic policies of governments. In the light of these analyses, the International Monetary Fund and the World Bank have advocated an increase in the role of free markets and private markets as far as possible, along with a diminution of the role of the state and a closer integration with the world economy, which in their view is necessary to achieve 'efficient' long-term economic growth in developing countries. This policy programme and, more importantly, its underlying analysis of the economic crises of developing countries in the 1980s, as well as the reasons why some countries have been successful and others not so, are vigorously disputed by a host of scholars.

To put this debate into a clearer perspective, it is useful to recall briefly the main stylized facts about Third World development since the 1950s. During the period between 1950 and 1980, developing countries made on average historically unprecedented economic and industrial progress. Even countries in sub-Saharan Africa, which started with extremely unfavourable conditions, managed to increase their share of world manufacturing production during the 1960s and 1970s. More significantly, a group of Asian and Latin American nations – the so-called newly industrializing countries (NICs) – were especially successful in the post-World War II period in establishing technical, scientific and industrial infrastructures, in training their labour forces, in creating managerial and organizational capacities and in developing broad-based industrial structures (Singh, 1989; Patel, 1992). Since 1980, however, this process has been interrupted (and, indeed, in many cases reversed) in Latin America and sub-Saharan Africa, whilst the industrial revolution has proceeded apace in the Asian countries. Not just the four little dragons (Hong Kong, Singapore, Taiwan and South Korea), but a number of other Asian countries have also achieved remarkable economic success. China's economic development during the last decade has been extraordinary, with a growth rate of nearly 10 per cent per annum in the 1980s. Even countries such as India were able to achieve an appreciable trend increase in their growth rates during the 1980s compared with their past records.

In the policy debate over the respective roles of the government and markets, and the desirable interrelationship between the two, the following have emerged as the central issues:

1. Why did the Latin American countries have such an abysmal economic failure in the 1980s whilst the Asian countries continued to have successful development? Was the inferior performance of the Latin American countries due to too pervasive a role of government in these economies and/or to the wrong policies which these governments followed?
2. How large or important a role did governments play in the extraordinarily successful development of the East Asian economies?
3. Is it really true, as commonly alleged, that public enterprises are invariably inefficient? To what extent can the economic failings of the unsuccessful countries be attributed to the high incidence of public enterprises in these economies?
4. To what extent can China's outstanding economic success during the last decade be ascribed to the marketization and the privatization of the economy?

In the remainder of this section we briefly comment on each of these questions in turn.

Asian Success and Latin American Failure in the 1980s

According to the mainstream view (see Maddison, 1985; Sachs, 1985; Balassa *et al.*, 1986; Corden, 1990; World Bank, 1991), the Latin American economic failure is due to internal causes such as excessive government interference, mismanagement (such as the misallocation of foreign borrowing to wasteful current consumption rather than for efficient investment in export industries) and inappropriate government policies (such as inefficient import substitution and overvalued exchange rates). The critics of this view (see Banuri, 1991; Fishlow, 1991, 1993; Hughes and Singh, 1991; Ros, 1993; Singh, 1992, 1993b; Taylor, 1992) argue, on the other hand, that although the Latin American governments made mistakes, the main reason for the economic failure was the debt crisis, which was caused by external economic forces over which these countries had no control and which had a disproportionate impact on Latin America as compared to the Asian countries.

Although a review of the evidence seems to support the latter view (see Singh, 1993a), given unfavourable external conditions, the Latin American states must improve their internal organization and resource utilization if they are to recover their long-term growth rates of 1950–80 and to resume fully their industrial revolution.

State and Economic Development in East Asia

From a policy perspective the issue of long-term economic strategies followed by the East Asian governments is also extremely important, given not only their successful experience in the 1980s but their spectacular economic record for the previous two decades. Here, the case of Japan is particularly relevant for several reasons. First, countries such as Taiwan and South Korea have tried to imitate the post-war Japanese model of development, and China is attempting to do so today. Secondly, although Japanese industrialization began in the 19th century, as late as the mid-1950s the country only produced five million tons of steel and 50,000 cars per annum. Many developing countries today have a much higher level of industrial production than Japan had at that time. Thirdly, there was influential opinion, both inside and outside Japan, which regarded the future economic prospects of the country in the late 1940s as extremely bleak.[12] Yet we know that it took Japan less than two decades to overtake the US in the production of steel, and less than three decades to overtake it in the production of cars.

In the analyses of longer-term economic development in the post-war period in Japan, Taiwan and South Korea,[13] the main issues concern the assessment of the roles of (1) state intervention in industrial development; (2) government policies towards integration with the world economy, and (3) government policies towards domestic and international competition. The mainstream perspective on the East Asian model has undergone substantial modification in recent years. It used to be argued (see Wolf, 1990) that the East Asian economic success arose from the fact that the government did not intervene and allowed a free play of market forces. In the light of the abundant evidence of heavy government intervention in the East Asian countries, this older neoclassical thesis has become increasingly implausible. The current orthodox view is to suggest that, although the government did intervene, these interventions were 'market friendly' or 'market conforming'. Moreover, it is argued that an essential ingredient of the East Asian economic success was the openness of these economies to international economic interchange. The role of domestic and international competition is also stressed.

The alternative heterodox interpretation of the East Asian experience emphasizes the fact that the governments in these countries followed strong, purposeful industrial policies. The interventions were designed to 'guide' the market rather than to conform to it (Amsden, 1989; Wade, 1990). Moreover, these countries did not have close integration with the world economy; rather they sought 'strategic' integration.

Singh's (1992) examination of the longer-term development strategies of the East Asian economies reveals that the state in these countries did not follow the World Bank's revised formulation of a 'market-friendly' approach to development. Rather, the governments in Taiwan, South Korea and Japan played a vigorous economic role and pursued a highly active industrial policy. The state did not supplant the market altogether, as the 'command' planning of production of the Soviet type did. But neither did it simply follow the market. Instead a whole plethora of government measures was used to guide the market towards planned structural change. Similarly, the East Asian countries did not seek or practise a close integration with the world economy during their periods of rapid growth; they integrated only in the directions and the extent to which it was useful for them to do so.

An interesting question in this context is, how does the *long-term* role of the state in the East Asian economies compare with that in Latin American countries such as Brazil and Mexico? Here there are a number of points which are relevant. First, as political scientists suggest, the state in Latin American countries is unable to act as effectively as a developmental state as the governments of the East Asian countries.[14] In view of its historical evolution and the nature of the relationships it has with various social groups (such as labour and landed interests), the Latin American state has much less autonomy than its counterpart in East Asia. Nevertheless, it is important to observe that the Mexican and Brazilian governments do have conspicuous economic successes to their credit. With heavy state intervention for three decades between 1950 and 1980, the Mexican economy expanded at a long term rate of nearly 6 per cent per annum – a highly respectable performance by comparative international standards. More significantly, with vigorous state involvement, the Brazilian economy recorded a growth rate of nearly 10 per cent per annum during 1965–80 – probably the fastest growth rate of any country over this period. The important point here is that although the nature and effectiveness of state intervention differed between East Asian states and countries such as Mexico and Brazil, the latter were performing very well until the debt crisis of the 1980s.

Public Enterprises

According to the International Monetary Fund–World Bank view, the public enterprise sector in developing countries is inefficient and overextended, and the privatization of public enterprises is an essential part of a programme to promote 'efficient' economic growth.

However, the results of the new developments in the theory of the firm and the theory of industrial organization (for example, agency theory, asymmetric information) do not provide a theoretical basis for the belief that public enterprises should necessarily perform less efficiently at the microeconomic level than the similar large management-controlled private enterprises operating in oligopolistic markets and subject to the imperfect discipline of the real world stock markets (see Chang and Singh, 1993). There is, in fact, a growing consensus among scholars in this field that as far as enterprise performance is concerned, it is not ownership *per se* which is the critical variable, but rather the nature of the competitive environment in which enterprises, whether public or private, operate (see, for instance, Vickers and Yarrow, 1988).

Turning to empirical evidence, the allegation that public enterprises are invariably 'inefficient' or that in general they perform badly cannot survive even an elementary examination of facts (see Chang and Singh, 1993). First, it should be appreciated that public enterprises are ubiquitous in mixed economies throughout the world – they have not simply been confined to left-wing regimes or poorly performing countries. Public enterprises play a significant role in the highly successful East Asian economies of Taiwan and South Korea; the public enterprise sector in these countries is at least as large, if not larger, than that in the leading Latin American economies of Argentina, Brazil and Mexico. Taiwan, hardly a left-wing regime, has one of the biggest public enterprise sectors among the developing mixed economies. Secondly, Kirkpatrick (1986) examined the relationship between the size of the public enterprise sector, per capita GDP and the rate of growth of GDP between 1961 and 1981 for a sample of 23 less developed countries, and found little relationship between these variables. Thirdly, the most efficient steel company in the world is the giant Korean enterprise Posco (Pohang Steel Company), which is state-owned. Although Posco is by no means typical of public enterprise in developing countries, evidence suggests that neither is it a total exception. Chang and Singh (1993) conclude that if one controls for the influence of variables such as age, size and industry, and if more appropriate criteria for measuring enterprise efficiency are employed rather than just private profitability, there is little reason to castigate public enterprises and to advocate large-scale privatization (see also Vernon, 1991, who arrives at a similar conclusion).

None of this is to suggest that public enterprise performance should not or cannot be improved. However, there are sound analytical reasons, as well as evidence, that it may often be cheaper to reform public enterprises than to privatize them (see Aylen, 1987; Rowthorn and Chang, 1991; Chang and Singh, 1993).

The Chinese Experience

It is common for the proponents of the market to interpret the recent spectacular economic performance of China in terms of the triumph of the markets and private enterprise over state control and state planning (World Bank, 1991). While it is true that the greatly improved performance of the Chinese economy in the 1980s coincides with the market-oriented economic reform introduced in the late 1970s, and that China has decisively moved away from Stalinist central planning and the command economy under the reform process, the extent of marketization and privatization, particularly the latter, is rather limited (Lo, 1993; Nolan, 1993; Singh, 1993c; Wang, 1993). Most of China's land and capital are still publicly owned; the economy appears to have been able to achieve high economic growth and to introduce markets in many areas of the economy whilst maintaining social ownership of the means of production, thereby demonstrating that privatization is not necessary for markets to operate. Moreover, China's integration with the world economy, though far greater than before the reforms, is still rather limited. Singh (1993c) stresses the extremely important complementarities between the plan and the market in China, and between the state-owned industries and market-oriented small-scale sector. He also argues that the Chinese development strategy resembles in important ways those of Japan, South Korea and Taiwan, in that the Chinese are seeking a 'strategic' rather than a 'close' integration with the world economy.

CONCLUSION

This chapter has argued that the mainstream neoclassical approach to states and markets is problematic. Although there have been some recent attempts to rectify this problem, the approach has tended to view states and markets as competing institutions, and has led to sharp shifts in opinion regarding the virtues of these institutions. At present the followers of this approach in academia, international institutions and in policy circles are showering their affection on markets and attempting to reduce the role of the state. In this chapter we have examined alternative economic theories, approaches to states and markets outside the narrow boundaries of economics, and the actual experience of developing countries, to argue both that the neoclassical dichotomy towards the state and markets is unjustified, and, *a fortiori*, the current shift in opinion towards markets and against the state is misplaced. It is hoped that this chapter, as well as the other chapters of this book, will help to convince readers that the virtues of both the state and markets need to be appropriately utilized to pursue the goals of economic development.

NOTES

1. There have, of course, been dissenters who have stood against these tides. For the earlier period, for instance, Bauer (1971) has been a strong advocate of free markets.
2. A few other recent books take a similar position. See Moran and Wright (1991) and Rueschemeyer and Putterman (1992).
3. This is not to deny, of course, the role of ideological factors (such as the view that increased state activity is undesirable because it infringes on individual rights), or the fact that the state–markets dichotomy has deep historical roots ranging at least as far back as the 16th century.
4. It may be noted that Wolf uses his vision of the US pluralist democratic system to develop his arguments about government failure, and does not consider other possible types of state or regime.
5. This description fits the mathematical new structuralist approach (see Taylor, 1983, 1991), but in fact is also consistent with less formalized earlier versions: the use of aggregative accounting relations refers to an 'overall' view; the use of given relations refers to given 'structures'; and the focus on stylized facts refers to specific characteristics relevant to the particular system being studied.
6. See, for instance, Carnoy (1984) for a review of Marxist theories of the state.
7. See Kohli (1986) for a brief discussion.
8. It is interesting to point out a dissimilarity between these approaches and the neoclassical economics approach. In the latter the state is *exogenous*; here the difficulty seems to be that the state is *endogenous*. But this dissimilarity is only superficial. By taking the state to be exogenous, economic approaches are not giving it a theory of exogeneity – that it depends on autonomous political forces, say. This means that the economist is left free to endogenize it, as has been done by public choice theorists with a vengeance, pushing the neoclassical approach to its logical conclusion.
9. See Swedberg (1990).
10. Economists using neoclassical methods have also made forays into this area by stressing transactions costs in what is called new institutional economics (see Williamson, 1975;

North, 1981), but they still do not embed economic behaviour in social structures (see Granovetter, 1985).
11. The discussion of this section is based on Singh (1993a, 1993b).
12. See World Bank (1991, pp. 13–14).
13. Hong Kong and Singapore, which have also been outstandingly successful, must be regarded as special cases as they are small city states.
14. See, for example, Evans (1992); Fishlow (1990, 1991).

BIBLIOGRAPHY

Abolafia, M.Y. and Biggart, N.W. (1991), 'Competition and Markets', in A. Etzioni and P.R. Lawrence (eds), *Socio-Economics. Toward a New Synthesis*, Armonk: M.E. Sharpe.

Amsden, A. (1989), *Asia's Next Giant: South Korea and Late Industrialization*, New York: Oxford University Press.

Amsden, A. (1992), 'A Theory of Government Intervention in Late Industrialization', in L. Putterman and S. Rueschmeyer (eds), *State and Market in Development. Synergy or Rivalry*, Boulder and London: Lynne Riener.

Aylen, J. (1987), 'Privatization in Developing Countries', *Lloyds Bank Review*, No. 163, January, 15–30.

Balassa, B. *et. al.* (1986), *Toward Renewed Economic Growth in Latin America*, Washington, D.C.: Institute for International Economics.

Banuri, T. (1991), *Liberalisation: No Panacea*, Oxford: Clarendon Press.

Bardhan, P.K. (1988), 'Alternative Approaches to Development Economics', in H.B. Chenery and T.N. Srinivasan (eds), *The Handbook of Development Economics*, 1, Amsterdam: North-Holland.

Bauer, P.T. (1971), *Dissent on Development: Studies and Debates in Development Economics*, London: Weidenfeld and Nicholson.

Bhagwati, J.N. (1978), *Anatomy and Consequences of Exchange Control Regimes*, Cambridge: Ballinger.

Bhagwati, J.N. (1982), 'Directly Unproductive Profit-Seeking (DUP) Activities', *Journal of Political Economy*, **90**(5), October, 988–1002.

Buchanan, J.M. and Tullock, G. (1962), *The Calculus of Consent*, Ann Arbor: University of Michigan Press.

Buchanan, J.M., Tollison, R.D. and Tullock, G. (eds) (1980), *Toward a Theory of Rent-Seeking Society*, College Station: Texas A&M Press.

Carnoy, M. (1984), *The State and Political Theory*, Princeton: Princeton University Press.

Chang, H.-J. and Singh, A. (1993), 'Public Enterprises in Developing Countries and Economic Efficiency: A Critical Examination of Analytical, Empirical and Policy Issues', *UNCTAD Review*, **4**, 45–82.

Chen, E. (1979), *Hyper Growth in Asian Economies: A Comparative Survey of Hong Kong, Japan, Korea, Singapore and Taiwan*, London: Macmillan.

Chenery, H.B. (1975), 'The Structuralist Approach to Development Policy', *American Economic* Review, Papers and Proceedings, **65**(2), May, 310–16.

Coase, R.H. (1960), 'The Problem of Social Cost', *Journal of Law and Economics*, **3**, 1–44.

Commons, J.R. (1959), *Institutional Economics*, Madison: University of Wisconsin Press.

Corden, W. (1990), 'Macroeconomic Policy and Growth: Some Lessons of Experience', Proceedings of the World Bank Annual Conference on Development Economics, Supplement to *The World Bank Annual Economic Review* and *The World Bank Research Observer*.

Dutt, A.K. (1992), 'Two Issues in the State of Development Economics', in A.K. Dutt and K. Jameson (eds), *New Directions in Development Economics*, Upleadon: Edward Elgar.

Evans, P. (1992), 'The State as Problem and Solution: Predation, Embedded Autonomy and Structural Change', in S. Haggard and R. Kaufman (eds), *The Politics of Adjustment: International Constraints, State Structures, and Distributive Conflicts*, Princeton: Princeton University Press.

Fishlow, A. (1990), 'The Latin American State', *Journal of Economic Perspectives*, 4(3), Summer, 61–74.

Fishlow, A. (1991), 'Some Reflections on Comparative Latin American Economic Performance and Policy', in Banuri (1991).

Fishlow, A. (1993), 'Economic Development in the 1990s', paper presented at the UNU/World Bank Symposium on Economic Reform in Developing Countries, Washington D.C., 6 February.

Granovetter, M. (1985), 'Economic Action and Social Structure: The Problem of Embeddedness', *American Journal of Sociology*, 91(3), November, 481–510.

Hughes, A. and Singh, A. (1991), 'The World Economic Slowdown and the Asian and Latin American Economies', in Banuri (1991).

Kirkpatrick, C. (1986), 'The World Bank's Views on State Owned Enterprises in Less Developed Economies: A Critical Comment', *Rivista Internazionale di Scienze Economiche e Commerciali*, 33(6–7), 685–96.

Kohli, A. (1986), 'Introduction', in A. Kohli (ed.), *The State and Development in the Third World*, Princeton: Princeton University Press.

Kohli, A. (1987), *The State and Poverty in India. The Politics of Reform*, Cambridge: Cambridge University Press.

Krueger, A. (1974), 'The Political Economy of Rent-Seeking Society', *American Economic Review*, 64, 291–303.

Lal, D. (1985), *The Poverty of 'Development Economics'*, Cambridge, Mass.: Harvard University Press.

Lo, D. (1993), 'Explaining Chinese Industrialization under Reform: A Structuralist Perspective on Growth and Retrenchment', unpublished, University of Leeds.

Lucas, R.E. (1988), 'On the Mechanics of Economic Development', *Journal of Monetary Economics*, 22, 3–42.

Maddison, A. (1985), *Two Crises: Latin America and Asia 1929–38 and 1973–83*, Paris: OECD.

Moran, M. and Wright, M. (1991), 'Conclusion: The Interdependence of Markets and States', in M. Moran and M. Wright (eds), *The Market and the State. Studies in Interdependence*, New York: St Martin's Press.

Murphy, K.M., Shleifer, A. and Vishny, R. (1989), 'Industrialization and the Big Push', *Journal of Political Economy*, 97(5), October, 1003–26.

Nolan, P. (1993), 'Politics, Planning and the Transition From Central Planning in China', unpublished, University of Cambridge.

North, D.C. (1981), *Structure and Change in Economic History*, New York: W.W. Norton.

Nozick, R. (1974), *Anarchy, State and Utopia*, Oxford: Basil Blackwell.

Patel, S.J. (1992), 'In Tribute to the Golden Age of the South's Development', *World Development*, **20**, May, 767–77.

Romer, P.M. (1986), 'Increasing Returns and Long-Run Growth', *Journal of Political Economy*, **94**, 1002–37.

Ros, J. (1993), 'The Development Crisis of the 1980s: A Review of Analytical and Policy Debates', in G. Vaggi (ed.), *From the Debt Crisis to Sustainable Development: Changing Perspectives on North-South Relations*, New York: St Martin's Press.

Rosenstein-Rodan, P.N. (1943), 'Problems of Industrialization in Eastern and Southeastern Europe', *Economic Journal*, **53**, 202–11.

Rowthorn, R. and Chang, H.-J. (1991), 'Public Ownership and the Theory of the State', paper presented at the Conference on International Privatization, St Andrews University, Scotland, September.

Rueschemeyer, D. and Evans, P.B. (1985), 'The State and Economic Transformation: Toward an Analysis of the Conditions Underlying Effective Intervention', in P.B. Evans, D. Rueschemeyer and T. Skocpol (eds), *Bringing the State Back In*, Cambridge: Cambridge University Press.

Rueschemeyer, D. and Putterman, L. (1992), 'Synergy or Rivalry', in L. Putternman and S. Rueschmeyer (eds), *State and Market in Development. Synergy or Rivalry*, Boulder and London: Lynne Riener.

Sachs, J. (1985), 'External Debt and Macroeconomic Performance in Latin America and East Asia', *Brookings Papers in Economic Activity*, **2**, 523–64.

Scitovsky, T. (1954), 'Two Concepts of External Economies', in M. Abramovitz *et al.*, *The Allocation of Economic Resources*, Stanford: Stanford University Press.

Sen, A.K. (1986), 'Adam Smith's Prudence', in S. Lall and F. Stewart (eds), *Theory and Reality in Development*, New York: St Martin's Press.

Singh, A. (1989), 'The Third World Competition and De-industrialization in Advanced Countries', *Cambridge Journal of Economics*, **13**(1), March, 103–20.

Singh, A. (1992), 'The Actual Crisis of Economic Development in the 1980s: An Alternative Policy Perspective for the Future', in A.K. Dutt and K. Jameson (eds), *New Directions in Development Economics*, Aldershot: Edward Elgar.

Singh, A. (1993a), 'Asian Economic Success and Latin American Failure in the 1980s: New Analyses and Future Policy Implications', *International Review of Applied Economics*, **7**(3), 267–89.

Singh, A. (1993b), '"Close" vs "Strategic" Integration with the World Economy and the "Market-Friendly Approach to Development" vs an "Industrial Policy": A Critique of the *World Development Report 1991* and an Alternative Policy Perspective', paper presented at the joint UN/World Bank Symposium on Economic Reform in Developing Countries: Issues for the 1990s.

Singh, A. (1993c), 'The Stock Market and Economic Development: Should Developing Countries Encourage Stock Markets?', *UNCTAD Review*, **7**(4), 1–28.

Skocpol, T. (1985), 'Bringing the State Back In: Strategies of Analysis in Current Research', in P.B. Evans, D. Rueschemeyer and T. Skocpol (eds), *Bringing the State Back In*, Cambridge: Cambridge University Press.

Stigler, G. (1975), *The Citizen and the State. Essays on Regulation*, Chicago: Chicago University Press.

Stiglitz, J. (1992), 'Alternative Tactics and Strategies for Economic Development', in A.K. Dutt and K. Jameson (eds), *New Directions in Development Economics*, Unpleadon: Edward Elgar.

Stiglitz, J. *et al.* (1989), *The Economic Role of the State*, Oxford: Basil Blackwell.

Stokey, N.L. (1991), 'Human Capital, Product Quality, and Growth', *Quarterly Journal of Economics*, **106**(2), May, 587–616.
Swedberg, R. (1990), *Economics and Sociology*, Princeton: Princeton University Press.
Taylor, L. (1983), *Structuralist Macroeconomics*, New York: Basic Books.
Taylor, L. (1991), *Income Distribution, Inflation and Growth*, Cambridge, Mass.: MIT Press.
Taylor, L. (1992), 'Polonius Lectures Again: The World Development Report, The Washington Consensus, and How Neo-liberal Sermons Won't Solve the Economic Problems of the Developing World', unpublished, Department of Economics, MIT.
Vernon, R. (1991), 'A Technical Approach to Privatization Issues: Coupling Project Analysis with Rules of Thumb', in R. Ramamurti and R. Vernon (eds), *Privatization and Control of State-Owned Enterprises*, Washington, D.C.: Economic Development Institute, World Bank.
Vickers, J. and Yarrow, G. (1988), *Privatization: An Economic Analysis*, Cambridge, Mass.: MIT Press.
Wade, R. (1990), *Governing the Market. Economic Theory and the Role of Government in East Asian Industrialization*, Princeton: Princeton University Press.
Wang, X. (1993), '"Groping for Stones to Cross the River": Chinese Price Reform Against "Big Bang"', unpublished, University of Cambridge.
Williamson, O. (1975), *Markets and Hierarchies*, New York: Free Press.
Wilson, T. (1979), 'Sympathy and Self-Interest', in T. Wilson and A.S. Skinner (eds), *The Market and the State. Essays in Honour of Adam Smith*, Oxford: Clarendon Press.
Wolf, C. (1990), *Markets or Governments. Choosing Between Imperfect Alternatives*, Cambridge, Mass.: MIT Press.
World Bank (1991), *World Development Report: The Challenge of Development*, Washington D.C.: The World Bank.

2. International Competitiveness: The State and the Market

Irfan ul Haque*

INTRODUCTION

The last decade witnessed a world-wide reassessment of the respective roles of the state and the market. Country after country in the developing world embarked on liberalization programmes and adopted pro-market approaches. With the collapse of communism in Eastern Europe, the former Soviet Union and other countries, central planning and dirigism started to give way to market prices and deregulation. And, in the developed world, there was the Reagan–Thatcher 'revolution' whose impact was felt well beyond the shores of the United States and Britain.

All the same, the state still remains alive and strong, showing few signs of withering away. In the United States, for example, despite the attempts to 'get the government off the people's back' during the 1980s, the government's share in the national economy, as measured by public expenditure, in fact continued to rise (along with a rise in fiscal deficits) to unprecedented levels. Given the now widely recognized need for government action and investment in such sectors as education, health, transport and general infrastructure in the USA, the imperative for a more active government remains strong, though in view of the difficulties the Clinton administration has faced in putting across its 'economic package', it may not translate into action. And if the US government were to invest rather than consume the $300 billion or so it collects in social security revenue – as any well-run pension fund should – the USA might very well see the rise of an elemental socialist state. But there is no issue that evokes more emotion or controversy in the media and the economics profession than the question of international competitiveness and what the government may or may not do to secure it, though again the pendulum seems to be slowly swinging back from the *laissez-faire* ideology of the 1980s.

*The views expressed in this chapter are those of the author given in his personal capacity, and are not necessarily those of the World Bank where he is employed.

This chapter attempts to show that while the market has a critical role in resource allocation, it needs to be actively supported by state action in several areas in order to secure competitiveness. It argues that as societies and economies develop and become more complex, the state's role increases ineluctably, and regulation and price signals or government and business need not be seen as adversarial alternatives but rather made to support each other. In successfully competitive countries, this support has been developed into a synergy.

The chapter first defines *international competitiveness*; it then discusses how the issue of competitiveness has been dealt with in traditional economics. The inadequacy of this framework to explain the evolution of world trade and its policy implications is discussed next. The final section attempts to define the role of the state in the context of a market economy. Whilst the discussion in the chapter is at a fairly general level, it draws upon the experience of the United States, as this country represents a case where traditionally government has played a minimalist role but where the nation is currently debating policies to deal with the crisis of competitiveness. At least in this case, it is hard to blame poor performance on price distortions, excessive protection or a lack of competition.

WHAT IS INTERNATIONAL COMPETITIVENESS?

Although the question of international competitiveness is centrally concerned with international trade, it is at its root one of a nation's capacity to maintain and increase its living standards without running into balance-of-payments problems. The ability to sell abroad is crucial to being able to acquire goods that cannot be produced at home, but this dependence on foreign trade need not be very great, as for example in the case of the United States, and yet the issue of competitiveness may be critical to the sustainability of living standards. International competitiveness therefore transcends the magnitude or sign of trade balance or the rate of expansion of exports and so on, though there is frequently confusion on this (Hatsopoulos *et al.*, 1988). Thus in the current debate on US competitiveness, the Japanese trade surplus is often blamed for lost jobs even though it is evidently helping to finance the excess of expenditure over income, while keeping the inflation low. The trade deficit is no more than the difference between domestic expenditure and output and is therefore basically a macroeconomic problem. Efficient production by itself cannot be expected to surmount the problem of inadequate savings in the USA. Obversely, international competitiveness, in the sense used here, may not be improved or attained simply by means of devaluation or deflationary macroeconomic policy which may stimulate exports and narrow the trade deficit because both policies entail a reduction in domestic income.

If the proper test of a country's competitiveness is taken to be its ability to raise living standards, then a crucial measure of competitive strength is the economy's productivity, both in relation to other countries and in terms of its improvement over time. Productivity in turn depends on the composition of output (as there tend to be systematic differences among sectors) and on its growth in individual sectors (some sectors are more dynamic than others). To put it differently, productivity can be raised by moving production towards higher productivity sectors (for example, from agriculture to manufacturing, from light manufacturing to more capital-intensive production) or by adopting increasingly efficient production processes. Economic progress entails that a country moves successively towards higher productivity sectors.

Several consequences follow from this proposition. First, from the viewpoint of the level and growth of living standards, it matters a great deal which products a country gets to produce: the prospects of growth crucially depend on whether a country specializes in the production of potato chips or microchips (Scott, 1985; Soete, 1991). A country specializing in low-productivity products, with little scope for improvement over time, can expect only modest increases in living standards. Secondly, a country must, while exploiting the existing productive capabilities, strive to become competitive in new lines of production, that is to *create* comparative advantage in new areas. In a competitive world, producers are constantly introducing new and improved products and more efficient processing techniques; a country (or a firm) that does not keep up with these developments faces the prospect of not just stagnant income, but actually a decline as it loses its market share to its competitors. Finally, the process of structural transformation entails new investment in plant and technology and the acquisition of needed skills. Even the simplest shifts in production patterns (for example, introduction of high-yielding crops) require new inputs and new practices that have to be learned.

The question, then, is to what extent market mechanisms alone can be relied upon to select and promote appropriate industries and to bring about necessary adjustments. Let us first see the answers provided by mainstream economics which continues to provide analytical underpinning to economic policy.

BASIS OF SPECIALIZATION: MAINSTREAM ECONOMICS

If competitiveness depends on the kind of products produced and traded, the question that then arises is: what determines international specialization in production? The neoclassical model does provide a generalized explanation for international trade; factor endowments determine a country's comparative advantage, and freely functioning markets can generally be relied upon to allocate factors of production efficiently and to determine the optimal pattern of product specialization. Trade policy intervention or any other form of government action is not only unnecessary, it might actually be harmful since the country could end up producing goods in which it has no comparative advantage. There is a large body of economic literature that attempts to show, theoretically and empirically, the harm policy intervention can do to economic performance (for example, most of the works of Balassa, Kreuger and Bhagwati). Paul Krugman notes:

> For one hundred seventy years, the appreciation that international trade benefits a country whether it is 'fair' or not has been one of the touchstones of professionalism in economics. Comparative advantage is not just an idea both simple and profound; it is an idea that conflicts directly with both stubborn popular prejudices and powerful interests. This combination makes the defense of free trade as close to a sacred tenet as any idea in economics (Krugman, 1987).

Mainstream economics, however, does recognize the case for state intervention when the market fails to perform its task properly, such as when there are increasing returns to scale or when there are important external economies. Intervention may also be justified when the market may not assign adequate weight to the process of learning, as in the case of the 'infant industry argument', but economists grant this concession grudgingly on the grounds that the infant may never grow up.

The 'New Trade Theory' explores situations where government action might yield better resource allocation than the market (see, for example, Grossman, 1986). It does not depart in any fundamental sense from the traditional theory, but rather within the same basic framework of production possibilities dictated by factor endowments addresses questions of government intervention, especially commercial policy, in economies characterized by monopolistic competition, increasing returns and external economies. However, the proponents of this theory are generally ambivalent, if not uncomfortable, about government intervention, particularly if it takes the form of output subsidy or trade policy which is not considered to be appropriate for correcting common market imperfections. They also argue that government would not know better than the market, that the benefits from intervention might be localized to specific industries or firms thereby creating pressure groups, or that it would risk inviting foreign retaliation and trade war (Krugman, 1987).

PROBLEMS WITH THE NEOCLASSICAL THEORY

There are, however, serious problems with traditional theory as an explanation for specialization in production. The so-called *Leontief paradox* – a finding that US exports were more labour-intensive than its imports – was the first formidable challenge to the validity of the theory. However, it is because of the difficulty the model has in explaining the successful experiences of Japan and other newly industrializing economies that questions are being now raised as to its adequacy and value. An increasing number of economists are coming round to the view that Japan and South Korea 'succeeded by doing everything wrong according to standard theory' (Blinder, 1990). The emphasis in their earlier industrialization was on import substitution, which was fostered by all manner of government intervention, covering commercial policy, fiscal incentives, credit allocation and so on. It is also hard to explain why significant differences exist in economic performance among developed countries with roughly comparable real wages and profit rates if they also face the same production functions (Fagerberg, 1988). The most serious problem with the model is that it does not really come to grips with the fundamental issues of competitiveness and growth, as there is always something that a country can produce and trade internationally. Competitiveness is not a real issue, nor is the model concerned with whether the area of specialization gives the country adequate earnings and income growth. Similarly, by treating production conditions as identical and technology-free and costless to move, the model suppresses some interesting issues of economic performance. What is more, the reality appears to be moving rapidly away from the neoclassical world. Consider the following stylized facts:

● Countries trade increasingly in a broadly similar range of products. This has been true for some time among the developed countries, but even in north–south trade the importance of primary products has declined with the rise of manufactured exports. The significance of natural resources as a basis for specialization has also declined.

● Direct labour cost has been declining in relation to the other costs of production, while the proportion of expenditure on research and development, design, marketing and distribution has been rising (Dahlman, 1991). In other words, the cost of labour is not an adequate indicator of the comparative costs of production, and the direct production cost is not an altogether satisfactory measure of how well an industry might do in the international market.

● Countries that use their labour efficiently (that is, have high labour productivity) also tend to be efficient users of capital and other resources (Dosi *et al.*, 1990). In other words, it is possible to rank countries on the basis of their overall efficiency where some countries can be said to be more competitive all around than others. The implication is that countries, far from operating on the same production function, as traditional theory posits, face quite different production conditions.

- Application of technology and innovation are principal determinants of a country's performance in terms of economic growth and labour productivity (Fagerberg, 1988), which in turn depend on the investment rate (Hatsopoulos *et al.*, 1988). However, technology is not a factor of production similar to (say) capital or labour or a scalar in a production function: what distinguishes technology (or knowledge) is its specificity in use (each in a group listening to the same lecture will employ their learning differently) and incremental nature (knowledge builds on itself) (Nelson, 1981). It is therefore not appropriate to view technology as an item that can be 'picked off the shelf' with a market like any other good. Nor would a firm, even after acquiring a particular technology, operate necessarily at the same efficiency as another. Indeed, firms tend to improve on what they happen to be doing – the so-called 'localized learning' – which leads to technological differences among firms being reinforced over time, resulting in firms or countries getting tied to different technology trajectories (Stiglitz, 1987; Dosi *et al.*, 1990).

- Over time the mobility of capital has increased, thanks to the removal of regulations on capital movement and the advances in communications and informatics. At the same time, however, the barriers to the movement of labour, if anything, have increased as the political climate in developed countries has become more hostile to immigrants from the developing countries. At the same time, the movement of capital from the developed north to the developing south (notably from the United States to Mexico) excites concerns similar to the movement of labour in the opposite direction.

The problem with the neoclassical model is not just that it fails to take these stylized facts into account, but rather that they call into question the model's very foundations. They imply that factor endowments, as conventionally viewed, do not provide an adequate basis for specialization in trade; that sales strategies rather than simple profit-maximization influence the outcome; that technology and innovation pose both a threat and a challenge to existing production; and that, with the freer movement of capital, it is no longer possible to equate the competitive advantage of a firm with that of a nation (individual firms may continue to do well while the economies where they are based get immiserized; witness the concern in the US with respect to

NAFTA) (Ostry, 1990). As capital accumulates, factor endowments should begin to converge among countries, thereby (according to the theory) diluting the advantages from international trade. There is no evidence of this happening; in fact, trade among industrialized and industrializing countries remains strong and is increasing in importance. Technology and innovation, and the capacity to imitate, seem to be key determinants of growth and competitiveness (Fagerberg, 1988).

Recent advances in the neoclassical theory attempt to respond to some of these concerns. The development of the 'New Trade Theory' has been noted earlier. The 'New Growth Theory' deals directly with the issue of technological progress, viewing it not as something falling from heaven as in the earlier models, but as an endogenous variable that the model tries to explain. The importance of R&D is brought out, and a country's pattern of trade is shown to be influenced, among other factors, by the resources devoted to research (Grossman and Helpman, 1992). But R&D is treated very much like any other economic activity, where costs and benefits can be evaluated to determine the optimal level of expenditure. Thus the model fails to deal with some of the essential features of the process of technological accumulation that make it different from other economic activities, that is, the costs of learning, the inherent unpredictability of the R&D outcomes, and the *impossibility* of meaningful optimization of expenditure decisions.[1] These points are pursued below.

A great deal of recent literature tries to identify sources of comparative advantage and competitiveness in a changing, dynamic world where technology is advancing, population is growing and new productive capacity is being created. The most notable example is, perhaps, Michael Porter's *Competitive Advantage of Nations*, where he develops his notion of the 'diamond of national advantage', which consists of factor conditions, demand conditions, supporting industries and firm strategies (Porter, 1990). These attempts do not pretend to provide an alternative *model*, which has probably been the major hurdle in their gaining respectability in mainstream economics. Relying instead on frameworks of analysis, these works tend to take a much broader view of competitiveness, bringing into focus such non-price factors as institutions, culture and government action (see also Dertouzos *et al.*, 1989 and Coriat and Taddéi, 1993).

THE STATE AND THE MARKET: ADVERSARIES OR COMPLEMENTS?

One reason for the neoclassical model's widespread appeal is its tight logical structure and its consequent capability to provide fairly definite policy conclusions: free markets can be generally relied upon to allocate scarce resources optimally, and state intervention by distorting price signals can end up hindering the market's functioning. The state's role has, in fact, been formalized in terms of certain basic theorems of neoclassical economics, which delineate acceptable and unacceptable areas for government intervention (Stiglitz, 1990). Where state intervention is required, it should take the form that least distorts prices or violates the *marginal equivalences* (for example, prefering lump-sum taxes over graduated taxes, or tariffs over quantitative controls). By abandoning the neoclassical framework, one loses an anchor that has given strength to economic analysis and provided plausible advice to policymakers, and enters a realm of uncertain outcomes and options. However, the definiteness of its policy conclusions rests essentially on the concept of the perfect market and disappears with ever so slight modifications to the basic framework. Since markets often do not work perfectly (how often is a debated point), the challenge for economists of all stripes has been to define the state's role and domain of public policy – *second-best* solutions – in this imperfect world.

In considering areas of consensus and debate, we explore here only the case for state intervention *in the market* and not the case for state ownership. This is a rather serious limitation because the latter also remains a keenly debated issue and is obviously central to the state's role. This means as a minimum that one is primarily interested in consumer welfare without regard to how it is increased.[2] However, in addressing the issue of competitiveness, the basic aim here is to examine how far the market can be relied upon to do the job, rather than who owns the assets. Only the *prima facie* case for state intervention is explored, not its form, which must be conditioned by the specific circumstances that call for policy action.

First we must look at the areas where there seems to be little disagreement. Most economists will agree that the market is usually an efficient and potent source of information for economic decision-making, and that the costs of ignoring its signals, as under central planning, can be enormous. There is also the consideration that the market permits exercise of individual freedom while the dictates of a bureaucratic agency clearly do not, though this point must not be pushed too far in cases of large unemployment and highly skewed income distribution. It needs to be stressed, however, that the market's role in resource allocation – be it for household, firm or government – is not derived from the neoclassical model; indeed a case for free trade can be made independently of this framework. Hla Myint, for example, argues for free trade and openness by putting forward such non-neoclassical arguments as the 'vent for surplus' and the educative effects of trade in introducing new wants, new technology and new forms of organization (Myint, 1987). In other words, if one does not subscribe to that model, one cannot be presumed to have rejected the market.

The state's role in maintaining employment and creating an environment where living standards can rise has a wide following in the profession, thanks to the Keynesian revolution. Notwithstanding the debate on discretionary fiscal policy and the influence of monetarism in the 1980s, economists would grant that macroeconomic policy is important and, as a minimum, needs to be conducted in a way that protects fiduciary while encouraging private initiative and investment. However, there is much debate on the components of the macro policy and the need for policy intervention (for example, trade policy) to support macro policy. There is also considerable difference of opinion on the effectiveness of policy in generating employment and controlling inflation.

Views also tend to converge on the several sources of market failure that might call for some form of state intervention. These instances typically occur when there are externalities, increasing returns, uncertainty, and information failures and so on (Stern, 1989). In the context of international trade, government intervention might be used to secure for the country concerned the monopoly rents arising out of market imperfections, a subject of principal interest to the 'New Trade' theorists. Nevertheless, there are many areas where the state's role is more ambiguous and controversial. In the absence of hard theory, this is a domain of prejudice, strong opinions and selective evidence. Let us consider these contested areas.

National interest

The state obviously is expected to intervene when national interest is perceived to be at stake, though this reason is easily abused and is liable to excite retaliation by other countries. Indeed, GATT was created primarily as an institution that could mediate on questions of national interest and prevent countries from pursuing the 'beggar thy neighbour' policies that were common during the inter-war period and did much to harm international trade. GATT has not been entirely successful in this, and recent years have witnessed a rising tension among the triad of the United States, European Community and Japan, with mutual 'bashing' of each other for not playing by the rules (Ostry, 1990). While the 'level playing-field' variety of argument, where the blame is passed on to the other side, is often self-serving, there are situations in real life when free trade may not be altogether beneficial for a country. This can happen, for example, when a country faces a rise in unemployment as a result of capital moving out of the country, or even when imports displace labour with few alternative employment opportunities for want of (say) investment in human and material capital.

This is not a case of market failure as conventionally understood, but one where one of the two countries is losing from the international exchange as the market tries to correct past inequality in incomes. These equilibrating forces operate also in the neoclassical model, where the factor rewards move towards equality with the opening of international trade. Clearly, as wages in the low-wage country rise, they *fall* in the high-wage country. The workers whose employment and living standards are threatened, as in the case of the United States *vis-à-vis* Mexico, are unlikely to be persuaded by the economist's argument that the market is allocating resources efficiently and that all that is needed is for them to move to higher productivity jobs. The situation in Russia and the rest of the former Soviet Union is ever more dramatic where, largely as a result of the sudden opening up to world trade, output and employment have fallen precipitously. Clearly, the market is not functioning to protect the living standards of the population, even when viewed in terms of the long run. Even if one grants that calls for blocking trade in the United States and other developed countries are unreasonable, the state clearly has a role in facilitating the reallocation of labour through macroeconomic policy as well as specific actions at sectoral level, such as worker training and investment incentives. State action may also be necessary in order to redress the balance where some are better able to take advantage of the market (in this case, investors) than others.

Development of the Non-tradable Sector

The efficiency of the non-tradable sector – which includes labour, infrastructure and public administration – is quite central to international competitiveness if for no other reason than the fact that producers can be expected to face roughly similar costs for traded inputs. There are few examples of countries that excelled in foreign trade where these sectors were neglected. What distinguishes the successful Far Eastern economies is the quality of their labour and infrastructure which, to a large extent, is a result of government policies and expenditure.

Among the non-tradable sectors, public administration must be included, for its effectiveness to a large extent determines the success of government intervention. Socialism failed in Eastern Europe and in the Soviet Union not just because of the weaknesses of the economic system itself, but more fundamentally because of the oligarchies – isolated, intolerant, and corrupt – that came to preside over it. On the other hand, the civil services of Japan, South Korea and Singapore, for example, have generally been regarded as highly efficient. Thus one observes that it is not always policies themselves that are good or bad, but rather the success or failure of government in implementing them. However, 'government failure' does not quite have the same dimensions as market failure, though they are usually juxtaposed. Most instances of market failure – such as increasing returns and external economies – are intrinsic to the market, that is, there are no market situations that can optimally deal with these failures. On the other hand, government failure arises out of problems of information, administrative capability, transparency, accountability and impartiality (Stern, 1989), which are aspects of governance and which vary a great deal among countries and over time.

Government failure is evidently a less serious problem in some countries than in others. According to one view, the success of the active state in Japan and other East Asian countries can be attributed to their 'hardness', a rather vague concept, but one that relates basically to the government's ability to govern (Briggs and Levy, 1991). It is then argued that countries with 'soft' states must not venture on the same road; for them the less government, the better. Apart from the rather circular reasoning behind this view, there must be degrees of 'softness' – some states being more soft than others – assuming that the term could be defined in an unambiguous way. Also, as Sen argued: 'Quite often what appears as softness is the responsiveness of the state to the public asserting itself and demonstrating that the state should take heed of the public's welfare. This need be no bad thing' (Sen, 1990).

Development of Technology

Technological progress implies new and better quality products and more efficient production processes; technology is therefore central to an economy's capacity to grow and compete internationally. The main question here is to what extent market mechanisms can be relied upon to tap the technological potential, and to promote innovation and product and process improvements. The experience of countries varies enormously in this respect, even when only the developed countries are considered. Japan, Germany and Switzerland are generally regarded as technologically the most dynamic, while the United States and the United Kingdom are among the least. Similarly, among the developing countries, the successful industrializers are also technologically far more dynamic than the others.

A key determinant of technological progress is the *effort* put into research and development. More dynamic countries tend to devote a higher proportion of their national income to R&D than others (Dosi *et al.*, 1990). Much of technological development and innovation in the industrial world occurs through R&D efforts at the enterprise level, not in government laboratories. In fact, one major reason why industry in Eastern Europe and the former Soviet Union remained backward was the concentration of R&D in centralized institutions in these countries and the inability of enterprises to avail themselves of the available technological knowledge (Pavitt, 1991). However, because of the inherent uncertainty of the outcome of R&D and the proprietary nature of technical knowledge, it represents a case of market failure (Nelson, 1981). Technology is not a product, or even a public good, that can be bought or sold in a standardized form; the cost of acquiring it and its effective use can vary enormously among firms. Thus, the market in technology either does not exist or, if it does, it is highly imperfect. But there is also a market failure on account of externalities, that is, a firm may lack the incentive to innovate, and be deterred from spending resources on R&D, if others can easily imitate. Patents, a state intervention, are intended to protect the monopoly rents of the innovator, but they do not completely prevent imitation. At the same time, because it sanctions monopoly, the use of patents runs rather counter to the free trade creed. However, if patents are tightly enforced, R&D would involve the waste of resources, as only the first one to make the discovery would reap the rewards, whilst others would gain little or nothing (Nelson, 1981). In short, the market causes either too much to be spent on R&D or too little, and it is not possible to strike the right balance by weighing the costs and benefits as the New Growth Theory attempts to do.

While the market cannot be relied upon to allocate resources to R&D, it is by no means certain that the government would do any better. There is an increasing support for government intervention in promoting hi-tech industries in the United States, but there is dispute over the cost of this involvement and the possible benefits that may arise. Nevertheless, government support to R&D, even in the United States, has been considerable and has been defended on the grounds of 'national interest' (defence, space programmes and so on). The case for government intervention basically turns on the technological effort that other countries might be making; the risk of falling behind dictates that the country make a commensurate effort. Beyond R&D, the state has a major role in building national technological capability, that is, the ability to develop and use technological knowledge which depends on both the general education level of the population and the orientation of education, specifically, the emphasis on science and engineering.

Industrial Policy

The case for industrial policy, which can be derived from any of the reasons discussed above, essentially rests on the importance of industry in the economy and its inability in certain situations to develop and survive in a competitive environment. Both of these premises are questioned, even though most economists would grant that productivity and its growth tend to be higher in manufacturing, and that service sectors – the hope of post-industrial economies – depend to a large extent on the manufacturing activity itself. The reason why an American barber costs so much more than one in a developing country is simply because of his opportunity cost, that is, the wages he may earn in higher productivity sectors. Whilst an increasing number of economists now accept that industry is the foundation of economic prosperity, there is little consensus on whether the government should intervene in its survival and growth.

The issue is not really whether or not there should be industrial policy, for all countries have policies that regulate and provide incentives to industries. The differences arise on whether governments take a *strategic* view of industry and select certain areas for promotion (Singh, 1991). The opponents of industrial policy reject it basically on grounds that government is driven by diverse objectives and is incapable of making economically 'rational' strategic choices: it tries to choose winners when it has neither the knowledge nor the ability to do so. Those who subscribe to this view find it difficult to explain why industrial policy has been successful in some countries and not in others. They also seem to have in mind a process of policy formulation that is confined to government bureaucrats who make arbitrary decisions without regard to market signals. This, however, seems to be a rather distorted view of how the successful countries fashioned their industrial policies and arrived at a choice of industries for promotion. The targeting of industries in Japan or South Korea was not done by bureaucrats working in isolation; in fact, there was a close involvement of all interested parties – businesses, trade unions and academics, as well as bureaucrats – in developing a 'vision' for the future. When industrial policy is formulated through such a consultative process, the choice of industries for development would generally be made on a sounder foundation than the decisions of isolated investors.

Even if it is accepted that the government cannot choose winners, it can certainly help to create conditions where they are born. There is a whole range of things that a government can do in a systematic and strategic way to support industry. This may include direct involvement in the development of some technologies (as discussed above), creation of an environment where long-term investments are encouraged, and facilitation of the movement of labour and so on. The point is rather well made in the following quote from *Business Week*:

> America needs a new growth policy for the 1990s, an industrial policy that acknowledges that ideas drive growth. Government should provide a fertile environment for individuals, companies, and industries to pursue new ideas and new techniques, and it should be willing to spend money and even lose money today in order to ensure more vigorous growth tomorrow (*Business Week*, 6 April 1992).

Government–Business Interaction

The state's role is usually articulated in terms of either government direction and regulation versus market signals, or public versus private ownership of the means of production. When put this way, government is necessarily cast as an adversary. And yet there are very different models of government–business interaction even among countries subscribing to the free enterprise system. The differences, which have become much more prominent with the end of the Cold War, seem to lie not so much in the extent of government involvement in the economy as in the nature of the relationship between government and business. In some countries, notably Japan, this relationship has been close and harmonious and has helped in securing competitive strength; whilst in others it is basically one of mistrust.[3]

Why such differences exist is a complex question, but it seems plausible that in societies where individualism is strong, the view that government encroaches on individual liberty will also tend to have greater support. It therefore cannot be an accident that neoclassical economics – whose basic aim it is to demonstrate conditions where atomistic competitive decision-making can yield optimal results – has thrived in countries where individualism is especially prized, viz. Britain and the United States, and in the latter more than in the first. Nevertheless, government's role in the economy has grown, as well as changed, virtually everywhere in the industrialized world. One major factor in this expansion perhaps has been that with economic development social structures also change, and many of the tasks previously performed communally get assigned to government, the most notable being the care of the sick and unemployed.

It can therefore be argued that societies that have relatively strong communal spirit would also be rather more receptive to, and less suspicious of, government, viewing it more as an agent of collective will. Where communal spirit is weak, government is more likely to be held responsible for protecting the weak and the unemployed (welfare state), and will neither have the mandate nor the resources to be active in the productive sectors. In the first type of society, there may also be a greater scope for strategic co-operation among otherwise competing firms, because they may take a rather different view of *competition* and *efficiency*. Instead of the dog-eat-dog variety of competition, it might be more goal-driven in a more socially conscious society (rather than competing to finish off the rival, competitors vie with each other in meeting a set goal). Similarly, instead of viewing efficiency as a strictly micro phenomenon, firms might take a society-wide view: before laying off workers to improve the bottom line, a firm might take into account the cost to society of feeding, clothing and sheltering the unemployed. There is, however, a certain irony in this: strong individualism calls for a strong government (to protect the weak, to internalize the *externalities*), but it also gives rise to an antipathy towards government. Although this might change, it seems at this point inconceivable that in Japan a big corporation could stage a hostile takeover of a small competitor, or that a big firm would lay off 75,000

workers, as General Motors is in the process of doing in the USA, without
causing a political crisis.

In short, the state's role cannot be settled in terms of the extent of government involvement in the economy, but rather by the possibilities of government and business (including both the owners and the labour) working together where businesses themselves are more cognizant of the social costs
and benefits of their actions. There obviously cannot be a standard formula
for structuring this relationship, but it is probably safe to conclude that as
long as the state's role remains unsettled, there cannot be an 'end to history'.

NOTES

1. The treatment of R&D as any other economic activity leads also to some implausible
   conclusions. Consider, for example, the following from Grossman and Helpman (1992):
   'Generally, when one country subsidizes R&D, this reduces the profitability of innovation
   abroad. If research contracts in a *country with comparative advantage in this activity*, there
   may be a slowing of aggregate (world) innovation. In the event the policy may reduce
   welfare levels worldwide' (p. 340) (Emphasis added).
2. See Lane (1991): 'Market economies do not require private ownership of means of production, but they inevitably place consumer welfare over worker welfare, derive their emphasis on efficiency from the interest in profits of managers and owners ... and allocate
   resources by the same acts that reward the owners of these resources' (p. 16).
3. There are, however, some serious problems also with a close business–government relationship, as is becoming evident from a series of political scandals in Japan and Korea.

BIBLIOGRAPHY

Blinder, A.S. (1990), 'There are Capitalists, Then There are the Japanese', *Business
    Week,* October 8, 21.
Briggs, T. and Levy, B. (1991), 'Strategic Interventions and the Political Economy of
    Industrial Policy in Developing Countries', in Dwight H. Perkins and Michael
    Romer (eds), *Reforming Economic Systems in Developing Countries,* Cambridge,
    Mass: Harvard Institute of International Development, Harvard University Press,
    365–401.
Coriat, B. and Taddéi, D. (1993), *Made in France: L'industrie Française dans la
    Competition Mondiale,* Paris: Brodard et Taupin, Libraire Générale Française.
Dahlman, C.J. (1991), 'Education Policy, Technical Change, R&D and Competitive
    Advantage', in Haque (1991).
Dertouzos, M.L. *et al.* (1989), *Made in America. Regaining the Productivity Edge,*
    Cambridge, Mass.: MIT Press.
Dosi, G., Pavitt, K., and Soete, L. (1990), *The Economics of Technical Change and
    International Trade,* Washington Square, N.Y.: NYU Press.
Fagerberg, J. (1988), 'Why Growth Rates Differ' in G. Dosi, C. Freeman, R. Nelson,
    G. Silverberg and L. Soete (eds), *Technical Change and Economic Theory,* London:
    Pinter Publishers.

Grossman, G.M. (1986), 'Strategic Export Promotion: A Critique' in P.R. Krugman (ed.), *Strategic Trade Policy and the New International Economies*, Cambridge, Mass.: MIT Press.

Grossman, G.M. and Helpman, E. (1992), *Innovation and Growth*, Cambridge, Mass.: MIT Press.

Haque, I. (1991), 'International Competitiveness: Interaction of the Public and Private Sectors', Washington, D.C.: The World Bank, EDT Seminar Series.

Hatsopoulos, G.N., Krugman, P.R. and Summers, L.H. (1988), 'US Competitiveness: Beyond the Trade Deficit', *Science*, **241**, 15 July, 299–307.

Havrylyshyn, O. (1990), 'Trade Policy and Productivity Gains in Developing Countries: A Survey of the Literature', *The World Bank Research Observer*, 5(1), January, 1–24.

Krugman, P.R. (1987), 'Is Free Trade Passé?', *Journal of Economic Perspectives*, 1(2), Fall, 131–44.

Lane, R.E. (1991), *The Market Experience*, Cambridge: Cambridge University Press.

Myint, Hla (1987), 'Neo-classical Development Analysis: Its Strengths and Limitations', in G.M. Meir (ed.), *Pioneers in Development*, Second Series, London: Oxford University Press.

Nelson, R. (1981), 'Research on Productivity Growth and Productivity Differences: Dead Ends and New Departures', *Journal of Economic Literature*, **XIX**, September, 1029–64.

Ostry, S. (1990), *Governments and Corporations in a Shrinking World*, New York: Council on Foreign Relations Press.

Pavitt, K. (1991), 'East-West Differences in National Systems of Innovation: Some Implications for Reform', mimeo, Science Policy Research Unit, Sussex University, Brighton, England.

Porter, M. (1990), 'Competitive Advantage of Nations', *Harvard Business Review*, March–April.

Scott, B.R. (1985), 'National Strategies: Key to International Competition', in B.R. Scott and G.C. Lodge (eds), *US Competitiveness in the World Economy*, Boston: Harvard Business School Press.

Sen, A.K. (1990), 'A panel contribution to the Roundtable Discussion, "Development Strategies: The Roles of the State and the Private Sector", *Proceedings of the World Bank Annual Conference on Development Economics*, Supplement to *The World Bank Economic Review* and *The World Bank Research Observer*, 421–5.

Singh, A. (1991), 'International Competitiveness and Industrial Policy' in Haque (1991).

Soete, L.L.G. (1991), 'National Support Policies for Strategic Industries: The International Implications', mimeo, January, Paris.

Stern, N. (1989), 'The Economics of Development: A Survey', *Economic Journal*, **99**, September, 597–685.

Stiglitz, J. (1987), 'Learning to Learn, Localized Learning and Technological Progress', in P. Dasgupta and P. Stoneman (eds), *Economic Policy and Technological Performance*, Cambridge: Cambridge University Press.

Stiglitz, J. (1990), 'A panel contribution to the Roundtable Discussion "Development Strategies: The Roles of the State and the Private Sector"', *Proceedings of the World Bank Annual Conference on Development Economics*.

3. State Intervention and the 'Market-Friendly' Approach to Development: A Critical Analysis of the World Bank Theses

Ajit Singh

INTRODUCTION

In the *World Development Report* for 1991, the World Bank economists put forward important theses concerning the appropriate role of the state in economic activity. The *Report* is a landmark document as, in the words of the then President of the Bank, Mr Barber Conables, it 'synthesises and interprets the lessons of 40 years of development experience'. In view of the World Bank's leading role in development financing for poor countries around the globe, the *Report's* analyses and recommendations are necessarily taken very seriously in policy-making circles throughout the developing world. It is therefore important that there should be a full examination of the *Report's* intellectual approach and the evidence underlying its conclusions.

This, indeed, is the main purpose of this chapter. It provides a critical assessment of the *Report's* theses concerning the role of the state in economic development, encapsulated in the *Report's* phrase, 'market-friendly approach to development'. The chapter also outlines an alternative perspective and argues that the best way to promote industrialization and economic development in many developing countries is for the government to pursue a vigorous 'industrial policy'. A central theme of the chapter is the contrast between these two concepts – the 'market friendly approach' and the 'industrial policy' – of the proper role of the state in economic development.[1]

THE MARKET FRIENDLY APPROACH TO DEVELOPMENT

The *World Development Report* sets out at the very start the question of the role of state intervention in economic activity in the following terms:

A central issue in development, and the principal theme of the *Report*, is the interaction between governments and markets. This is not a question of intervention versus *laissez-faire* – a popular dichotomy, but a false one. Competitive markets are the best way yet found for efficiently organising the production and distribution of goods and services. Domestic and external competition provides the incentives that unleash entrepreneurship and technological progress. But markets cannot operate in a vacuum – they require a legal and regulatory framework that only governments can provide. And, at many other tasks, markets sometimes prove inadequate or fail altogether. This is why governments must, for example, invest in infrastructure and provide essential services to the poor. It is not a question of state or market: each has a large and irreplaceable role (p. 1).

The issue, then, is what should be this 'large and irreplaceable role' of the government? The *Report* asserts: 'Economic theory and practical experience suggest that [government] interventions are likely to help provided they are market-friendly' (p. 5). 'Market-friendly' is a seductive phrase and it can mean all things to all people. To save the analysis from therefore becoming totally tautological, to its credit, the *Report* defines the concept with some precision. 'Market-friendly', it is explained, means the following:

a. Intervene reluctantly. Let markets work unless it is demonstrably better to step in... [It] is usually a mistake for the state to carry out physical production, or to protect the domestic production of a good that can be imported more cheaply and whose local production offers few spillover benefits.
b. Apply checks and balances. Put interventions continually to the discipline of international and domestic markets.
c. Intervene openly. Make interventions simple, transparent and subject to rules rather than official discretion.

The state's role in economic development in this 'market-friendly' approach is thus regarded as being important, but best limited to providing the social, legal and economic infrastructure for the market to operate, and to creating a suitable climate for private enterprise. An important function of the government in this concept is to promote domestic and international competition, as these are thought to best generate 'efficient economic growth' (see 'The Government and Competition in Domestic Markets'). The *Report* implicates other development economists in its policy recommendations by suggesting that there is now a growing consensus around the 'market-friendly approach' to development (p. 1).

THE 'MARKET-FRIENDLY' APPROACH TO DEVELOPMENT AND THE EAST ASIAN EXPERIENCE

The basic methodological approach of the 1991 *World Development Report*, which I completely concur with, is to draw analytical and policy lessons by comparing the experience of successful and unsuccessful countries during the last four decades of economic development. The recent economic history of the highly successful East Asian economies therefore rightly plays an extremely important role in the *Report's* analysis. The *Report* draws specific attention to the state of Japanese society and the country's economy in the late 1940s, and its extraordinary progress since then. The *Report* observes (pp. 13–14):

> Extraordinary progress is possible even when countries seem doomed to fail. Forty-three years ago an influential government report in an important developing country observed that labour today shunned hard, productive jobs and sought easy, merchant-like work. The report showed that workers' productivity had fallen, wages were too high, and enterprises were inefficient and heavily subsidized. The country had virtually priced itself out of international markets and faced a severe competitive threat from newly industrializing China and India. It was overpopulated and becoming more so. This would be the last opportunity, concluded the prime minister in July 1947, to discover whether his country would be able to stand on its own two feet or become a permanent burden for the rest of the world. That country was Japan. *The central question of the report is why countries like Japan have succeeded so spectacularly while others have failed* (emphasis added).

The *Report* is quite right to stress the case of Japan, since the experience of that country in the period following World War II is highly relevant to the developing countries, particularly the large semi-industrial economies. In the early 1950s, Japan produced less steel (about five million tons) and fewer cars (about 50,000) than countries such as Brazil, India and Mexico do today, and it was largely an exporter of labour-intensive products. The US annual steel output at that time was about a hundred million tons and the American automobile industry produced around six million cars every year. Yet less than two decades later, Japan was producing more steel and, by 1980, more cars than the US. The Japanese workers, starting from Asian wage levels in the 1950s, were well on their way to reaching European standards of living 25 years later (Singh, 1989).

In analysing this, arguably the most spectacular case of successful industrial development in the history of mankind, the relevant question in the present context is to what extent, if any, the Japanese followed the *Report's* prescriptions and a 'market-friendly' approach to development. Did the Japanese government intervene in the markets 'reluctantly': did it, for example, leave prices and production priorities to be determined mostly by market forces and simply provide the necessary infrastructure for private enterprise to flourish? How 'transparent' was government intervention in Japanese industry? To achieve this colossal economic success, how closely did the Japanese economy integrate with the world economy? The *Report* does acknowledge the inescapable fact that there was considerable government intervention in the course of post-war Japanese development. The important issue, however, is whether the *Report's* characterization of this intervention and the lessons to be drawn from it are valid.

There is overwhelming evidence, and it is generally accepted among scholars in the field, that the government in Japan did not intervene in the markets 'reluctantly'. On the contrary, it pursued a forceful and aggressive industrial policy to change the unsatisfactory economic situation faced by that country so eloquently described in the paragraph quoted previously. The cornerstone of this industrial policy was the so-called 'structural policy' aimed at adaptation and technological development of certain specific industries (steel, chemicals, machinery and other heavy industries) thought to be vital for the rapid growth of productivity and per capita incomes. The role of the government in promoting these industries, and hence bringing about Japanese economic success, has been so crucial that, as the Japanese industrial economist Professor Nino (1972) remarked: 'whereas [the] USA is said to be a country of [the] military industrial complex ... in this sense, Japan may be called a country of the Government industrial complex'.

At the end of World War II, the bulk of Japanese exports consisted of textiles and light manufactured goods. In the view of the Ministry of International Trade and Industry (MITI), although such an economic structure may have conformed to the theory of comparative advantage (Japan being a labour-surplus economy at the time), it was not viable in the long run. It is worth quoting in full Vice-Minister Ojimi's rationale for the Ministry's industrial policy:

> The MITI decided to establish in Japan industries which require intensive employment of capital and technology, industries that in consideration of comparative cost of production should be the most inappropriate for Japan, industries such as steel, oil-refining, petro-chemicals, automobiles, aircraft, industrial machinery of all sorts, and electronics, including electronic computers. From a short-run, static viewpoint, encouragement of such industries would seem to conflict with economic rationalism. But, from a long-range viewpoint, these are precisely the industries where income elasticity of demand is high, technological progress is rapid, and labour productivity rises fast. It was clear that without these industries it would be difficult to employ a population of 100 million and raise their standard of living to that of Europe and America with light industries alone; whether right or wrong, Japan had to have these heavy and chemical industries. According to Napoleon and Clausewitz, the secret of a successful strategy is the concentration of fighting power on the main battle grounds; fortunately, owing to good luck and

wisdom spawned by necessity, Japan has been able to concentrate its scant capital in strategic industries (OECD, 1972).

The government used a wide variety of instruments to bring about this extraordinary structural transformation of the Japanese economy between 1950 and 1973, the period of its most rapid growth. The most important of these were bank finance and directed credit; import controls and protection; restrictions on entry and exit of firms in the domestic market; control over foreign exchange, and importation of foreign technology (OECD, 1972; Nino, 1972; Boltho, 1975; Caves and Uekusa, 1976; Dore, 1986; Yamamura, 1988).

The significance of these policies, and particularly the economic rationale underlying them, will be considered further in the next two sections. In the meantime we note that the Japanese government did not only use these methods of intervention to concentrate resources to promote specific industries, its role in the country's industrial development was deeper and even more intrusive. It extended to the level of the individual firm: MITI accorded favourable treatment in a variety of ways to the specific firms which were thought best to fulfil its aims and were therefore in its good books. As for the 'transparency' of this intervention, it was the exact opposite of the 'market-friendly' specification. Thus Professors Caves and Uekusa (1976) on the operations of the Japanese industrial policy:

> Each sector of the Japanese economy has a cliental relation to a ministry or agency of the government. The ministry, in addition to its various statutory means of dealing with the economic sector, holds a general implied administrative responsibility and authority that goes well beyond what is customary in the United States and other Western Countries. While the Ministry of International Trade and Industry (MITI) plays the most prominent role, its operations are not distinctive. The industrial bureaus of MITI proliferate sectoral targets and plans; they confer, they tinker, they exhort. This is the economics by admonition to a degree inconceivable in Washington or London. Business makes few major decisions without consulting the appropriate governmental authority; the same is true in reverse.

Moreover, as we shall see in the next section, the Japanese government did not seek a 'close', but rather what may be called a 'strategic', integration with the world economy. For example, it made extensive use of formal or informal import controls and protection. It also restricted foreign direct investment by multinationals. These points will be taken up further when the concept of 'strategic integration' is developed below.

As several scholars have noted, the other East Asian tigers, notably South Korea and Taiwan, have also each followed a purposive and comprehensive industrial policy (see, among others, Johnson, 1987; Amsden, 1989a; Wade, 1990). These countries have been greatly influenced by the Japanese example and practice. In view of their relative backwardness compared with Japan, state intervention in these economies has been even more far-reaching than in Japan. Very briefly, in the case of South Korea, attention may be drawn to the following aspects of that country's industrial policy:

1. The use of long-term credit at negative real interest rates to foster particular industries.
2. The 'heavy' subsidization and the 'coercion' of exports.
3. The strict control over multinational investment and foreign equity ownership of South Korean industry.
4. A highly active state technology policy.
5. State promotion of large-scale conglomerate firms, government encouragement of mergers of specific corporations and, in general, state restrictions on the free entry and exit of firms.

Table 3. 1 summarizes the industrial policy instruments used in the development of core South Korean industries (as well as textiles) in the late 1960s and 1970s.

Similarly, for Taiwan, Wade (1990) documents the widespread and intensive use of state industrial policy to guide purposefully the market economy. It is certainly not a picture of some night-watchman state intervening 'reluctantly'. Until the early 1980s, both South Korea and Taiwan had nationalized banks, and in both countries state-directed credit to favoured sectors and firms was an important device for planned industrial development. Moreover, the authors of the *Report* overlook the fact that the public enterprise sector in Taiwan is one of the largest among the developing mixed economies. It is bigger than India's or that of Argentina, Brazil or Mexico. Public enterprises have contributed a third of gross fixed capital formation in Taiwan throughout the years from 1950 to 1975, a period which witnessed the most rapid economic and industrial growth in that country (Short, 1984; Chang and Singh, 1993). Wade (1990) observes that:

> In many sectors public enterprises have been used as the chosen instrument for a big push. This is true for the early years of fuels, chemicals, mining, metals, fertilizer, and food processing; but even in sectors where public enterprises did not dominate, such as textiles and plastics, the state aggressively led private producers in the early years.... Later, during the late 1950s and 1960s, public enterprises accounted for a large part of total investment in synthetic fibres, metals, shipbuilding, and other industries.... To say that public enterprises have often played a central role in creating new capacities is not to say that private firms have been left alone. Incentives and pressure are brought to bear on them

Table 3.1 *The chief provisions of industrial promotional laws in South Korea*

Major Content	Machinery	Shipbuilding	Electronics	Petrochemical	Iron and Steel	Non-ferrous metal	Textile
(year of enactment)	(1967)	(1967)	(1969)	(1970)	(1970)	(1971)	(1979)
REGULATIONS							
Entry restriction	x	x	x	x	x	x	x
Capacity Regulations							
Setting up facility standard	x	x					
Capacity expansion approval				x	x		x
Incentives to use domestically produced facilities	x		x				
Production Regulation							
Regulation of material imports					x	x	
Production standard and its inspection	x	x	x		x	x	
Restrictions on technology imports	x		x				
Price Control				x	x		
Reporting and inspection	x	x	x	x	x	x	x
RATIONALIZATION							
Rationalization programmes	x	x	x	x			x

R & D SUPPORT						
Subsidies to R&D	x			x		x
Joint R&D projects						x
FINANCIAL SUPPORT						
Special purpose fund	x	x		x		x
Financial assistance	x	x		x		x
Subsidies						
Direct subsidy	x					x
Reduced public utility rates	x			x		
Tax Preferences						
Special depreciation	x					x
Tax reduction exemption	x	x	x	x		x
SPECIAL INDUSTRIAL COMPLEX	x		x	x		x
ADMINISTRATIVE ASSISTANCE						
Facilitating overseas activities		x			x	
Purchase of raw materials				x	x	
PRODUCERS' ASSOCIATION	x	x				x

Source: Reproduced from Chang (1992), p. 153

through such devices as import controls and tariffs, entry requirements, domestic content requirements, fiscal investment incentives, and concessional credit. Even in the case of machine tools, a small-scale industry relatively neglected until recently, the state nevertheless has provided subsidized design help, subsidized credit, and quantitative import restrictions. And large-scale private firms are often exposed to more discretionary government influence, taking the form of what in Japan is called 'administrative guidance' (pp. 110–11).

In view of the useful and important role played by public enterprises in Taiwan, as well as in South Korea, the *Report's* blanket admonition to the states in developing countries not to engage in 'direct production' – not to produce steel and cement (p. 31) – would appear to be misconceived. The reference to steel is particularly inappropriate since Posco, the Korean state-owned steel company, is the most efficient steel producer in the world. In 1986, Posco produced 467 tons of crude steel per person, compared with an average of 327 tons for Japan's five biggest steel producers. The company's efficiency advantage was passed on to its Korean customers. It charged domestic steel consumers $320 per ton – far less than American or Japanese car-makers who (according to Posco) paid $540 and $430, respectively. (See *The Economist*, 21 May 1988; for a more detailed discussion of Posco's efficiency advantage over other steel producers, see Amsden, 1989a, pp. 298–99.)

To sum up, Japan, South Korea and Taiwan between them did all the things which the 'market-friendly' approach to development is not supposed to do. Above all, all three countries followed an 'industrial strategy' – a set of policies to change deliberately the market prices and production priorities – which is explicitly ruled out by this approach. The *Report* acknowledges that there was heavy state intervention in all three countries, but argues that 'these economies refute the case for thoroughgoing *dirigisme* as convincingly as they refute the case for *laissez-faire*' (p. 5). The experience of these countries is certainly an argument against *laissez-faire*; further it does not provide any support for 'command' planning of production of the Soviet type which, in effect, supplants the market altogether. However, for mixed economy Third World countries with a strong government, it is unequivocally an argument for adopting an industrial strategy, for guiding the market, and for not follow-ing a hands-off 'market-friendly' approach as enunciated in the *Report*. More-over, as mentioned in the case of Japan, it will be suggested below that the experience of all three East Asian countries is an argument against seeking 'close integration' with the world economy; rather, it is an argument for choosing 'strategic integration' with the latter. These concepts of 'guiding' the market and of 'strategic integration with the international economy' will become clearer when we discuss the role of domestic and international competition in these economies in the following sections.

Other neoclassical economists, not just the authors of the report, also have a difficult task in accommodating the facts of pervasive interventions of the East Asian states in their internal and external economies with the theoretical and policy framework used in such analysis. Some have even argued that these countries would have grown faster still if the state had not intervened in these economies (Lal, 1983). Others have suggested that, in countries such as South Korea, the state has followed a 'prescriptive' rather than a 'proscriptive' policy, and that this accounts for the success of state intervention in that economy. Still others have suggested that the essential reason for the state's success in these countries is that it has followed the market, rather than leading or guiding it. Such arguments have been carefully analysed by Wade, Amsden and others, and found to have very little merit.

What does distinguish the industrial policy of Japan, South Korea and Taiwan from that of many other countries, both developed and developing, is the ability of the state in the former countries to use not only 'carrots' (incentives, subsidies, and so on) but also 'sticks' (punishments) to influence firm behaviour. In that sense, the state in these countries has been much more powerful and has what the political scientists call greater 'autonomy' than many other economies (see, further, Amsden, 1989a; Wade, 1990; Fishlow, 1990).

THE STATE AND THE PROMOTION OF ECONOMIC OPENNESS

The analytical foundation of the *Report* is the total factor productivity approach to economic growth. It is suggested that inter-country and inter-temporal variations in growth rates are caused by variations in total factor productivity of capital and labour. Changes in the latter variable are thought to be determined mainly by government economic policy – the degree of openness of an economy, the extent of competition in the product and factor markets, and investment in physical and human capital (education), particularly the latter. The underlying chain of causation is that competition and education promote technical progress and therefore total factor productivity, and hence economic growth. Free mobility of people, capital, and technology and free entry and exit of firms are regarded as being particularly conducive to the spread of knowledge and technical change.

The role of 'openness' and international competition, as well as domestic competition, as critical determinants of productivity growth are repeatedly stressed throughout the *Report* (see Chapters 1, 2, 4, 5 and 8). In relation to domestic competition, the *Report* notes:

...systems of industrial licensing, restrictions on entry and exit, inappropriate legal codes concerning bankruptcy and employment, inadequate property rights, and price controls – all of which weaken the forces of competition – have held back technological change and the growth of productivity (p. 7).

In the analysis which follows I shall concentrate mainly on the *Report's* arguments with respect to the role of competition. Questions of external competition, 'openness' and the 'integration of countries with the global economy' will be examined in the rest of this section, and those relating to domestic competition in the product, labour and financial markets in the next.

The *Report's* assertions with respect to the role of openness, external competition and closer integration with the world economy in promoting economic growth do not stand up to serious examination either at a theoretical level or empirically, particularly in terms of the experience of the East Asian countries it holds up as models of successful development. In the discussion below, I shall first comment on the empirical evidence presented by the *Report* itself to support its contention of an important positive relationship between these variables. Next, I shall provide information bearing on these issues for the East Asian economies. It was suggested earlier that these countries had sought a 'strategic' but not a 'close' integration with the global economy – that is, they integrated up to the point where it was useful for them to do so for promoting national economic growth. I shall put forward an alternative theoretical paradigm with respect to the relationship between openness, international economic integration and economic growth. This will help to provide an analytical rationale for the 'strategic integration' path pursued by Japan, South Korea and Taiwan.

The *Report's* own empirical analysis of the relationship between trade openness, 'distortions' from international prices and productivity growth is presented in Chapter 5. This evidence (see Figure 5.3 on p. 100 and Table Note 5.3 in the technical Appendix, p. 163), even in its own terms is extremely weak. Notwithstanding countless permutations of the indicators used to denote distortions and openness, only 12 of the 37 regression coefficients reported in Table Note 5.3 are statistically significant at the 5 per cent level. The R^2s range from between 0.03 and 0.3. The interpretation of the econometric results on p. 164 is less than exemplary: it is implied, for instance, that it makes no difference to the verification of the economic hypotheses under discussion whether one considers 'levels' of or 'changes' in the values of some of the independent variables. The tentative character of this empirical evidence is acknowledged in the text of Chapter 5 of the *Report*, but despite

Table 3.2   Import penetration in manufactures in advanced industrial countries, 1961–78 (ratio of manufactured imports to GNP)

	1961	1965	1969	1973	1978
USA	1.5	2.1	3.4	4.0	4.5
UK	4.6	6.7	8.0	11.7	14.2
Rest of EC	6.1	7.6	10.1	13.0	15.8
Japan	1.8	1.5	2.2	3.0	2.4

Source: CEPG (1979).

this far-reaching and firm policy conclusions are drawn from it in the *Report's* overview chapter.[2]

With respect to the nature and extent of 'openness' practised by the East Asian economies, I provide here some relevant data on Japan. Table 3.2 gives comparative figures on imports of manufactures into Japan and other industrial countries between 1961 and 1978. During this period, as a proportion of GDP, Japanese imports rose by 66 per cent. This compares with a three-fold increase in the corresponding US imports, a more than tripling of the UK imports, and a nearly 250 per cent growth in the imports of other European Community countries. In 1978, manufactured imports constituted only 2.4 per cent of the Japanese GDP; the corresponding proportion in Britain and the other countries of the EC was five to six times larger. Even in the United States which, because of its continental size, traditionally has a relatively closed economy, the volume of imported manufacturing goods in the late 1970s was proportionally almost twice as large as in Japan. Clearly, during the 1960s and 1970s (and even more so in the 1950s), the Japanese economy operated under a regime of Draconian import controls, whether practised formally or informally.

With respect to the questions of overvalued exchange rates and distortions, the Japanese government maintained exchange controls and kept a steady nominal exchange rate with respect to the US dollar over almost the whole of the period of that country's most rapid growth (1950–73). Purchasing power parity calculations by Sachs (1987), using Japanese and US price indices, show a 60 per cent real appreciation of the exchange rate between 1950 and 1970. As for close integration with the international capital markets and foreign direct investment, Sachs notes that domestic capital markets were highly regulated and completely shut off from the world capital markets for most of this period. Only the government and its agencies were able to borrow from and lend abroad. Foreign direct investment was strictly controlled.

Foreign firms were prohibited, either by legal or by administrative means, from acquiring a majority ownership in Japanese corporations.

To appreciate how the Japanese policy of protection worked at a microeconomic level, consider the specific case of the celebrated Japanese car industry. Magaziner and Hout (1980) point out that, 'government intervention in this industry was characterized by three major goals: discouragement of foreign capital in the Japanese industry and protection against car imports, attempts to bring about rationalization of production, and assistance with overseas marketing and distribution expenditure.' They point out that the government imposed comprehensive import controls and adopted a variety of measures to discourage foreign investment in the car industry. Quotas and tariffs were used to protect the industry; the former were applied throughout the mid-1960s, and prohibitively high tariffs until the mid-1970s. Moreover, 'the government controlled all foreign licensing agreements. To make technology agreements more attractive to the licensor, it guaranteed the remittance of royalties from Japan. The policy stipulated, however, that continued remittances would be guaranteed only if 90 per cent of the licensed parts were produced in Japan within five years – about as powerful a domestic content arrangement as you can get.

The *Report* acknowledges that the Japanese protected their industry (as did Taiwan and South Korea), but it is silent on the question of restrictions on foreign direct investment and government controls over foreign capital inflows for industrial development. Even with respect to protection, the *Report* does not tell you how large and pervasive its use in effect was in a country such as Japan. Moreover, the *Report* is embarrassed by the East Asian protection; its overall tone is to suggest that it is a miracle that these economies did as well as they did despite the protection.

There is little recognition of the fact that protection has played an extremely important, positive role in promoting technical change, productivity growth and exports in a country such as Japan. Protection provided the Japanese companies with a captive home market, leading to high profits which enabled the firms to undertake higher rates of investment, to learn by doing and to improve the quality of their products. These profits in the protected internal market, which were further enhanced by restrictions on domestic competition (see the final section), not only made possible higher rates of investment but also greatly aided exports. Yamamura (1988) explains the mechanism involved:

> Because increased output meant reduced cost per unit it translated into increased profits on the product sold at high fixed prices in the domestic market, even if the increased output had to be exported at no profit or even at a loss. ...Manufacturers enjoyed a margin of error when making ... major investment decisions. Essen-

tially, even in the face of the high probability that the increase in output would have to be sold unprofitably on the international market the expansion was still worth the risk. The stronger the 'home market cushion' – or the more effective the cartels and protection on the domestic arena – the smaller the risk and the more likely the Japanese competitor was to increase capacity boldly in anticipation of demand growth. This can give the firm a strategic as well as a cost advantage over a foreign competitor operating in a different environment who must be more cautious (p. 177).

The *Report* echoes the view of some neoclassical analysts who suggest that, although the governments in East Asian countries imposed protection, they were careful to 'offset the bias against exports that is usually a feature of trade protection'. This suggests that the governments maintained a rough neutrality of incentives between selling in the home and the foreign markets, that is, despite intervention, there were 'level playing-fields' between different sectors of the economy and between internal and external markets.[3] However, as Scott (1991) rightly points out, this is simply an incorrect characterization of the commercial and industrial policies pursued in the East Asian economies. Scott notes that the level playing-fields between selling in the national and international markets prevailed in the US and UK economies, which have, however, been relatively unsuccessful in world competition. Countries such as Japan and South Korea, on the other hand, particularly during their periods of rapid growth, had a positive bias in favour of exports through the wide panoply of industrial policy instruments discussed above, including notably the use of performance criteria on exports and market share. The Japanese and South Korean corporations could only receive favoured government treatment in terms of loans, foreign exchange allocations and so on if they met such criteria. Thus, despite often low short-run financial returns on exports, they were obliged to fulfil their export targets.

To sum up, the experience of Japan contradicts comprehensively the *Report's* central thesis that the more open the economy, the closer its integration with the global economy, and the faster its rate of growth. Although, for reasons of space, the cases of other East Asian countries (Taiwan and South Korea) have not been considered above, their stories, subject to certain modifications, point in the same direction.[4] If, as stated, the *Report's* central purpose was to find out why countries such as Japan have been so successful in economic development during the last 40 years, it has clearly been using the wrong paradigm for examining Japanese economic history. The basic problem is that the underlying assumptions of this paradigm are greatly at variance with the real world of static and dynamic economies of scale, learning by doing and imperfect competition. In such a world, even neoclassical analysis now accepts that the optimal degree of openness for an economy is not 'close' integration with the global economy through free trade.[5] In that case, what is the optimal degree of openness for the economy? This extremely important policy question is, however, not seriously addressed by orthodox theory.

Chakravarty and Singh (1988) provide an alternative theoretical paradigm for considering this issue. Very briefly, they argue that 'openness' is a multidimensional concept; apart from trade, a country can be 'open' or not so open with respect to financial and capital markets, in relation to technology, science, culture, education, inward and outward migration. Moreover, a country can choose to be open in some directions (say, trade) but not so open in others, such as foreign direct investment or financial markets. Chakravarty and Singh's analysis suggests that there is no unique optimum form or degree of openness which holds true for all countries at all times. A number of factors affect the desirable nature of openness: the world configuration, the timing, the sequence, the past history of the economy, its state of development. They point out that there may be serious irreversible losses if the wrong kind of openness is attempted or the timing and sequence are incorrect. The East Asian experience of 'strategic' rather than 'close' integration with the world economy makes perfect sense within this kind of theoretical framework.

THE GOVERNMENT AND COMPETITION IN THE DOMESTIC MARKETS

Contrary to the *Report's* homilies about the virtues of 'free mobility of capital and labour' and 'free entry and exit of firms' and the importance of competition in the domestic markets, the practice of the successful East Asian countries has been rather different. As in relation to the question of integration with the world economy, these countries appear to have taken the view that from the dynamic perspective of promoting investment and technical change, the optimal degree of competition is not perfect or maximum competition. The governments in these countries have therefore managed or guided competition in a purposeful manner: it has been encouraged, but notably also restricted, in a number of ways.

In Japan, although after World War II the *Zaibatsu* were disbanded and anti-trust laws of the US type were enacted under the tutelage of the occupation authorities, these pro-competition measures were greatly diluted over time. The government permitted or encouraged a variety of cartel arrangements in a wide range of industries – export and import cartels, cartels to combat depression or excessive competition, rationalization cartels, and so on. Table 3.3 provides information on cartels which were exempted between 1964 and 1973 from Japan's anti-monopoly laws. According to Caves and

Table 3.3 Japanese cartel agreements exempted from anti-monopoly law by the Fair Trade Commission or competent ministry, by exempting statute, 1964–73[a]

Statutory basis for exemption	1964	1965	1966	1967	1968	1969	1970	1971	1972	1973
Depression cartels	2	2	16	1	0	0	0	0	9	2
Rationalization cartels	14	14	14	13	13	12	10	13	10	10
Export cartels	201	208	211	206	213	217	214	192	175	180
Import cartels	1	2	3	4	3	4	4	3	2	2
Cartels under Medium and Small Enterprises Organization Act	588	587	652	634	582	522	469	439	604	607
Cartels under Environment Sanitation Act	106	122	123	123	123	123	123	123	123	123
Cartels under Coastal Shipping Association Act	15	14	16	15	22	22	22	21	19	19
Cartels under other statutes	43	50	44	44	47	48	56	53	34	42
Total	970	999	1 079	1 040	1 003	948	898	844	976	985

[a] Number in force in March of each year.

Source: Japanese Fair Trade Commission, Staff Office, *The Antimonopoly Act of Japan* (1973), p. 27. Reproduced from Caves & Uekusa (1976), p. 158.

53

Uekusa (1976), cartels accounted for 78.1 per cent of the value of shipments in textiles; 64.8 per cent in clothing; 50.0 per cent in non-ferrous metals; 47 per cent in printing and publishing; 41.2 per cent in stone, clay and glass; 34.5 per cent in steel products, and 37.2 per cent in food products. Caves and Uekusa note that although these cartels varied in their effectiveness, 'their mere presence in such broad stretches of the manufacturing sector attests to their importance' (p. 147).

More importantly, the Japanese government has regarded the anti-trust laws as a part and parcel of its overall industrial strategy. As Magaziner and Hout (1980) point out, in young industries, during the developmental phase, the government discouraged competition. When these industries became technologically mature, competition was allowed to flourish. Later, when industries were in competitive decline, the government again discouraged competition and attempted to bring about an orderly rationalization of the industry. Magaziner and Hout observed that 'MITI's greatest strength appears to be its understanding of the competitive stages through which an industry moves and its ability to fashion appropriate policy' (p. 38).

Students of the Japanese economy provide many examples of the above pattern from a number of different industries. In steel, for example, Scott (1991) observes that during the expansion phase of the industry individual companies were not allowed to build new plants except on a world-class scale. This meant:

> spacing out investments to build large-scale plants without at the same time generating an excess capacity. Japanese firms were required to wait their turn to build a new plant while a competitor built new capacity and achieved high volumes. Next time the roles will be reversed. This kind of coordination was carried out under the aegis of the government – by MITI. Later the system required the scrapping of old capacity as a condition for permission to build new. As a result Japan with a smaller home market than the US built ten plants larger than any in the US.

Yamamura (1988) provides a useful model of Japanese industrial policy and the role of competition within it. The government essentially organized an 'investment race' among large oligopolistic firms in which exports and world market share were significant performance goals. As in the real world, markets are always incomplete, and such a race without a co-ordinator will lead to ruinous competition, price wars and excess capacity, inhibiting the inducement to invest. In the Japanese economic miracle, MITI provided this crucial co-ordinating role and orchestrated the dynamic combination of collusion and competition which characterizes Japanese industrial policy. 'In a nutshell,' Yamamura (1988) observes:

what MITI did was to 'guide' the firms to invest in such a way that each large firm in a market expanded its productive capacity roughly in proportion to its current market share – no firm was to make an investment so large that it would destabilize the market. The policy was effective in encouraging competition for the market share (thus preserving the essential competitiveness of the industrial markets) while reducing the risk of losses due to excessive investment. Thus it promoted the aggressive expansion of capacity necessary to increase productive efficiency in output (p. 175).

Again for reasons of space, I briefly note here that South Korea also did not follow a policy of maximum domestic competition or unfettered market-determined entry and exit of firms. The South Korean government, if anything, went one step further than the Japanese in actively helping to create large conglomerates, promoting mergers, and exit of firms (see Table 3.1). It also helped to organize the 'investment race' among the Korean giant conglomerates along Japanese lines. It is sometimes argued that competitive market forces have played a greater role in Taiwan's domestic economy, but I note that both Taiwan and South Korea possess some of the most highly concentrated industrial structures among market economy countries (see Table 3.4).

Turning to the factor markets, in Japan both the domestic labour and capital markets have operated rather differently from those envisaged in the *Report's* recipes for faster economic growth and successful development. Although in South Korea and Taiwan the labour market may have worked with 'minimum labour laws', as the *Report* approvingly notes (p. 80), the situation in Japan has been quite different. A large proportion of the labour force has effectively a lifetime security of employment. Many leading scholars of the Japanese economy ascribe the international competitive success and technical leadership of the Japanese corporations precisely to these 'rigidities' in the labour market. Security of employment encourages workers to undertake firm-specific investments in human capital, to promote technical change rather than to thwart it (for fear of being made redundant). Not least, it also lets workers identify their interests with those of the corporation (see, further, Dore, 1986; Aoki, 1990, among others).

Similarly, in relation to the capital market, a growing number of scholars in the US and the UK today believe that the Japanese economic success is also in part due to the fact that the Japanese industrial corporations have been spared, unlike their Anglo-Saxon counterparts, the tender mercies of a stock market and a freely functioning market for corporate control. There are powerful analytical and empirical reasons for believing that stock market-based competitive financial systems are not conducive to promoting industrial investment, technical progress and productivity growth.[6] In none of the

Table 3.4   Per cent distribution of manufacturing value-added[a] by firm size, selected countries, 1973

Country	Number of Workers			
	1–9	10–99	100–499	500 or more
Korea	5.8	13.8	27.7	52.7
Taiwan[b]	4.4	16.7	22.5	56.4
Hong Kong	7.4	30.2	32.1	30.2
Brazil	3.4	23.7	36.1	36.6
Turkey[c]	11.7	10.1	27.5	48.4
Peru	4.0	23.9	46.4	25.7
Japan[d]	8.7	28.4	24.9	37.9
Canada[d]	2.0	21.1	37.4	39.3
Czechoslovakia	0.2	5.4	18.2	76.11
Austria	0.8	21.5	36.2	41.5
United Kingdom	15.7[e]		24.4	60.0
United States[d]	2.4	18.3	30.5	48.7

[a]   Generally, value added in producers' values
[b]   Value added in factor values, 1971.
[c]   1970
[d]   Net value added in factor values
[e]   1–99

Source: All countries except Taiwan: United Nations (1979). Taiwan: Executive Yuan, *The Report of Industrial and Commercial Census of Taiwan and Fukien, District of the Republic of China, 1971*, quoted in S. Ho (1980). Reproduced from Amsden (1989).

exemplar East Asian countries did a competitive capital market play a significant role in financing industrial growth. South Korea had a government-controlled banking system until the early 1980s; Taiwan's leading banks continue to be under state ownership even today. The Japanese financial system during the period of the economic miracle (1950–73), although not under state ownership, was bank-based, oligopolistic and subject to considerable state direction.

Finally, I turn to the *Report's* argument that (government) 'intervention in the market in East Asian economies was, in an overall sense, more moderate than in most other developing economies' (p. 39). How does one quantify the extent of government intervention – for example the crucial coordinating role of MITI in Japanese industrial investment outlined above? Such government support for the industry is much more significant than cash expenditure or subsidies. Moreover, as Magaziner and Hout (1980) note: 'The process of discussion and debate between MITI and the companies in response to developments in the marketplace creates a dynamic decision making process. MITI aptly refers to Japan as a "plan-oriented market economy"' (p. 39).

CONCLUSION AND POLICY IMPLICATIONS

This chapter has argued that the principal lesson to be drawn from the experiences of Japan, South Korea and Taiwan – countries which the *World Development Report* holds up as models of successful development – is not that they had some neutral, passive state with a 'market-friendly approach to development'. Nor is it that these nations sought or practised a deep integration with the world economy during their periods of rapid growth. Rather, the state in these economies played a vigorous role and followed a highly active industrial policy. The government did not supplant the market altogether, as the 'command' planning of production of the Soviet type did; nor did it simply follow the market. Instead, in line with MITI's description of Japan as a 'plan-oriented market economy', the government guided the market towards planned structural change. Moreover, the three East Asian countries integrated with the world economy in the directions and extent to which it was useful for them to do so.

It has been emphasized here that in a world of imperfect competition, economies of scale and learning by doing, there are sound analytical grounds for following such policies to promote technical change and economic growth. In such a world, the optimal degree of openness or the optimal degree of domestic competition for an economy is not maximum openness or perfect competition. The *Report* seems to have been led into a misinterpretation of the East Asian experience because it is wedded to a theoretical paradigm whose assumptions do not correspond to the real world of manufacturing. Its analysis and the lessons it purports to draw from the last 40 years of development experience are not therefore helpful to developing countries.[7]

From a policy perspective, the foregoing analysis raises the following central question: can the East Asian experience be replicated by other countries? This question of course deserves a paper in its own right, but very briefly, for the sake of completeness, the short answer is: not in all respects but in many important ways; not everywhere but in important semi-industrial countries such as China, India, Mexico and Brazil. Let us consider specifically the case of India, where many intellectuals believe that the state lacks 'autonomy' to implement a Japanese-style industrial policy. Today, the Indian government is indeed very weak, but this is not a static situation. There have been periods of greater autonomy – for example, the Nehru era in the 1950s, when there was a national consensus on certain developmental goals.

To give some examples, I believe the following kinds of lessons could have been learned and implemented in India during various phases of strong government in the last 40 years. Once implemented and successful, they could have generated positive feedback dynamics of their own, leading to further autonomy for the state:

1.   *The need to complement import substitution with export promotion.* This would have permitted the country to achieve current account balance on a higher growth trajectory.
2.   *The ruling élite's attitude towards technology imports and technological development.* The country was prone to invent its own wheel – this is not to deny that such a policy had some positive benefits in terms of the development of technological 'know-why' as opposed to just 'know-how', but clearly the process was very wasteful. India should have been humbler and borrowed technologies, as Japan and other late-industrializers were doing.

These were intellectual failures of the ruling élite to appreciate correctly the world around it, rather than problems which arose from the lack of autonomy of the state. Of course, India could plead extenuating circumstances for these failings in terms of its colonial history, and so on, but that does not alter the fact of these failures. Similarly, it may be that the Indian state did not have the autonomy to orchestrate oligopolistic investment races or to set export targets in the East Asian manner – even that is not certain – but it definitely could have learned other useful lessons from MITI, particularly the latter's role in continuously building a social consensus around the required developmental policies as world circumstances changed. In other words, the essential point is not that a subset of MITI-type sensible policies could not have been implemented because of lack of autonomy of the state, but rather that they were not implemented.

NOTES

1.   This chapter draws on material from my longer paper, Singh (1993a). The latter also examines the *Report's* theses in other areas.
2.   In relation to other empirical studies on this subject, the *Report* states in the text on p. 98: '*Most of the studies* which have analysed GDP growth and openness to trade have found a positive relation (Box 5.3)' (emphasis added). However, when one turns to Box 5.3 the conclusion is much more tentative. We are told: 'The *majority of the evidence* now available shows a positive relation between openness – however measured – and growth' (p. 99, emphasis added). For the record, I note here that other recent surveys of the empirical evidence on this issue by independent scholars (see Pack, 1988; Rodrik, 1991) are even more sceptical about a positive relationship between openness and economic growth.

3. Some neoclassical economists take this argument even further and suggest that government intervention in the East Asian economies did no more than what the market would have done anyway, that is, the government policy was simply simulating the market. There are serious analytical and empirical flaws in this market simulation thesis (see Wade, 1990).
4. For a detailed analysis, see Wade (1990) and Amsden (1989a).
5. See, for example, Krugman (1987) and Rodrik (1992).
6. There is a large literature on the subject. For the UK, see Cosh, Hughes and Singh (1990) and Singh (1992b). For the US, see, for example, MIT Commission on Industrial Productivity (see Dertouzos *et al.*, 1989). See also Singh (1993d). For a discussion of stock markets and economic efficiency in developing countries, see Singh (1993c).
7. For an analysis of other issues raised in the *Report*, and particularly for a critical examination of the *Report*'s discussion of the experience of the unsuccessful Latin American economies during the last decade, see the fuller version of this chapter, Singh (1993a). See also Singh (1993b).

BIBLIOGRAPHY

Amsden, A. (1985), 'The State and Taiwan's Economic Development', in P. Evans, D. Rueschemeyer and T. Skocpol (eds), *Bringing the State Back In*, Cambridge: Cambridge University Press.

Amsden, A. (1989a), *Asia's Next Giant*, New York: Oxford University Press.

Amsden, A. (1989b), 'Big Business and Urbanisation in Taiwan: The Origins of Small and Medium Size Enterprise and Regionally Decentralised Industry', mimeo, Massachusetts Institute of Technology. Cambridge, Massachusetts.

Aoki, M. (1990), 'Toward an Economic Model of the Japanese Firm', *Journal of Economic Literature*, 28(1), March, 1–27.

Bhagwati, J. (1988), *Protectionism*, Cambridge, Massachusetts: The MIT Press.

Boltho, A. (1975), *Japan: An Economic Survey*, London: Oxford University Press.

Caves, R. and Uekusa, M. (1976), *Industrial Organisation in Japan*, Washington, D.C.: The Brookings Institution.

CEPG (Cambridge Economic Policy Group) (1979), *Economic Policy Review*, no. 5.

Chakravarty, S. and Singh, A. (1988), 'The Desirable Forms of Economic Openness in the South', Helsinki, WIDER, mimeo

Chang, H.-J. (1992), *The Political Economy of Industrial Policy – Reflections on the Role of State Intervention*, Unpublished PhD Dissertation, Faculty of Economics and Politics, University of Cambridge.

Chang, H.-J. and Singh, A. (1993), 'Public Enterprises in Developing Countries and Economic Efficiency', *UNCTAD Review*, No. 4, 45–82.

Cosh, A., Hughes, A. and Singh, A. (1990), *Takeovers and Short-termism in the UK*, Industrial Policy Paper no. 3, London: Institute for Public Policy Research.

Dertouzos, M., Lester, R. and Solow, R. (eds) (1989), *Made in America*, Cambridge, Massachusetts: The MIT Press.

Dore, R. (1985), 'Financial Structures and the Long Term View', *Policy Studies*, July, 10–29.

Dore, R. (1986), *Flexible Rigidities: Industrial Policy and Structural Adjustment in the Japanese Economy 1970–80*, London: The Athlone Press.

Fishlow, A. (1990), 'The Latin American State', *Journal of Economic Perspectives*, 4(3), Summer, 61–74.

Glyn, A., Hughes, A., Lipietz, A. and Singh, A. (1990), 'The Rise and Fall of the

Golden Age', in S. Marglin and J. Schor (eds), *The Golden Age of Capitalism*, Oxford: Clarendon Press.

Helpman, E. and Krugman, P. (1989), *Trade Policy and Market Structure*, Cambridge, Massachusetts: The MIT Press.

Johnson, C. (1987), 'Political Institutions and Economic Performance: The Government–Business Relationship in Japan, South Korea, and Taiwan', in F. Deyo (ed.), *The Political Economy of New Asian Industrialism*, Ithaca: Cornell University Press.

Krugman, P. (1987), 'Is Free Trade Passé?', *Journal of Economic Perspectives*, 1(2), Fall, 131–43.

Lal, D. (1983), *The Poverty of Development Economics*, London: The Institute of Economic Affairs.

Lockwood, W. (1965), 'Japan's "New Capitalism"', in W. Lockwood (ed.), *The State and Economic Enterprise in Japan*, Princeton: Princeton University Press.

Magaziner, I. and Hout, T. (1980), *Japanese Industrial Policy*, London: Policy Studies Institute.

Nino, K. (1972), 'On Efficiency and Equity Problems in the Industrial Policy – with Special Relation to the Japanese Experience', *Kobe University Economic Review*, no. 19, 1–80.

OECD (1972), *The Industrial Policy of Japan*, Paris: OECD.

Pack, H. (1988), 'Industrialisation and Trade', in H. Chenery and T.N. Srinivasan (eds), *The Handbook of Development Economics*, Vol. 1, Amsterdam: North-Holland.

Rodrik, D. (1991), 'Closing the Productivity Gap: Does Trade Liberalisation Really Help?', in G. Helleiner (ed.), *Trade Policy, Liberalisation, and Development: New Perspectives*, Oxford: Clarendon Press.

Rodrik, D. (1992), 'The Limits of Trade Policy Reform in Developing Countries', *Journal of Economic Perspectives*, 6(1), Winter, 87–106.

Sachs, J. (1987), 'Trade and Exchange Rate Policies in Growth Oriented Adjustment Programme', in V. Corbo, M. Goldstein and M. Khan (eds), *Growth Oriented Adjustment Programme*, Washington, D.C.: The World Bank.

Scott, B. (1991), 'Economic Strategy and Economic Policy', a paper presented at the World Bank, 21 November 1991.

Short, R. (1984), 'The Role of Public Enterprises: An International Statistical Comparison', in R. Floyd, C. Gary and R. Short (eds.), *Public Enterprises in Mixed Economies: Some Macroeconomic Aspects*, Washington, D.C.: International Monetary Fund.

Singh, A. (1979), 'North Sea Oil and the Reconstruction of UK Industry', in F. Blackaby (ed.), *De-Industrialisation*, London: Heinemann Educational Books.

Singh, A. (1984), 'The Interrupted Industrial Revolution of the Third World: Prospects and Policies for Resumption', in *Industry and Development*, June, 43–68.

Singh, A. (1989), 'The Third World Competition and De-Industrialisation in Advanced Countries', *Cambridge Journal of Economics*, 13(1), 103–20.

Singh, A. (1990), 'Southern Competition, Labour Standards, and Industrial Development in the North and the South', in S. Herzenberg and J. Perez-Lopez (eds.), *Labour Standards and Development in the Global Economy*, Washington, D.C.: US Department of Labour, Bureau of International Labour Affairs.

Singh, A. (1992a), 'The Actual Crisis of Economic Development in the 1980s: An Alternative Policy Perspective for the Future', in A. Dutt and K. Jameson (eds.), *New Directions in Development Economics*, Aldershot: Edward Elgar.

Singh, A. (1992b), 'Corporate Takeovers', in J. Eatwell, M. Milgate and P. Newman (eds.), *The New Palgrave Dictionary of Money and Finance*, London: Macmillan, 480–86.

Singh, A. (1993a), '"Close" vs "Strategic" Integration with the World Economy and the "Market-Friendly Approach to Development" vs an "Industrial Policy": A Critique of the World Development Report 1991 and Alternative Policy Perspective', paper presented at the joint United Nations–World Bank Symposium on Economic Reform in the Developing Countries: Issues for the 1990s. University of Duisburg, INEP Report Heft 4/1993. A revised version of this paper will also be published in the Proceedings of the Symposium.

Singh, A. (1993b), 'Asian Economic Success and Latin American Failure in the 1980s: New Analyses and Future Policy Implications', *International Review of Applied Economics*, 7(3), 267–89.

Singh, A. (1993c), 'The Stock-Market and Economic Development: Should Developing Countries Encourage Stock-Markets?', *UNCTAD REVIEW*, No. 4, 1–28.

Singh, A. (1993d), 'The Anglo-Saxon Financial System, The Market for Corporate Control and International Competitiveness', paper presented at the Notre Dame Conference on US International Competitiveness, March.

Wade, R. (1990), *Governing the Market*, Princeton, New Jersey: Princeton University Press.

World Bank (1991), *World Development Report, 1991. The Challenge of Development*, Washington, D.C.: The World Bank.

Yamamura, K. (1988), 'Caveat Emptor: The Industrial Policy of Japan', in P. Krugman (ed.), *Strategic Trade Policy and the New International Economics*, Cambridge, Massachusetts: The MIT Press.

4. Public Enterprises, Private Enterprises and the State: Prospects under Post Socialism

Lance Taylor

INTRODUCTION

To a great extent, economic performance in post-socialist nations will be driven by interactions between the state and the private sector. Standard theory gives some insight into sectoral prospects, but ultimately is beyond its depth when dealing with profound institutional change. This chapter draws lessons from structuralist and mainstream models about likely interactions between state-owned and privately-owned enterprises (SOEs and POEs, respectively), and suggests how broader considerations will finally determine the nature of post-socialist economic growth.[1]

THEORIES OF ENTERPRISE

Defining a 'firm' and describing how it intersects with the rest of the economy are not easy tasks, as debate over decades among both neoclassical and institutional economists attests. Recent neoclassical models follow Coase (1937) as refined by Williamson (1985) in emphasizing trade-offs between difficulties of arranging transactions in the market and the inefficiencies of undertaking them within the firm, with different forms of enterprise emerging via the minimization of transactions costs. In a related literature initiated by Jensen and Meckling (1976), how firms function depends on the limits of information available to and the types of transaction between their potential owners ('principals') and managers/workers ('agents'). As will be seen presently, SOE–POE interactions are often modelled in these terms.

In the first instance, the distinction between SOEs and POEs rests on who controls (the larger part of) their financial liabilities – the state or the private sector. Under socialism, of course, almost all enterprises in the industrial sector were in the hands of organs of the state. With exceptions such as three-quarters of the farmland in Poland, the government controlled most productive capacity in the service and agricultural sectors as well.

In the mainstream view, their differences in ownership lead SOEs and POEs to *behave* differently. Public firms are consistently accused of being less efficient than their counterparts in the private sector, for a variety of reasons. An initial attack on planning, and by implication SOEs, was launched from Vienna in the 1920s by von Mises (1935), reflecting the anti-socialist tradition of Austrian economics. Von Mises argued that a complete set of market exchanges is required to generate prices which will underwrite the efficient allocation of resources. If planners interfere with even a few fundamental price linkages (in particular the profitability calculus underlying investment decisions), their bungling can badly upset the production process.[2]

Complete 'market freedom' was inflated into a prior condition for 'political freedom' by von Hayek (1944), another member of the Austrian school (Milton Friedman is his best-known intellectual disciple). Von Hayek's *Road to Serfdom* would be paved by public interventions in the private market – once bureaucrats begin to usurp citizens' rights to act in a completely unregulated economy, they will soon move against other forms of liberty as well. One key rationale for the global shock reform programmes initiated in Eastern Europe in the early 1990s follows directly from von Mises and von Hayek. Unless *all* the preconditions for *laissez-faire* are created at one shot, Kornai's (1990) *Road to a Free Economy* can never open up. Unfortunately for this theory, the experience of post-socialist economies during 1990–93 suggests that global shocks put the road blocks more firmly into place.[3]

At a less hysterical level of discourse, recent authors conflate SOEs' 'wrong prices' and consequent resource misallocation with a principal/agent problem (Chang and Singh, 1993). SOE managers typically report to politicians, who in turn report to 'the public'. In a market system, this two-tier delegation of authority is replaced by an ownership link between principals and agents (or shareholders and managers), which is supposed to pressure the latter to behave efficiently.

Under socialism, Kornai (1981) pointed to a specific capital market manifestation of this problem. Because they have 'soft' budget constraints underwritten by the state, SOEs can (or under the administrative system could) be gleefully unconcerned about wasting resources. Because it really didn't have the public's interest in mind and wanted to build up its own comfort, the *nomenklatura*/Party apparatus encouraged this inefficiency to persist.

A key question addressed here is to what extent the foregoing arguments about the potential inefficiency of SOEs make practical sense. The answer will not be clear-cut. In terms of Hirschman's (1970) famous distinction, a principal's threat to 'exit' from owning an inefficient POE may not be more effective than a politician's or bureaucrat's 'voice' in threatening SOE managers with dire retribution unless they shape up. Along Weberian lines, much depends on how owners and bureaucrats, managers and workers, fit into the overall socio-economic system.

INTERACTIONS BETWEEN STATE-OWNED AND PRIVATE FIRMS

In traditional economists' fashion, we can begin to explore these patterns by asking how the two forms of enterprise influence each others' demands and supplies over time. Not too many people have been concerned with the directly practical question of how SOEs and POEs fit into the process of economic growth. Among structuralists, for example, Kaldor (1957) and Pasinetti (1962) concentrated on distributional strife between workers and capitalists owning liabilities (bonds) of the *same* productive firms. They did not ask how outputs and profit levels of different kinds of producer get determined. Gibson and Dutt (1993) do raise this question, but under socialist as opposed to post-socialist institutional conditions.

On the neoclassical side, Aghion and Blanchard (1993) take up the potential sustainability of post-socialist growth, emphasizing two deficiencies of post-socialist SOEs. First, they are alleged to pay excessively high wages and/or have relatively high unit labour costs.[4] Secondly, they may well run losses *à la* soft budget constraint and require subsidization from the fiscal deficit or state-controlled banks (enforced bank loans to loss-making state enterprises are 'quasi-fiscal' deficits in the jargon). Figure 4.1 illustrates the implications of these assumptions for how private and state enterprises affect one another in the short run.

In the north-east of the four-quadrant diagram, the line labelled D_s shows that higher POE activity (X_p) stimulates output of state enterprises (X_p), by income generation (which adds to consumer demand) and by intermediate purchases – both are familiar channels. A steep D_s implies that these demand linkages are weak, that is, POEs have marginal effects on the state sector, which still accounts for most of GDP (see the data in Table 4.1).

For reasons stemming from the supply side, the line D_p for the effect of X_s on private sector activity slopes downwards. The ruling hypotheses are that: (1) a lower X_s creates unemployment by forcing SOEs to lay off their high wage labour and thereby reduces the wage level overall; so that (2) POEs are stimulated to raise their output, X_p, by lower labour costs.

POE activity will also be affected by the overall level of demand, determined in other quadrants of the diagram. In the south-east, the public sector borrowing requirement (PSBR) goes up with X_s: greater activity on the part of loss-making state enterprises forces their subsidy inflows to rise. In the

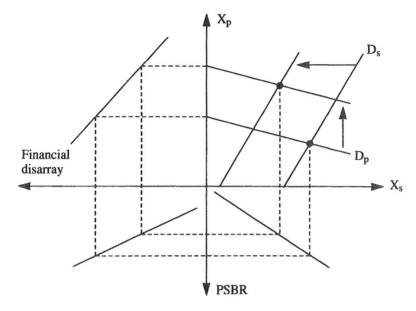

Figure 4.1   The orthodox view of SOE/POE interaction in the short run

south-west, this fiscal (or quasi-fiscal) problem is reflected in more 'financial disarray', that is inflation may speed up, interest rates rise and contractionary policy be pursued due to the bigger PSBR. In the north-west quadrant, these responses to adversity cut demand for POE products, and the intercept of the D_p locus slides down.[5]

Now we can ask what happens as SOEs are shut down by state actions such as winding-up subsidies, forced restructuring, and so on. The line describing their activity level, D_s, shifts to the left by *force majeure*. Via a softer labour market and lower wages, POE output is crowded-in directly along the downward-sloping line, D_p. At the same time, the intercept of D_p shifts upwards due to a lower PSBR and reduced financial disarray. Both linkages imply that getting rid of public enterprises is a sensible policy to pursue.

This scenario seems superficially plausible, but reveals problems on closer inspection. First, SOEs on the whole pay taxes. Indeed, increasing fiscal deficits in post-socialist economies in 1991–92 were in large measure due to reduced receipts from SOEs as they *began* to run losses in stagnant macro-economic environments.

Secondly, the supply-side cheap labour story presented above can easily be offset by demand factors, in part because supply responses to lower wages are likely to be negligible, for reasons elaborated in AKT. On the demand side, many POEs sell intermediate goods to state enterprises – higher output for the latter means more revenue for the former. Also, consumer expenditures from SOE-generated incomes may, at the margin, flow strongly towards private firms, especially in the previously under-supplied service sectors in which they thrive.

Figure 4.2 illustrates the implications of a dominant demand linkage. Now D_p slopes upwards as a higher X_s raises X_p via stimulating increased sales (the standard assumption, at least in most models). In the south-east quadrant the PSBR declines due to higher tax revenues when X_s goes up. Cutting back on SOEs and shifting the D_s schedule to the left means that POE activity is crowded out, as the economy veers towards stagnation. In the world of Figure 4.2, shutting down SOEs on a large scale is not good medicine for the private sector, even if the state firms are inefficient in comparative terms.

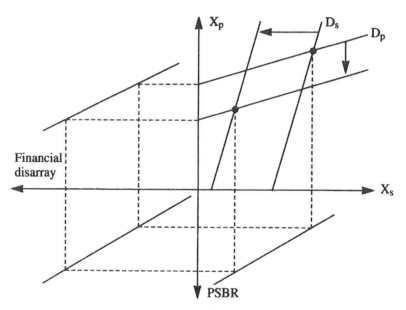

Figure 4.2   A more realistic view of SOE/POE interaction

Unsurprisingly, these cautions carry over to the medium and long runs. The key questions are how capital formation and technological change respond to changes in short-run activity levels. Along the lines of growth models developed in Taylor (1991), Figure 4.3 shows how shutting down SOEs may influence resource allocation and the steady-state growth rate of capital stock under the orthodox hypothesis that higher state enterprise activity crowds out POEs. The diagram embodies two plausible assumptions to

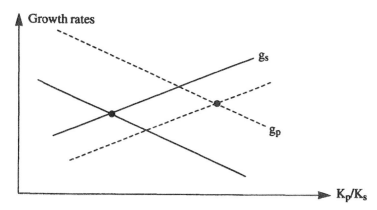

Figure 4.3   The orthodox view of SOE/POE growth

determine levels of capital formation in each sector, utilizing the ratio of sectoral capital stocks, K_p/K_s, as plotted on the horizontal axis in Figure 4.3.

First, when the ratio shifts towards sector i, its rate of profit, r_i, falls, that is r_p (r_s) is a decreasing (increasing) function of K_p/K_s. In other words, a sector's profit rate (the ratio of its profit income to its capital stock) decreases as its relative capital stock increases, a thoroughly standard assumption. The second hypothesis is that each sector's capital stock growth rate, g_i (the ratio of its net investment to capital stock in place), is stimulated by a higher profit rate, r_i. Together with the first assumption, this means that g_s (g_p) rises (falls) with K_p/K_s, as shown. If SOE investment is insensitive to profitability, the line for g_s would be roughly horizontal; profit-conscious POEs might have a strongly negatively sloped schedule.

When SOEs are shut down and POE output and profitability are crowded-in, the lines shift to the dashed positions. SOE profit rates fall as they are curtailed and they invest less, moving down g_s. POEs respond to higher short-term activity levels by investing more. A new long run or steady-state growth rate (with $g_s = g_p$) is determined by the point at which the two dashed schedules intersect. As Figure 4.3 is drawn, capital shifts towards the private sector (K_p/K_s rises) and the long-term capital stock or potential output growth rate speeds up.

As one might suspect, this growth rate result can reverse when state enter-prises crowd in private sector activity, as illustrated in Figure 4.4, where both the g_s and g_p loci shift downwards when SOEs are shut down. Output con-traction in both sectors in the short run frustrates investment demand, leading to slow growth over time.

The moral of these scenarios is that it makes sense to look at how state-owned and private firms relate to each other in the economy at large. SOEs

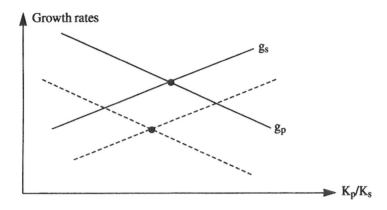

Figure 4.4   A more realistic view of SOE/POE growth

may well stimulate POEs by one channel and hold them back by another (various combinations of crowding-out and -in can be put together in the toy model just presented). These differential influences could go one way at low levels of activity and the other way at high levels, that is, the lines in Figures 4.1 and 4.2 could change slopes.

Crowding-in effects *do* appear to be important at the current range of sectoral output levels (evidence supporting this conclusion is presented in AKT), so that keeping SOEs healthy looks like a useful strategy to pursue. This goal in turn involves continuing roles for a government Ministry of Industry and Development Bank of the traditional kind, especially under present post-socialist circumstances in which SOEs account for the bulk of economic activity overall.[6]

PUBLIC AND PRIVATE ENTERPRISE SECTORS

Table 4.1 supports the last point by providing numerical information about the continuing importance of state enterprises under post-socialism. It is clear that progress in privatization has been slow, for many reasons. Initially, establishing various levels of government in the democratic successor states to socialism as the *de jure* owners of land, productive capital and the housing stock, was a non-trivial legal task. Estimating the asset values of the SOEs was difficult, as was their 'corporatization' or creation of Western-style organizational and financial structures. Large firms, on the whole, ended up in the hands of 'privatization agencies' of diverse forms. Their main tasks are to continue operating the companies that they inherited and ultimately to turn them over to the private sector, another tricky manoeuvre, as will be seen.

Table 4.1   Official estimates of the private sector share of GDP (%)

	1990	1991	1992
Bulgaria	–	5	10
CSFR	5	9	–
Czech Republic	–	–	20
Slovak Republic	–	–	20–21
Hungary (1)*	10	27	35
Hungary (2)	14	16	25
Poland	31	42	45–50
Romania	–	–	26
Russia	–	–	7

* The two estimates for Hungary are based on tax returns and labour force data, respectively.

Source: UNECE (1993).

Small firms in many cases were sold off fairly quickly, but there have been complex and lengthy negotiations regarding restitution of assets confiscated by previous regimes, transfer of title to housing units, and reorganization of agriculture (UNECE, 1993).

The shares of GDP accounted for by the different national private sectors in Table 4.1 are on the low side and are bound to rise as the difficulties just listed are gradually overcome. However, it is important to recognize that a goal of 100 per cent private sector operation of the economy does not make sense. Despite a recent wave of privatization of public companies, no country at post-socialist income levels has gone so far as to turn its entire economy over to private operators.

Indeed, if the numbers in Table 4.1 set upper bounds on SOE shares of production, data through the 1980s show that in semi-industrialized econo-mies lower bounds on shares in GDP and gross fixed capital formation fell in the ranges of 10–15 per cent and 20–40 per cent, respectively (Chang and Singh, 1993). Public enterprises included the most efficient steel plant in the world in South Korea (Amsden, 1989), a bevy of state firms in Taiwan used at different times to spearhead sectoral big pushes (Wade, 1990), and well-known, productive companies in almost all developing nations.

SOE shares of output were cut back drastically after the late 1980s in a few countries, notably in Latin America under the strong ideological influence of the World Bank and International Monetary Fund – the Bretton Woods insti-tutions, or BWIs. This rush to privatize may well reflect what Hirschman (1982) called a 'public–private cycle', due to inevitable disappointments

General perspectives

with whatever means happen to be in place for addressing the socio-economic problems of the day. The Thatcher government made privatization the vogue in the United Kingdom around 1980; as lagging indicators of global political trends, developing economies took about a decade to join the pack.

There is no reason to expect the cycle to remain in an extreme privatization phase. Public companies were originally set up under capitalism to remedy perceived deficiencies of the unencumbered market, which private enterprise has historically been unable to resolve. They include failures to seize economies of scale or stake out leading sectors; the ability of state-controlled firms to generate countercyclical investments along with stable savings flows; and goals of achieving social equity through pricing policy and employment creation. All these factors have to be weighed in any serious decision about privatization, even starting from a situation of high public enterprise shares like those in Table 4.1.

Next we turn to the details of ownership structures *per se*. Table 4.2 gives a bird's eye view of the patterns that exist. The main points to be observed are the following:

Table 4.2   Different ownership structures

Types of ownership	Types of Enterprise	
	SOEs	POEs
Arm's length (outsider)	Success cases in many countries	United States United Kingdom
Hands-on (insider)	White elephants (?)	
Bank-centered		Germany Japan
Groups		South Korea Taiwan Many LDCs

First, 'outside' or 'arm's length' ownership of firms by households who transact shares in a stock market (either directly or by way of financial intermediaries such as pension plans and mutual funds), is a somewhat special case, largely restricted to the UK, US and other economies which inherited the British financial system. For its defenders such as Jensen (1986), the stock market provides an ideal vehicle for enterprise owners to solve the principal/agent problem by exerting their 'exit' option. Since firms are always open to hostile takeovers, the argument goes, their managers will act in efficient fashion to avoid losing their jobs.

The one trillion dollar corporate merger and acquisition (M&A) wave in the United States in the 1980s constitutes an important test of this proposition. Did the efficiency of the American economy rise as a consequence of the ownership exit options exerted during these financial manoeuvres? The results will take years to be assessed, but early estimates place social *losses* in the range of hundreds of billions of dollars, due to lower wages, increased unemployment, business failures, huge debt burdens, and stagnant investment and R&D spending (Crotty and Goldstein, 1993). Managers became obsessed with their firms' short-term survival as opposed to sustained output growth, and many enterprises' stakeholders were severely hit. The takeover premiums that Wall Streeters gained during the M&A decade came not from squeezing out poor managers, but from the paper increases in asset valuations and rising debt that accompany any speculative boom.[7] As will be seen, similar frenzies are a clear and present danger under post-socialism.

Secondly, under outside ownership, 'free rider' problems easily arise. Rather than aggressively disciplining the management whose salaries they pay, individual owners may be lax in their supervision. There is not much incentive for a minor shareholder to intervene in corporate affairs, so that poor managers can go their own way. As many commentators have pointed out, 'insider' or 'hands-on' enterprise finance can help keep management on its toes.[8]

In Continental European and Japanese practice, for example, firms partially control each other through cross-shareholdings. Each enterprise's large stake in several others reduces temptation for free-riding. An individual firm will typically have close relationships with external sources of finance such as a specific bank or (in Germany, for middle scale firms) state or local government. Such large investors will often have representatives on the Board. With insider knowledge and their own institutional income flows in mind, bankers or government officials can impose discipline on managers while at the same time providing credit (often by rolling over short-term loans) at moderate cost.[9]

In the Anglo-American model, firms first pay for investment by borrowing from banks (or, more recently, by entering the money market), and then refinance short-term debt from internal saving and by issuing long-term liabilities in the capital market. One implication is that the final cost of funds tends to be higher in the US, since German and Japanese shareholder banks can internalize information flows and exploit scale economies in credit provision. A broad, liberalized capital market along Anglo-American lines may

provide allocative efficiency by equalizing returns to different sorts of holdings, but it can also be productively *in*efficient, creating high costs of finance
and shortening economic horizons.

One major risk with hands-on ownership is insider speculation. For example, in Chile in the mid-1970s firms previously nationalized under the Allende
regime were privatized rapidly, with financial 'groups' linked to the government being the major buyers. These conglomerates started borrowing from
banks under their control to bid up their own shares' prices as the stock
market boomed. Total financial holdings ballooned in comparison to real
output and capital stock in a characteristic signal of financial fragility of the
sort that Minsky (1986) describes.

After the inevitable crash, a quarter of the assets of the banking system
were non-performing and the two biggest banks (each central to a conglomerate) lost more than five times their capital. Refinancing the conglomerates'
bad debt required creation of stocks of liabilities amounting to one-third of
GDP – externally (from the government to foreigners) and within Chile
(from the central bank to households, and from the government to the central
bank). Associated payments obligations will cost taxpayers several per cent
of GDP per annum well into the next century.

A clear implication of this history is that as private wealth builds up under
post-socialism, a combination of strict regulation and productive investment
outlets will be needed to prevent its financially unsophisticated owners from
replicating Chile's excellent adventure. Particularly risky will be rapid wealth
transfers such as those that result from voucher privatization schemes of the
sort perhaps getting under way (after several false starts) in the Czech Republic in 1993. Claims and counterclaims supported by 'confidence' and Ponzi
schemes (shrewd operators borrowing ever more from naive lenders on the
one hand to pay off their expanding interest payment obligations on the
other) could easily balloon under such circumstances.

A third observation from Table 4.2 is that insider control of companies is
not confined to Continental Europe and Japan. As Leff (1979) pointed out
long ago, company 'groups' or conglomerate enterprises are ubiquitous in the
developing world. The South Korean *chaebols* are prominent examples, nour-
ished by 'rents' created by state industrial policy interventions to become
production powerhouses. Chang (1993) argues that the conglomerate structure can create transaction efficiencies, holding down proliferation of both
free-riders and rent-seekers because the state and the groups deal among
themselves as large entities. They can 'bundle' issues, permitting a bargaining solution to be devised because there is room for side-payments on many
related questions.

Theoretical explanations aside, the world-wide presence of company groups
suggests that they will appear under post-socialism as well. Privatization

schemes such as those discussed in the following section should be designed with this eventuality in mind. Conglomerates' benefits in terms of reducing transactions burdens and costs in terms of creating monopoly power (with a corresponding need for regulation or creation of internal or external competition) are likely to be important policy concerns.

Fourthly, Table 4.2 suggests (somewhat whimsically) that ownership structures affect SOEs' performance as well. Arm's length public ownership combined with other incentives may push SOEs towards efficient operation, but there are no sure guarantees; along with good performers, public sector white elephants and employment patronage havens are notorious far and wide. For the enterprises that will remain under state control for extended periods in post-socialist economies, one can think of several policies to encourage their productivity:

1. Objectives can be clarified, especially with regard to provision of social services. Social safety nets will be sorely needed during the transition, but to what extent should they remain the responsibility of firms? How should provision of services trade off in enterprise planning with building up retained earnings and undertaking badly needed capital formation?

2. Incentives have to be modified in line with rethinking SOE goals. The day of the soft budget constraint may have ended, at least for enterprises that cannot claim big political favours. But that does not mean that public (or nominally private) company managers do not have to be pushed to perform. Experience in East Asia and elsewhere demonstrates that an ongoing role of the state in encouraging, reorganizing, and at times eliminating, firms can play an integral role in economic success.

3. The task of creating incentives, however, should not be allowed to overwhelm the government, assuming that the bureaucracy's tendencies toward aggrandizement of its writ can be contained. Creation of (or directed evolution of the current privatization entities towards) small, élite agencies to monitor SOEs may contribute to this end.

4. Finally, competition can play a role. Within a country, SOEs can be forced to compete with other public or private firms in markets where economies of scale and 'natural monopolies' are not dominant. Participation in export markets can be a stimulating test. However, it is worth recalling that Japanese and Korean planners consistently steered clear of 'excessive competition', especially in industries with big sunk costs which tend to engage in short-term price wars and extreme investment cycles over time (Chang, 1993). A role for licensing and regulatory policy opens up, as discussed more fully in AKT.

The moral of the foregoing observations is that there is no single road to capitalism, let alone the size of the public sector or the patterns of ownership of firms. The Anglo-American institutional model dominates received theory and the advice that BWIs and associated advisers are imparting to post-socialist and other economies in transition. However, economies with relatively large shares of GDP and investment in the hands of SOEs, and with insider organization of corporate control, have performed better economically in several dimensions than Britain or the United States since World War II. Further implications are taken up below.

MODES OF PRIVATIZATION

None of the transition countries have chosen coherent, easily traceable paths towards privatization. As noted above, control of large SOEs has been consolidated in the hands of privatization agencies which now have to run the firms while at the same time trying to sell them off (or else pass them along to still other agencies set up to do the same thing). Small enterprises (especially in the service sector) are in the process of being sold to the public at large or to previous stakeholders such as managers and/or employees through auction or buy-out schemes.[10] In many cases, immobile assets such as housing were simply transferred to occupants for nominal charges, in a form of social restitution.

The major privatization issues centre around farms and large public enterprises. How can titles and/or rights to exploit these assets be transferred? Only three methods (each with many variants) are at hand:

1. Rental arrangements are possible, including leases and such extensions as franchises, management contracts, and so on.
2. Equity of firms can gradually be sold off, through buy-outs, auctions, share flotation, and so on. All these methods involve *flows* of funds, in the sense that buyers pay for their purchases from current incomes or else by running down their existing financial assets or running up liabilities. Privatization in industrialized and developing nations has uniformly been done in flow fashion.
3. New financial assets can be created by fiat for households, which they can then trade in directly or indirectly for the liabilities of the companies held by privatization agencies. This approach boils down to transferring a *stock* of wealth from the state to the private sector. There have not been many examples under Western capitalism. One was the wholesale distribution of Western land in the US in the 19th century, when 160 acres went to each eligible farm family, and millions of acres to railroad

companies, universities and other worthy institutions. Two-thirds of the hopeful farmers failed to stay on their new homesteads for the five years required to obtain clear title; swindlers and speculators reaped the gains.

In post-socialist agriculture, few people are homesteading their way into private farming (UNECE, 1993). Rental, as opposed to other forms of transfer, appears to be the rule. The reason is risk. Market prospects are weak, and banks are unable to provide credit. Most Western farms are subsidized, but post-socialist governments are unwilling to take up this standard practice (at least until worries about food self-sufficiency begin to vex policy-makers' minds). Peasants are wisely adopting a 'wait and see' attitude about land transfers, and opting for contract arrangements, cultivation without clear title, or maintaining ties with state farms and co-operatives whose potential fates are anything but clear.

Flow transfers may ultimately prove important in industry, but they pose problems of mobilizing finance. If we assume for the moment that only citizens or national firms acquire public enterprises,[11] then Fanelli, Frenkel and Rozenwurcel (1990) observe that they can pay for their acquisitions in just four ways: (1) an increase in private saving; (2) a fall in private investment; (3) a decrease in private sector flow demand for financial assets; and (4) an increase in private sector flow demand for credit.

Alternative (1) could be helpful for output growth if accompanied by a jump in investment. The public sector would probably have to be the motor, taking into account the crowding-in effects of public on private capital formation that appear throughout the semi-industrialized world (Taylor, 1993). In other words, privatizing governments should reinvest the proceeds instead of cutting the current fiscal deficit. This observation becomes doubly relevant if the private sector reduces its own capital formation to take over public firms.

Alternative (3) is more likely than (4), especially in post-socialist economies with primitive financial markets. But then the government will find it difficult to place its own liabilities, provoking it to emit money or bear higher interest burdens, or both. There will be strong pressures to use the proceeds of privatization just to cover the PSBR with no spill-over to capital formation.

Finally, to the extent that public firms can be sold to foreigners, is their direct foreign investment 'additional' to what would have arrived in any case? What about remittance obligations in the future? It *is* true that transnational corporations which are doing more than simple sourcing do not readily leave a country once they have entered and built up sunk capital, and that they can serve as vehicles for technology acquisition. But even in this area, East Asian experience suggests that in the long run an economy may be better off if it strives for technological competence on the part of its own firms (Amsden, 1989; Chang, 1993).

These financial flow concerns will be macroeconomically important if practical difficulties turn privatization into a long, drawn-out process. Flow transfers could amount to several per cent of GDP for many years, given the levels of POE activity documented in Table 4.1. They also describe processes of 'liquidation' (Poland) or 'transformation' (Hungary) via which companies are wound up and their assets sold at scrap value. The effects on public investment and potential private sector output growth of these operations cannot be promising, especially in the absence of a coherent industrial policy.

At the level of rhetoric, at least, post-socialist governments as of 1993 were committed to stock transfers. Potential claims on the productive assets of the large firms held by privatization agencies were to be issued *gratis* to the public, typically as 'vouchers'. These pieces of paper could then be converted into equity of newly privatized enterprises directly, or else into shares of mutual funds. In other words, an Anglo-American type of financial system was supposed to be created at one stroke.

Free-rider and principal/agent conundrums instantly raise their ugly heads. In contrast to their role under flow privatization, people trading in vouchers for shares are not adjusting portfolios of assets and liabilities built up over time – if 'serious' resources are not involved, their decision-making can veer towards the frivolous. To avoid such risks, Eastern European reformers are creating a layer of financial intermediaries – 'holdings' – between house-holds and the firms that they will ostensibly own.[12] These entities are sup-posed to be large and powerful enough not to free-ride. Either by takeover threats or by voicing the power of their big blocks of shares, they may force the management of newly privatized SOEs to maximize owners' returns. The theory sounds good, but there are concerns about how effectively the hold-ings will function in practice.

First, they could just behave like the pension funds, mutual funds and life insurance companies which own 70 per cent of outstanding equity in the United Kingdom. These entities exert scant leverage on the companies whose shares they own, and are essentially a veil for widespread free riding (Corbett and Mayer, 1991). On the whole, American financial intermediaries are no more aggressive. During both the financially quiescent 1970s and the turbu-lent 1980s, their takeover threats failed to impose efficient management on many corporations.

On the other hand, holding companies might take an activist role, restruc-turing firms and trying to stimulate entrepreneurship and technology acquisi-tion directly. How these activities would be co-ordinated with national indus-trial policy is not clear. Are we talking about *chaebols* which interact with national planners along co-operative lines, or conglomerates with tendencies towards excessive competition or cosy cartels? The regulatory problems that these possibilities raise cannot be addressed by simply creating the holdings.[13]

Thirdly, destabilizing insider speculation is always a risk in stagnant economies with many financially inexperienced actors. If they see little room for gain by pushing production, the people in charge of the holdings may seek to raise their own incomes by playing financial games. Small cases of speculation and fraud (involving only thousands of people losing their wealth) broke out in several countries during 1992–93. In laxly regulated financial markets hypnotized by the *laissez-faire* ideology, can a 'big one' *à la* Chile be far behind?

Finally, if the holdings do become more than a veil, and the regulatory and instability problems that they create are adequately addressed, then they will almost certainly evolve in the direction of becoming the conglomerate groups that flourish in middle income capitalist environments. Economically, such a 'normal' course is perhaps to be welcomed, because relatively well-defined enterprise groups can provide a means of embedding progressive capitalism into the socio-economic system.

Socially and politically, however, group formation could raise problems. In many countries, conglomerates are based on close control of productive companies by small, homogeneous sets of people, united by kin or confession. Especially in Eastern Europe, as ancient communal animosities suppressed under socialism for 40 years are reappearing (or flaring into civil wars in Yugoslavia), the tendency towards formation of community-anchored economic power may become cause for unrest among the vast army of economic losers that the current pattern of transition seems certain to create.

THE EMBEDDING OPERATION

Such political risks are only an aspect of a more fundamental difficulty that the transition presents: how is capitalism to be embedded in societies in which for decades it has not been able to fit?

Deeper minds than von Hayek's and von Mises's have grappled with this question, without clear-cut success. Nonetheless, one can learn from the attempts at synthesis made by Marx, Weber, Polanyi and others. For example, in his theory of the origins of capitalism, Marx stressed the importance of the institutions supporting accumulation, which have not reappeared in Eastern Europe and Russia under allegedly 'market friendly' reform programmes.

The mature Weber (1968) pointed to a complex causal pattern underlying capitalism's original appearance: 'All in all, the specific roots of Occidental culture must be sought in the tension and peculiar balance, on the one hand, between office charisma and monasticism, and on the other between the contractual character of the feudal state and the autonomous bureaucratic hierarchy'. All were essential in setting up capitalism as a system of institutionalized strife among shifting but well-defined social groups (Collins, 1980). At a more practical level, all successful or semi-successful reform programmes in semi-industrialized countries in recent decades – Spain, Chile, Turkey, Korea, Taiwan – have involved complex causal patterns and contingent historical events.

Polanyi's (1944) great insight was that institutions supporting the market system have to arise from within society, which also defends itself against the worst excesses of capitalism – child labour laws were passed early in the 19th century and the collapse of real wages in Eastern Europe was arrested at 30–40 per cent late in the 20th century. 'Double movements' of this sort will continue to occur under post-socialism, in a peaceful fashion if the tensions of change do not become unbearable.

As society's superordinate actor, the state will have to play a central role in forcing both sides of the double movement – markets will be neither created nor regulated without public action. Developing country experience also shows that states can fail in several dimensions (Evans, 1992). They operate under fundamental uncertainty, and may or may not respond to the uneven advances of different sectors, disproportionalities, and balance-of-payments and inflationary pressures that will inevitably arise (Hirschman, 1958). They can try to do too much, thereby achieving little. They can become purely predatory, as in countless petty dictatorships around the world (and in the successor states to Yugoslavia, when war finally ends there?). Nonetheless, as theoreticians of backwardness from Gerschenkron to Amsden have pointed out, when backward economies do catch up the process is mediated by the state, in particular by an autonomous bureaucracy accepted by (or embedded in) the society overall.

In post-socialist as well as developing economies, policies proposed by the Bretton Woods institutions will have very little to do with putting these institutional prerequisites for modern capitalism into place.

NOTES

1. Arguments presented in outline form in this chapter appear in more detail in Amsden, Kochanowicz and Taylor (1994), abbreviated to AKT in what follows.
2. In arguing that socialism is bound to be inefficient, von Mises ignored a long line of conservative scholars from Pareto and Barone through to Schumpeter who asserted that a planning system *could* replace (or certainly supplement) the market – it just had to get the marginal conditions right. Credit von Mises with a degree of common sense that his colleagues lacked. Computational and informational gaps alone would soon overwhelm

any potential super-Gosplan, as the failure of its incarnations under Leninist planning amply confirmed.

3. Shapiro and Taylor (1990) point out that market friendly economists who followed von Hayek kept up his *Road to Serfdom*'s theorizing about how perfectly *laissez-faire* fits with vanishing states, benevolent dictatorships, and other impossible political configurations. They also conveniently forgot von Hayek's (1949) almost Burkean insistence that if market institutions develop, they only do so in a historical, organic fashion.

4. The two concepts are not the same – see AKT for more details. Under post-socialism, the second accusation holds more water than the first.

5. Implicit assumptions are that tax and subsidy flows associated with POEs are minor, and that demand for SOE output is relatively autonomous, in part because many of them produce intermediate goods and deal with one another.

6. Aghion and Blanchard (1993) draw different conclusions from a model incorporating labour market crowding-out (plus other standard mainstream paraphernalia such as Say's Law as modified to incorporate dole to the unemployed, determination of POEs' investment by their available saving, and generalized perfect foresight about wage and employment changes – all a bit alien to observable post-socialism). They conclude that: '...the equilibrium speed of transition is likely to be too slow, justifying measures by the government to accelerate the transition. These measures may include restraints on wages in the state sector, and top-down privatization and restructuring, imposed on firms rather than chosen by them'. To be fair, they also recognize that: 'Going too fast may lead to too high unemployment and derail the transition' along the lines of Figure 4.4's growth stagnation.

7. The theory of speculative finance of the sort that underlay the M&A episode and the insider manoeuvres in Chile discussed later is set out by Minsky (1986). In a typical scenario, a financial intermediary (for example, a bank or a brokerage firm) might offer liabilities (insured deposits or junk bonds) to acquire speculative assets (shares of companies undergoing M&A action). So long as the prices of the speculative assets go up (feeding back into expectations of future capital gains), both sides of the intermediary's balance sheet expand, along with the ratio of its debt to real asset holdings (essentially the real capital stocks of the companies concerned). When the speculative asset prices stabilize or start to decline, the intermediary's liabilities become bad debt. Cleaning it up may be essential for saving the financial system, with the taxpayers typically picking up the cost. During the course of the speculative excursion, the principals of the intermediary are often guilty of fraud and theft, but the real problem is the public's willingness to hold dubious claims because of self-delusion about the possibilities for limitless financial gain.

8. Corbett and Mayer (1991) and Akyuz (1993) present useful surveys of this issue in the context of the post-socialist transition.

9. Germany's bank-based financial system is solidly built into the socio-economic structure, having emerged in the 19th century as a response to the challenges posed by 'economic backwardness', as Gerschenkron's (1952) celebrated essay pointed out.

10. Definitions and details vary enormously across countries, but the UNECE (1993) reports that during 1992 well over half of 'small' production units had been privatized in the Czech and Slovak Republics, and the ex-GDR *Länder*. The share in Russia was about one-third. Public receipts from these sales have been tiny shares of GDP.

11. In fact this hypothesis is not far off the mark. Apart from Eastern Germany, post-socialist economies have not proven attractive for foreign investors. Hungary's share of foreign control of capital is the highest in the region – at about 3 per cent (UNECE, 1993).

12. In 1992–93, holdings were being established by the state in Poland and Romania, while 'investment privatization funds' organized by entrepreneurs arose spontaneously in the CSFR. Russian schemes went in all the Eastern European directions, but with more opportunity for inside ownership.

13. Nor can they be circumvented by stating *ex ante* that the holdings will have to sell themselves out to create a decentralized capital market after five or ten years, as Blanchard and Layard (1991) propose. *Ex post*, if sufficiently powerful holding units emerge, they will find ways to reconstitute themselves as did German and Japanese conglomerates after

World War II, or the law can simply be changed! If powerful units don't emerge, then the whole experiment will be pointless.

BIBLIOGRAPHY

Aghion, P. and Blanchard, O.J. (1993), 'On the Speed of Transition in Eastern Europe', mimeo, Cambridge, MA.: Department of Economics, Massachusetts Institute of Technology.

Akyuz, Y. (1993), *Financial Liberalization: The Key Issues*, Geneva: UNCTAD.

Amsden, A. (1989), *Asia's Next Giant: South Korea and Late Industrialization*, New York: Oxford University Press.

Amsden, A., Kochanowicz, J. and Taylor, L. (1994), *The Market Meets its Match: Reindustrializing Eastern Europe*, in press.

Blanchard, O.J. and Layard, R. (1991), *How to Privatise*, London: Centre for Economic Performance, London School of Economics.

Chang, H.-J. (1993), 'The Political Economy of Industrial Policy in Korea', *Cambridge Journal of Economics*, **17**, 131–57.

Chang, H.-J. and Singh, A. (1993), 'Public Enterprises in Developing Countries and Economic Efficiency', *UNCTAD Review*, **4**, 45–82.

Coase, R. (1937), 'The Nature of the Firm', *Economica*, **4**, 386–405.

Collins, R. (1980), 'Weber's Last Theory of Capitalism: A Systematization', *American Sociological Review*, **45**, 925–42.

Corbett, J. and Mayer, C.P. (1991), *Financial Reform in Eastern Europe: Progress with the Wrong Model*, London: Centre for Economic Policy Research.

Crotty, J.R. and Goldstein, D. (1993), 'Do US Financial Markets Allocate Credit Efficiently? The Case of Corporate Restructuring in the 1980s', in G.A. Dymski, G. Epstein and R. Pollin (eds), *Transforming the US Financial System*, Armonk, N.Y.: M. E. Sharpe.

Evans, P. (1992), 'The State as Problem and Solution: Predation, Embedded Autonomy, and Structural Change', in S. Haggard and R.R. Kaufman (eds), *The Politics of Economic Adjustment*, Princeton, N.J.: Princeton University Press.

Fanelli, J.M., Frenkel, R. and Rozenwurcel, G. (1990), *Growth and Structural Reform in Latin America: Where We Stand*, Buenos Aires: CEDES.

Gerschenkron, A. (1952), 'Economic Backwardness in Historical Perspective', in B. Hoselitz (ed.), *The Progress of Underdeveloped Countries*, Chicago, IL.: University of Chicago Press.

Gibson, W. and Dutt, A.K. (1993), 'Privatization and Accumulation in Mixed Economies', *Journal of Comparative Economics*, **17**, 1–22.

Hirschman, A.O. (1958), *The Strategy of Economic Development*, New Haven, CT.: Yale University Press.

Hirschman, A.O. (1970), *Exit, Voice, and Loyalty: Responses to Decline in Firms, Organizations, and States*, Cambridge, MA.: Harvard University Press.

Hirschman, A.O. (1982), *Shifting Involvements: Private Interest and Public Action*, Oxford: Basil Blackwell.

Jensen, M. (1986), 'Agency Costs of Free Cash Flow, Corporate Finance, and Takeovers', *American Economic Review*, **76** (2), 323–9.

Jensen, M. and Meckling, W. (1976), 'Theory of the Firm: Managerial Behavior,

Agency Costs, and Ownership Structure', *Journal of Financial Economics*, **3**, 305–60.

Kaldor, N. (1957), 'A Model of Economic Growth', *Economic Journal*, **67**, 591–624.

Kornai, J. (1981), *Growth, Shortage, and Efficiency: A Macrodynamic Model for the Socialist Economy*, Oxford: Basil Blackwell.

Kornai, J. (1990), *The Road to a Free Economy*, New York: W.W. Norton.

Leff, N.H. (1979), '"Monopoly Capitalism" and Public Policy in Developing Countries', *Kyklos*, **41**, 718–38.

Minsky, H. (1986), *Stabilizing an Unstable Economy*, New Haven, CT.: Yale University Press.

Pasinetti, L.L. (1962), 'Rate of Profit and Income Distribution in Relation to the Rate of Economic Growth', *Review of Economic Studies*, **29**, 267–79.

Polanyi, K. (1944), *The Great Transformation*, New York: Farrar and Rinehart.

Shapiro, H. and Taylor, L. (1990), 'The State and Industrial Strategy', *World Development*, **18**, 861–78.

Taylor, L. (1991), *Income Distribution, Inflation, and Growth*, Cambridge, MA.: MIT Press.

Taylor, L. (1993), *The Rocky Road to Reform*, Cambridge, MA.: MIT Press.

UNECE (United Nations Economic Commission for Europe) (1993), *Economic Survey of Europe in 1992–93*, New York: United Nations.

von Hayek, F. (1944), *The Road to Serfdom*, Chicago, IL.: University of Chicago Press.

von Hayek, F. (1949), *Individualism and Economic Order*, London: Routledge & Kegan Paul.

von Mises, L. (1935), 'Economic Calculation in the Socialist Commonwealth', in F. von Hayek (ed.), *Collectivist Economic Planning*, London: Routledge & Kegan Paul.

Wade, R. (1990), *Governing the Market*, Princeton, NJ: Princeton University Press.

Weber, M. (1968), *Economy and Society* (edited by G. Roth and C. Wittich), New York: Bedminster Press.

Williamson, O. (1985), *The Economic Institutions of Capitalism*, New York: The Free Press.

Part II

Empirical Studies

5. Sisyphus Among the Neoliberals: On Privatization and Rolling Back the Latin American State[1]

David Felix

INTRODUCTION

Privatizing public assets is a recent addition to the efforts over the past decade to restructure the debt-ridden Latin American economies so as to enable them to resume normal servicing of their foreign debts and regain access to foreign capital for sustaining a revival of economic growth. It was not stressed in the initial IMF-guided restructuring programmes. These focused rather on achieving macroeconomic stability through slowing monetary emission and reducing the fiscal deficit, and on improving the trade balance and overall resource allocation by 'getting prices right', that is, by altering the structure of relative prices through decontrolling markets.

Import-substituting industrialization (ISI), which had shaped the development effort of the larger Latin American economies since the 1930s, was put forward as the primal cause of their price 'distortions' and macroeconomic disorders. And when successive programmes failed to produce the expected revival on schedule, the failures were explained away for a time by enlarging the indictment of ISI. Redoubled efforts were needed because ISI had left the economies in even worse shape than originally estimated.

But as macroeconomic disorders persisted, output stagnated and debt servicing arrears spread through the region, the adequacy of the ISI *leyenda negra* as a cover story for the failures weakened. A supporting villain was therefore added – the state itself. It was oversized, overstaffed and overextended in areas better done privately, and its deficit financing was fuelling inflation and crowding-out private investment. From 1987 onwards, rolling back the state by selling public firms and various infrastructural and social services to private operators became more prominent components of the restructuring programmes.

The improved cover story fitted in with Washington's broader goal of eliminating national barriers to the international movement of goods, services, capital, enterprise and everything else except labour, drugs, subversive ideas and unfair foreign trading practices. Flushed with the triumphs of Reaganomics, the White House turned the Department of State, the Agency for International Development and sympathetic foundations and think-tanks loose on Latin America in an ideological full-court press to promote privatization, the liberating of markets and the unleashing of entrepreneurs. The campaign was also backed by tangible inducements. Eligibility for Baker Plan loans and Brady Plan debt writedowns was restricted to the heavily indebted countries willing to undertake free market restructuring and to privatize, while pliant international financial institutions (IFIs) such as the IMF, World Bank and Inter-American Development Bank, were much more generous to clients on Washington's approved list.

The desire of foreign banks to liquidate their Latin American loan portfolios added to the external pressures to privatize. Latin American lending, a honey-pot to foreign banks in the 1970s, had become in the 1980s a morass of negotiations, reschedulings and involuntary new loans to stave off open defaults. Notwithstanding these efforts, interest arrears began accumulating after 1986, plunging the market prices of Latin American loan paper to levels that made debt-equity swaps an appealing alternative to selling the loan paper outright. Swapping for public assets had the greater potential since few private assets remained available at distress prices, as most large Latin American firms and their owners had been reliquified by governmental bail-outs and 'international portfolio diversification', that is, capital flight.

Within Latin America the standard rhetoric of market liberalization and rolling back the state that anoints the spread of privatization covers a varying mix of concerns. Hunger for immediate fiscal and foreign exchange revenue has largely shaped the response of Latin American economies teetering on the brink of hyper-inflation, such as Argentina, Brazil and Peru. With their tax base and real tax revenue diminished by capital flight, the Tanzi–Olivera effect[2] and the diversion of economic activity to the untaxable 'informal' sector, and with dollarization eroding the 'inflation tax',[3] one-off revenue injections from the sale of public assets have had desperate appeal. Longer-run objectives, for example, efficiency gains from the privatized firms, preferential economic ties with the US and a strengthened ideological climate for private investment by shrinking the public sector, have been the more important moulders of privatization in some of the other countries.

My general thesis is, however, that the macroeconomic benefits from privatization are likely to be disappointing, and the rolling back of the state impermanent. The centre of gravity of development policy will, over the long term, remain the mixed economy with a large interventionist public sector, rather than the small, open competitive economy norm that informs the current push to roll back the state. I now elaborate on the main reasons for this conclusion, beginning with political–ideological ones.

THE FRAGILE POLITICAL BACKING FOR ROLLING BACK THE STATE

In contrast to Eastern Europe, where disaffected intelligentsia and plant managers (initially with broad popular backing), have been pressing for wholesale privatization and market liberalization in order to dismantle command economies and the Communist Party's monopoly of power, disaffection among leading power groups in Latin America with the economic scope of the state is merely partial. The collapse of Eastern European illusions that market liberalization and capital inflows can quickly elevate consumption to Western European levels may well reorient the policy dynamics of that region towards the mixed economy – whether under the aegis of fascism or social democracy is unclear – but is unlikely to bring back the command economy. The *status quo ante* in most Latin American economies, on the other hand, has been for many decades the mixed economy. Until the 1980s, business, the salariat and a large segment of the urban working class prospered as the public sector expanded. Public investment 'crowded-in' private investment, sparking the sustained growth of GDP and formal sector employment, while the accompanying public subsidies and protective barriers sheltered private gain. Because of these ties, political support for efforts to extricate the economy from the current crisis by market liberalization and privatization is fragile, with none of the major power groups unequivocal ideological converts. The business élites and intelligentsia are split on privatization and free trade, the unions and the public sector salariat mainly hostile.

One business split is between equipment manufacturers (both locally owned and subsidiaries of multinational companies), who had prospered supplying the domestic market, and firms primarily oriented to external markets. The former are wary of free trade and the broad-scale sale of public firms, since import protection and privileged transactions with the public sector and its parastatals nurtured their past growth and current survival. During the heyday of ISI, such public–private linkages were viewed benignly in the mainstream development literature as the growth pole approach to economic development, a way of exploiting external economies and of focusing entrepreneurial efforts in technologically backward economies. Today, the privileged relationships are dismissed by many development economists as mere 'rent-seeking'. The revisionism derives, however, more from changing ideological fashion than from warranted fact or theory, neither of which, as is argued further on, justify categorical rejection.

Moreover, privatization is often being structured to protect the 'rent-seekers'. Major Argentine materials and equipment firms have been allowed to buy shares on generous terms in privatized public utilities, railroads and highways, continuing thereby as preferred suppliers to the privatized enterprises. Privatized Argentine petrochemical firms dissuaded the government from privatizing its ethylene plant so as to protect the subsidized pricing of their main feedstock.[4] Privatization need not mean rolling back the state as economic actor and protector.

The 'cosmopolites' are the industrial exporters: export–import mercantile firms, financial and service firms with international ties, agribusinesses and multinational company consumer product subsidiaries. The last became especially prominent in Latin America during the expansionary decades of ISI, when Brazil and Mexico were the first and second highest recipients of private foreign investment of all the newly industrializing countries (NICs). Some US multinationals in consumer products viewed President Bush's hemispheric free trade initiative favourably, because it would enable them to close some of their Latin American production lines and import directly from lower cost plants.[5] Others have joined privatizing consortia where the operator of the privatized enterprise is a European government corporation, thus manifesting a pragmatic perspective on free trade and private versus public ownership. Both locally-owned 'cosmopolites' and large ISI firms survived the 'Lost Decade' in relative comfort because they were the main beneficiaries of government bail-outs earlier in the decade. Rolling back the state does not include rolling up these generous safety nets.[6]

Organized labour and the salariat, on the other hand, have strong reasons to oppose free market restructuring, since the economic burden has fallen most heavily on real wages, salaries and employment in the public and private formal sectors, and on public social and educational services built up during the ISI era. Privatization threatens to expand inequality by further shrinking public sector *'conquistas sociales'* that have survived the restructuring programmes.

Income inequality in Latin America has increased secularly, but until the 1980s with pauses and occasional reversals. It rose during prosperity, when there were more gains to trickle down, and levelled off or declined in depressions, when rents and profits tended to take the relatively greater hits.[7] The 'Lost Decade' breaks with this pro-cyclical pattern; it is the first extended depression in which income inequality continued to worsen. Between 1980 and 1987 average real income of wage–salary earners fell 15 per cent in the Latin American private formal sector and 30 per cent in the public sector, while the combined employment of the two sectors rose a bare 3 per cent. Concurrently, in the urban informal sector the economically active rose 55 per cent, and average real income fell by 42 per cent.[8] The prolonged deterioration of income and employment and downward mobility would seem to be an especially explosive political mixture. That the explosions have been sporadic thus far is a puzzle.

Some of the answer may lie in the demoralization of the Latin American intelligentsia. Generally critical of the inequities of the restructuring efforts, they have not been able as yet to produce a persuasive alternative paradigm around which to mobilize the discontented; a paradigm that gives political pizazz and seeming coherence to an alternative revival strategy, as the Prebisch Doctrine had once given to ISI. Victor Urquidi, a long-time doyen of the Latin American development theory class, sums up the malaise in his plaintive observation that 'no one in Latin America thinks anymore about development, but only in a limited way about how to recover some growth'.[9]

Still, the patience of the economically squeezed is a fragile asset. For longer-term survival, neoliberal restructuring must begin compensating the patient classes materially. Basic contradictions in the structural adjustment strategy, exacerbated by adverse conjunctural factors, however, make the imminence of sustained trickling down unlikely.

CONTRADICTIONS IN THE NEOLIBERAL STRUCTURAL ADJUSTMENT STRATEGY

A persistent dilemma of neoliberal restructuring concerns exchange rate policy. To restore balance-of-payments equilibrium and debt-servicing capacity, the strategy calls for exchange rate devaluations proportionately greater than the increases of the price level and money wages, in order to sustain a real devaluation and so increase the relative profitability of investing in internationally traded goods.[10] But if devaluation accelerates non-traded goods prices and money wages unduly, it becomes incompatible with another *sine qua non* of neoliberal restructuring of the inflation-ridden Latin American economies – reducing the inflation to international rates. In such circumstances, minimizing devaluation becomes a tempting anti-inflation tool, albeit one that appreciates the real exchange rate and depresses the relative prices of traded goods. 'Getting prices right' retrogresses to 'getting prices wrong'.

This dilemma plagued the neoliberal restructuring of Chile, Argentina and Uruguay in the 1970s. Each began by 'getting prices right', deregulating domestic financial markets, lifting exchange and import controls, lowering tariffs and letting nominal exchange rate depreciation bring down the real exchange rate. Chile was alone in vigorously privatizing, but all three vigorously pursued complementary anti-inflationary measures: strike suppression, union purges, reductions of fiscal deficits and tightened central bank lending. However, when inflation appeared to bottom out at or near three-digit rates, each country began retarding devaluation below the inflation rate to pull down the rate.

In the second act of this neoliberal drama, inflation declined, but real exchange rates continued to appreciate and the relative prices of importables and exportables kept deteriorating. Import demand surged, exports sagged and foreign borrowing financed rapidly expanding trade and current account deficits. High domestic real deposit and lending rates, lagging exchange rates and foreign banks avid to lend, encouraged foreign borrowing – most of it by private banks and large non-bank firms – with governments encouraging the process by lifting capital controls in the hope that foreign borrowing would force down home interest rates. The ensuing debt-financed economic booms were brief.

The disastrous final act began when speculation against the exchange rate surged, foreign banks cut off new loans and the exchange rate went into free fall. Cascading financial crises and collapsing output and employment enveloped each country. Massive government bail-outs of the over-leveraged firms and banks, with Chile renationalizing most of its privatized banks in the process, drove up fiscal and quasi-fiscal deficits. Concurrently, the creditor governments, intent on rescuing their over-exposed lending banks, forced the debtor governments to guarantee *ex post* private foreign bank debts, adding to the fiscal burden of the debtors.[11] The desperate initial conditions facing the current neoliberal restructuring were products in large part of the preceding collapse of neoliberal restructuring.

Currently, most of Latin America is again in the second act. Exchange rate policy has shifted from devaluing to 'get prices right' to minimizing devaluation to bring down inflation. By 1991 the region's real exchange rates had appreciated by 15 per cent on average from their 1980s lows. The rebound was greatest in Peru (73 per cent), Argentina (45 per cent) and Mexico (30 per cent), with all but five small countries appreciating.[12] Additional appreciation is indicated by the incomplete data for 1992 and 1993. As before, 'getting prices wrong' is slowing exports as well as inflation, while imports have been surging. Thus far, however, the current account deficits are being financed by capital inflows embodying a smaller proportion of borrowed funds than in the 1970s. The monetary authorities also appear more alert to financial cowboying by domestic banks and firms than were their predecessors. This may keep the final acts less explosive than the early 1980s dénouements, but probably not much less unhappy.

This is because the structural characteristics of less developed economies (discussed later) make stabilizing the price level by 'getting prices wrong' incompatible with neoliberal restructuring absent, uniquely favourable, external conditions – for example, sharply rising terms of trade or major natural resource discoveries – that encourage foreign capital to keep financing rising current account deficits in the expectation that rising exports will in time start closing the deficits. Such prospects are rare today. Indeed, because of major adverse factors, current conditions are much less supportive of neoliberal restructuring than those prevailing during the rise and fall of the earlier Southern Cone neoliberal efforts.

KEY ADVERSE FACTORS

One adverse factor is the foreign debt overhang, which still casts a large shadow. In nominal dollars the regional debt has, despite debt-equity swaps and Brady writedowns, scarcely fallen from its 1987 peak; and, deflated by the regional terms of trade, the real debt burden remains above the 1982 level, the year the crisis exploded. Debt rollovers and falling international interest rates have helped bring most of the debt service/export ratios below 1982 levels, but with a few exceptions they are still well above the pre-crisis year ratios. With the debt transformed into predominantly fixed interest obligations, the vulnerability of debt service to interest rate shock is much reduced, but so also are benefits from future falling rates. And three of the largest debtors, Argentina, Brazil and Peru, are further burdened with working off large interest arrears.[13] In sum, the debt overhang is still large enough to deter full reaccess to international financial markets.

Decapitalization, the result of prolonged public and private underinvestment during the 'Lost Decade', is another key adverse factor. Table 5.1 shows that the net stock of non-residential fixed capital per worker, which had risen strongly in most of the cited countries prior to 1980, tumbled in the 1980s. The stock of machinery and equipment, crucial determinants of productivity, aged and shrank the most.[14] The partial exceptions are also revealing. The decline of Chile's equipment stock during the 1970s probably reflects the substantial deindustrialization that accompanied the neoliberal restructuring.[15] Colombia, which had moderated its debt accumulation by limiting private foreign borrowing during the 1970s, was the only one of the six that could service its debt out of exports, stay with its ISI strategy and accumulate in the 1980s. These exceptions and the rising capital/labour trends prior to the 1980s suggest that the neoliberal indictment of ISI is overdrawn. In any event, the decapitalization of the 1980s augments supply-side bottlenecks to sustaining recovery in the 1990s by depressing capacity and increasing the import intensity and foreign exchange requirements of investment and output.

Other adverse factors are the global asset price deflation and the accompanying world-wide slowdown of output growth. Falling real prices of capital assets are the downside of the puncturing of the prolonged post-war boom of

Table 5.1　Growth of net stock of non-residential fixed capital relative to
　　　　　　the labour force, 1951–89

	Ke/L	K/L	Ke/L	K/L	Ke/L	K/L
			(Per cent change per decade)			
	Argentina		Brazil		Chile	
1951–60	43.9	30.7	56.4	137.1	70.8	20.3
1961–70	81.6	42.2	26.0	57.9	28.0	33.6
1971–80	47.8	46.0	114.1	108.3	–3.3	–1.1
1981–89	–34.3	–18.6	–30.8	–2.9	–2.2	–11.4
	Colombia		Mexico		Venezuela	
1951–60	73.2	6.8	58.1	48.7	185.7	130.0
1961–70	1.8	8.2	216.2	26.2	–26.3	–6.0
1971–80	65.0	27.1	60.1	28.3	67.5	38.8
1981–89	4.2	7.5	–18.8	–5.2	–25.1	–19.5

Definitions:
Ke = the net stock of machinery and equipment.
K = Ke plus the net stock of non-residential structures.
L = the economically active population.

Source: Computed from data series in Andres A. Hofman, 'The Role of Capital in Latin America: A Comparative Perspective on Six Countries for 1950–1989', Working Paper No. 4 (United Nations, Economic Commission for Latin America and the Caribbean, Santiago, Chile, December, 1991).

capital values that peaked toward the end of the 1980s. Thus the real value of household wealth, which between 1982 and 1989 rose 37 per cent in the US and 83 per cent in the UK, fell in 1990 by 8 per cent in the US and 15 per cent in the UK.[16] Comparable declines have been under way in other Anglophone countries, Japan and Western Europe. The asset price deflation is producing widespread financial stress and rising bankruptcies because it uncovers the substantial debt-leveraging that firms and households had resorted to in purchasing and constructing the capital assets. For example, the liabilities of US and British households during 1982–89 grew nearly twice as fast as their assets.[17] Falling values of loan collateral and debt defaults have in turn put at risk banks and other financial intermediaries, who have reacted by credit tightening. This has increased the financial trauma of highly leveraged firms, forcing them to sell off more assets in declining markets, and to curb investment, current production and employment, which in conjunction with falling real household wealth depresses consumption, *und so weiter*.

How long the asset–debt deflating persists depends in part on whether the United States, Germany and Japan can co-ordinate their fiscal–monetary actions to halt it. This is a tall order, requiring the respective governments to override deeply conflicting domestic priorities and pressures. In any event, a quick turnaround would be unlikely even were astute international co-ordination attainable, given the enormous expansion of financial claims and liabilities since 1970 relative to real output, trade and investment, as shown in Tables 5.2 and 5.3.

Table 5.2 International financial deepening: international banking in relation to world output, trade and investment, selected years

	1964	1972	1980	1983	1985	1987
	As a percentage of world output[a]					
Net international bank loans[b]	0 7	3.7	8.0	12.0	13.2	14.8
Gross size of international banking market[c]	1.2	6.3	15.5	21.8	25.3	27.9
	As a percentage of world trade[a]					
Net international bank loans[b]	6.4	25.7	35.2	57.3	63.9	72.9
Gross size of international banking market[c]	10.6	43.8	67.8	104.0	122.2	137.2
	As a percentage of world gross fixed investment[a]					
Net international bank loans[b]	4.0	18.0	39.2	66.3	72.4	78.2
Gross size of international banking market[c]	6.7	30.6	75.4	120.5	138.7	147.3

Note:
The Table relates the stock of bank loans outstanding at the end of the year to world output, trade and gross fixed investment in current dollars during the year.
[a] Excluding Eastern European countries.
[b] Claims of banks in the BIS reporting area, excluding inter-bank redepositing.
[c] Claims of banks in nearly all European countries, the Bahamas, Bahrain, Canada, Cayman Islands, Hong Kong, Japan, Netherlands Antilles, Panama, Singapore and the United States, including inter-bank redepositing.

Source: UNCTAD secretariat estimates; BIS, *Annual Report* (various issues) and Morgan Guaranty, *World Financial Markets* (various issues).

Table 5.3   Size and structure of world financial markets in 1982 and 1988

	1982		1988	
	Value of assets ($ billion)	Per cent of total assets	Value of assets ($ billion)	Per cent of total assets
Bank assets[a]	8 887	64.1	17 005	46.6
Domestic	6 218	44.8	11 500	31.5
International	2 669	19.3	5 505	15.1
Capital markets	4 977	35.9	19 507	53.4
Euroequity	—	—	40	0.1
International bond markets[b]	259	1.9	1 085	3.0
Stock markets	1 591	11.5	9 563	26.2
Bond markets	3 127	22.5	8 819	24.1
Total	13 864	100.0	36 512	100.0

Notes:
[a] Gross size of banks' balance sheets.
[b] Eurobonds and foreign bonds.

Source: UNCTAD secretariat estimates; BIS, *Annual Report* (various issues) and Morgan Guaranty, *World Financial Markets* (various issues). Capital market information has been supplied by Salomon Brothers International. All data are end-year.

Table 5.2 shows that international bank loans, exclusive of inter-bank credits, rose from negligible percentages of the nominal values of world trade and world gross fixed investment in 1964 to about 75 per cent of each by 1987. They also rose over 20 times faster than the nominal dollar value of world output. Yet Table 5.3 shows that during 1982–88 the rapid growth of international bank and bond lending was overtaken by the expansion in the values of domestic bank assets and equities. It is easy to understand why Latin American governments strapped for hard currency might mistake this prolonged financial bubble for a permanent condition on which they could confidently base their restructuring strategy. But bubble it is proving to be, whose deflating is likely further to hamper the flow of long-term finance to Latin America as well as the growth of world output and trade, thereby dampening the exporting prospects on which the restructuring is also premised.

SWEETENING THE POT FOR FOREIGN CAPITAL

Thus far the reaction of most Latin American governments to the darker international scene has been to enhance inducements to foreign capital. Minimizing devaluation is assigned the added function of reducing exchange rate risk for foreign financial investors. Privatization has been expanded, partly for the direct revenues, but also as an ideological surety to encourage portfolio capital inflows and more IFI loans. To stimulate direct foreign investment, patent and copyright laws have been strengthened, foreign investment codes liberalized, and free trade negotiations initiated with the United States and intra-regionally. Throughout 1992, capital inflows – some of it returning flight capital – sufficed to finance much of the region's modest resurgence of private investment and immodest resurgence of current account deficits. Short-term loans and portfolio capital led the inflows, with privatization revenues and direct investment in third and fourth place. But by the end of the year strains were visible in each of the major flows.

The short-term lending primarily exploited the large spreads between interest rates on domestic currency government bills and the US and Eurocurrency short-term rates. Since the domestic bills carried virtually zero default risk, and their short maturity – typically 30 days or less – minimized liquidity risk, the large spreads (when combined with free currency convertibility and a relatively stable nominal exchange rate) offered quick, low-risk yields in hard currency. But the inflowing capital was also poised to pull out if return/risk expectations worsened. When mid-1992 expectations that the minimal devaluations would soon give way under the stress of rising current account deficits set off anticipatory outflows, the governments were impelled to counter with monetary tightening to raise home interest rates. This staunched the exodus but discouraged portfolio capital flows and has slowed output growth.

Portfolio capital has been mainly drawn to shares of privatized entities and local firms that might benefit from ownership or other special links to the privatized firms. US and British mutual funds and US banks intermediated much of the portfolio capital, enabling small as well as large investors to become indirect shareholders of the Latin American firms. In the thin Latin American bolsas the inflows fuelled spectacular booms in stock prices, which the mid-1992 interest rate upsurge brought to a halt. Since then bolsa prices have flattened, as have the yields of the intermediating mutual funds and on-depository receipts. (The latter are tradeable paper issued by US banks against shares of the Latin American firm held in custody by the bank.) Portfolio inflows have accordingly shrunk.

The direct revenues from privatization have generally been modest. At the end of 1991 the region's receipts from privatization – half of it accruing to

Mexico – merely totalled about $16 billion,[18] whereas Mexico's foreign debt in 1991 was $98 billion and the entire region's $430 billion. Net front-end receipts were smaller still. Since marketable public assets necessarily exclude irremediably unprofitable entities, pre-privatization restructuring has been not uncommon. Governments have assumed the debts of the enterprise, weakened labour agreements, and raised controlled prices before taking bids. Some terms of sale have included tax rebates and, in the case of utilities and public goods, long-term exclusive franchises with ample rate-setting freedom. The foreign exchange receipts from the sales will also be overtaken in time by profit repatriation; how quickly depends in large part on the terms of sale. And apart from the terms of sale, privatization receipts, which necessarily decline as the stock of unsold marketable assets dwindles, can do little to sustain rising current account deficits in the long term.

The indirect pay-offs, on the other hand, have often been substantial, with the rewards for ideological good behaviour seemingly more important thus far than the efficiency gains stressed in the conventional economic literature on privatization. The contrasting Argentine and Chilean privatizations illustrate the point.

There is broad consensus among academic observers that Argentina's wholesale privatization has been especially poorly executed. Assets have been badly underpriced, private ownership concentration and monopoly power have been considerably augmented, performance requirements have been nebulous, and so on.[19] Major embarrassments have forced the government to renegotiate its highway privatization contracts and to resume ownership of the privatized national airline. And, paradoxically, the designated operators of the privatized telephone company and the main electric utility are Spanish, Italian and French state companies

Surely, efficiency and human capital justifications don't fit these privatizations. Competition has been reduced, and management merely transferred from Argentine to Mediterranean bureaucrats. Since Argentinians are mainly literate offspring of European immigrants, if Argentina's public sector has been in demoralized disarray, the rationale for turning management over to European government firms cannot be human capital shortfalls or the innate inefficiency of public management. One likely cause of the disarray, an economic élite with a deficient sense of national commitment,[20] is not being cured by the privatization. Rather, it shows up in the gross sleaze and corruption that has enveloped the Menem government's economic programme from its inception.[21]

Yet the Menem regime is the recipient of a generous Brady Plan workout and Paris Club rollover of its official debts, substantial IFI loans, and frequent accolades from official Washington, the financial press and the IFIs. Thus, the President of the World Bank, disregarding the vastly overvalued exchange rate and fast growing current account deficits, took pains on his recent visit to Argentina to reaffirm that the World Bank 'will continue to support this great effort'.[22] These indirect rewards for a badly flawed privatization and unsustainable exchange rate policy suggest that right intentions matter more than results for the 'international community'.

Chile's privatization during 1985–89 illustrates a different aspect of the same point. To the Pinochet regime, putting its free market strategy back on track after the embarrassment of having to renationalize much of the private sector as part of the financial bail-outs of 1982–84 was more important than maximizing the sales revenue to offset their domestic and foreign exchange costs to the government. Extra special treatment from the Washington-based IFIs – during 1983–86 Chile's share of IFI loans to Latin America was 2.5 times its share of the region's foreign debt[23] – facilitated the choice by easing the fiscal and foreign exchange pressures. Thus the banking system was reprivatized on subsidized terms[24] and non-financial firms sold at well below present value.[25] The desire to strengthen ideological defences against a recrudescence of socialism by defusing share ownership accounted for some of the subsidization. For example, the 'popular capitalism', in which shares of the privatized firms were sold to employees at low prices with generous credit terms and resale guarantees, was a much publicized feature. In contrast to the 1970s (and Argentina and Mexico currently) Chile's 1985–89 privatizations sought to deter ownership concentration and, in particular, the formation of large conglomerates. The diffusion effort, while only partly successful in checking concentration, contributed to a related goal of the government, that is, more active and thicker securities markets, although again only partially; 65 per cent of the turnover on the Santiago bolsa in 1989 was in shares of firms that had been privatized in 1985–89, which were also responsible for 74 per cent of corporate bonds outstanding in 1990.[26]

However, while Chile's privatization has received comparatively high marks, the efficiency gains have been meagre. Ironically, this is because, apart from the renationalized banks, the firms privatized during 1985–89 were already well run, profitable and an important source of government revenue. During the 1970s they had been on hard budgets, cut off from tax and credit subsidies and denied access to foreign loans by the hostile 'Chicago Boys'. As relatively 'lean and mean' enterprises they survived the 1982–84 crisis without need of bail-outs. Saez's data show no employment drop the year after privatization for any of these firms, nor any general upward trend in profits thereafter.[27] Rather, the privatized firms apparently crowded out rather than augmented private investment, since the acquisition financing was mainly diverted from other investible projects and the companies were distributing most of their profits as dividends while funding capital projects with debt.[28] Again the indirect rewards were derived more from ideology than efficiency.

Can free trade compacts reinforce foreign direct investment enough to ease significantly the growing current account deficits? The Mexican government fervently hopes so. President Salinas, who had repeatedly stated that Mexico's economy was not yet suited for more than selective trade compacts with the United States, abruptly changed his tune when his May 1990 European trip to drum up lending and investment commitments drew blanks. On returning he immediately initiated the NAFTA negotiations. His main motive was, according to press reports, to reassure foreign capital that Mexico's free market restructuring was irreversible. It's a tall bet. Since foreign investors expect to repatriate profits in excess of the foreign exchange they bring in during the project's gestation, foreign direct investment produces net foreign exchange gains for the host country over time only if it keeps expanding exponentially, or if it directly and indirectly expands exports and/or import substitutes sufficiently to service the rising profit outflow. Despite Mexico's liberalized border zone and general opening up to foreign investment, the net foreign exchange gains from foreign direct investment, excluding debt-equity swap privatization, has been miniscule. When Salinas initiated NAFTA negotiations, Mexico's current account deficit was $7.5 billion; by 1992 it had risen to $23 billion in relation to international reserves of $12 billion. The hope that Mexico's efficiency wages are low enough for NAFTA to spark a flood of investment into export production sufficient to halt the rising current account deficits despite the rising real exchange rate seems rather unreal.

If foreign financing levels-off or falls, it is doubtful that the rising current account deficits of the Latin American countries can be reversed by other means that are both compatible with neoliberalism and allow a trickling down of benefits to pacify the discontented. Monetary-fiscal tightening to reduce imports by depressing aggregate demand might, in tandem with a money wage freeze, permit the return to a 'get prices right' exchange rate policy. But while in the spirit of neoliberal restructuring, this offers the discontented classes not bread but more stones. Southern Cone military dictatorships dared not take their neoliberalism so far; today's democratic regimes are hardly in a position to be more ruthless. The alternative – controls and export subsidies to reduce the current account deficit – is compatible with sustaining 'getting prices wrong', but not with neoliberalism. Some backsliding is being tolerated; for example, Argentina's recent reverting to thinly disguised controls and subsidies on a modest scale has not upset Wall Street or the IFIs. But the impact on its mounting deficit has also been modest. More aggressive resort to controls, on the other hand, would deter private and IFI financing of the deficit, and could also open the door to populist controls to redress the burden-sharing inequities. That would mean pacifying the discontented by giving up on the neoliberalism.

THE DUBIOUS DEVELOPMENTAL CASE FOR MINIMALIZING THE PUBLIC SECTOR

Latin America is a heterogeneous economic region, and the conjunctural factors are having a varying impact on the region's economies. From an economic development perspective, however, the economies share various structural shortfalls that have kept their productivity and material welfare levels well below the economically advanced economies. These have been the analytic focus of the literature on late development, and overcoming them the objective of the *dirigiste* industrialization policies – including ISI – which 20th century late industrializers have all pursued, albeit in different combinations and with varying success.[29] If the free market and privatization momentum in the region is truly a permanent rejection of the *dirigiste* path rather than a limited crisis-driven deviation, it should have a convincingly superior theoretical paradigm to guide the strategy.

The closest to such a normative paradigm is probably the small competitive open economy model, which purports to demonstrate that the most effective way to offset developmental shortfalls is to give domestic markets full freedom to integrate with world markets. This would allow the forces of competition to 'get prices right', that is, unify the internal with the world relative prices of all internationally traded goods and factors, so that domestic effective demand is fully met (regardless of shortfalls) by foreign and domestic sourcing in proportions determined by comparative costs and profitability.

The defects of the model as a comprehensive paradigm are well recognized in the economic theory literature. Even the formulators of free market policy in the IFIs and Latin American economic ministries use it more as a promotional tool to sell policy to the public than as a serious guide to designing policy. Nevertheless, since *dirigiste* policies play off the defects of the model, it is useful to identify major ones that *dirigisme* is intended to offset.

One is that the model is merely an exercise in comparative statics. Having no time dimension, it can offer no insights on process, policy priorities, speed of change and other essential policy questions having to do with dynamic relationships. This flaw belatedly caught the attention of economists enthused by the Argentine, Chilean and Uruguayan free market programmes of the 1970s, when those economies crashed in the early 1980s. The crashes spawned a post-mortem debate on the correct sequencing of liberalization measures. The debate showed a new awareness among free market economists that the path to a stable, free market outcome is narrow and slippery, but no consensus on which sequences of liberalizing reforms can make it through and which would crash. The debate is on again today with the main focus shifted

to Eastern Europe. Again the outcome is inconclusive, though a further
analytic advance has emerged in that some participants concede that initial
conditions in the East European economies may preclude more than a mixed
economy outcome. This belated recognition of a commonplace of the hard
sciences – that initial conditions affect final outcomes as well as transitional
paths – is also a rejection of the claim that the small competitive open
economy model is a relevant normative paradigm for all Third World economies, regardless of their heterogeneity.

The model's incompleteness is further manifested by the exclusion of
international labour market integration from its optimal arrangements or, for
that matter, from its analytic purview. Although advanced economies closely
regulate immigration from low wage countries, the proponents of free market
restructuring, while vigorously attacking policies that restrict domestic labour mobility, are singularly silent about policies that restrict international
labour mobility. The reticence is probably because free international migration opens up a can of worms about welfare and political stability limits to
the speed and level of migration in both emigrating and receiving regions.[30]

Price formation is another shaky feature of the open economy model. Free
markets are assumed to act as pure auction markets in which trades are made
only at market clearing prices, these 'right' prices appearing to each market
agent as parameters that he is powerless to manipulate. This view is at odds
with the main thrust of modern market analysis, in which auction markets are
a relative rarity and firms in the more typical markets, rather than being
passive 'price-takers', manipulate prices as part of their market strategy.
Price as a strategic variable means not merely that individual firms have
some price-setting power, but also that announced prices typically have fringes
of side terms – publicized as well as unannounced quantity discounts, re-
bates, bonuses and penalties – that may vary between rival firms and dis-
criminate between classes of client, which blurs the operational meaning of
'right prices'. Strategy also implies that market competition is a bargaining
game in which asymmetries of information and bargaining power between
rival firms and between sellers and buyers shape the bargaining outcomes.

Collective action by Latin American economies to offset some of these
asymmetries dates well back into the *laissez-faire* era, taking three main
forms. One was price-fixing agreements between domestic primary goods
producers, with the government brought in as enforcer during depressed
periods when free-riding tended to get out of hand. The inter-governmental
commodity agreements of more recent vintage are extensions that seek to
overcome international free-riding by primary producing countries.

The second was action to tilt towards the host country the Ricardian rents
associated with foreign-owned production for export of primary products. Dif-
ferentially heavier taxation of such rents dates well back in Latin America: to

the taxing of Peruvian guano in mid-19th century and Chilean nitrates later in the century. The motivation was not necessarily developmental. In the Chilean case the landed oligarchy, then in full control of the state, substituted nitrate taxes for land taxes, and spent the tax relief primarily on consumption. Later, the developmental motive for nationalizing Ricardian rents– to expand the nation's investible surplus, elevate skills by requiring foreign firms to employ and train nationals for technical and managerial positions, and so on – became more prominent. The consumption motive also persisted, but with some democratizing of the gains, usually stemming from a democratizing of politics that helped workers of the foreign firms get state neutrality and even support for their efforts to exact higher wages and fringe benefits. Nationalizing the foreign firms was often the final stage of a prolonged struggle over Ricardian rents. It is not clear why reselling to foreign investors should remove these rents as a future bone of contention between the investors and the host country.

Such Ricardian rents, which derive from the disparate quality and accessibility of natural resources between countries, have also as a dark side the 'Dutch Disease' to which resource-rich primary exporters are prone. The term was coined to label the adverse effects on the competitiveness of Dutch industry brought on by the Netherlands' natural gas export bonanza in the 1970s. By pushing up the exchange rate, the gas exports had cheapened competitive industrial imports and squeezed industrial exports. In this case, the 'Disease' was mild and short-lived; Dutch industry was able to draw on its ample technological and managerial prowess to adjust and recover. In primary exporters lacking such prowess, the 'Dutch Disease' is more chronic and virulent. It limits the ability of market forces to diversify the economy during export bonanzas, contributing to the 'growth but not much development' outcome characterizing many such export bonanzas. The potential cures for the 'Disease' are all interventionist.[31]

A third form of intervention, government banks set up to lower the cost and increase the availability of credit to private borrowers, also dates back in Latin America to the 19th century. Initially these were state mortgage banks, established at the behest of the landowning élite to tap the lower cost London bond market and relend on generous terms against land as collateral. In the past half century, the gamut of state banking has been enlarged to provide easier credit for industry, construction, peasant agriculture, and so on. Though usually a response to particularistic demands, there is a broader theoretical legitimacy to using state banking as a development tool, if not to many of the ways it has actually been used. For reasons inherent in loan contracts, international financial markets tilt against less developed economies, creating opportunities for collective action to reduce capital costs.

Opportunities exist because financial markets are inherently non-clearing markets, loan contracts being inter-temporal and the future uncertain.

Lenders use various criteria, based ultimately on subjective judgement, to reduce default risk. They screen borrowers, quantity-ration credit to those that pass the screening, collateralize loans, appraise spending and cash flow projections of borrowers, and incorporate default risk premia in their lending terms. Conservative lenders rely more on screening and credit rationing; risk-taking lenders screen more loosely but raise the risk premia. The lending terms also incorporate liquidity premia to protect against inflation, interest rate changes and other market risks that raise the opportunity cost of being locked into long-term loans. Liquidity premia are therefore lower in financial centres that are rich in specialized institutions and instruments and have thick resale markets for spreading the liquidity risk in long-term lending. The greater availability of long-term credit, and the lower liquidity premia in such markets relative to those in less developed financial markets, provide the economic rationale for using the greater visibility of the state to the foreign financial markets to overcome informational barriers that exclude private supplicants from less developed countries.

Liberating the thin, financial markets of less developed countries does not eliminate the tilt. Local firms continue to incur a higher cost of capital than their advanced country competitors, because high risk premia still need to be paid to keep local financial capital from draining to the more diversified and liquid financial centres and to attract loans from these centres. The motive for using the state as financial intermediary therefore persists. And in Latin American countries, where financial asset holdings are especially highly concentrated,[32] the motive is reinforced by equity concerns. A policy that strengthens the power of financial capital to keep domestic interest and tax rates hostage to capital flight, would augment the already highly concentrated wealth and income distribution of the region and exacerbate its endemic instability.

The acquisition and production of new technology, so central to the economic development process, also offers important opportunities for collective action to offset market biases. The international market for technology is inherently monopolistic and two-tiered. In the top tier are the leading innovators of each industry, large firms that have also ample reverse engineering capacity and skills for replicating the innovations of rival firms. Such firms have a mutual incentive to share technologies in order to minimize duplicative technological research, pre-emptive patenting and other costly stratagems of technological competition. They typically join in cross-licensing agreements, and organize joint R&D ventures for sharing costs and risks of major technology projects. The lower tier consists of the remaining firms of each industry who, lacking the innovative threat capability needed to crash the top tier, have more circumscribed access to innovations of the top tier firms, for which they have to pay monopoly prices.

Since Third World firms are generally in this lower tier, there is from the development perspective a strong case for their governments to try to improve the terms of access by limiting licensing fees, decoupling technology packages, and so on. The effectiveness of such efforts has varied greatly. South Korea has had considerable success;[33] Latin American countries, with the partial exception of Brazil, much less. Indeed, in their current anxiety to entice foreign investors, Latin American governments have suspended virtually all such efforts. But the centrality of technological progress for sustaining economic development is unlikely to allow the current submissiveness to the dictates of the technology-producing countries to be permanent.

This is because heavy dependence on foreign sourcing of domestic technology retards the ability of domestic producers to adjust their production processes and output mixes flexibly and denies them and the economy earnings from technological rents. Using the state to overcome various technology market failures that impede the development of an indigenous innovative capacity has been prominent in the economic history of today's developed economies; this has given it grudging intellectual respectability among free market economists. They accept the theoretical case for state financing of research, viz. that market forces alone will encourage only bankable projects: those whose contribution can be privatized and marketed profitably by the innovating agent. They also accept the two main theoretical justifications for protecting and subsidizing new ventures: that learning curves lower production costs and 'learning by doing' stimulates technological innovation. Their argument against interventionist policies to promote technology is, rather, that governments for various political economy reasons are likely to do it badly. The small open economy model reduces to a second-best development model, but remains the best in town.

Setting aside political economy complications, the aforementioned flaws of the small competitive open economy model imply that, in the language of complex systems analysis, *dirigisme*, not *laissez-faire*, is the attractor towards which late developing economies will gravitate if their policy dynamics are governed primarily by economic efficiency and a reasonable consensus on growth and distribution. *Dirigisme* and mixed economy are, of course, flabby concepts used also to describe the policy stance of advanced capitalist economies. However, the key market biases that work against late developing economies mean that the economic logic rationalizing their *dirigisme* goes well beyond the public goods arguments used to support state interventions in advanced economies. It impels less developed economies towards a more comprehensive economic role for the state than in advanced economies.

Two political economy complications emphasized by free market economists do, however, roil the policy dynamics. The first is that, since the human capital shortfalls that keep labour productivity in less developed economies relatively low should also depress the efficiency of the public bureaucracy, assigning that bureaucracy more comprehensive economic responsibilities than is required of their advanced country counterparts, is an inconsistent strategy that is likely to overload the public sector's administrative capacity and retard rather than advance economic development. The second complication is that interventionist policies get diverted from their developmental functions to become merely protected sources of income for rent-seeking groups with economic and political clout. To free market economists, the two forms of government failure suffice to offset the market failures, leaving the small competitive open economy model with its minimalist state as the guiding star for developing economies.

The evidence, however, supports merely the existence, not the sufficiency, of the government failures. The differences between Asian and Latin American NICs in the scope of their *dirigisme* are too small to account for the greater macroeconomic stability and accumulation rates, and lesser technological dependency and income concentration of the Asians.[34] The inference is that development is to an important degree path-dependent, with institutional and cultural differences in initial conditions between countries accounting for some of the differences in effectiveness with which similar development strategies are being implemented.[35]

What does this imply for the long term? One possibility is a paradigmatic stand-off. Latin American élites remain narrow rent-seekers, and the masses are prone to salve their discontent at the worsening inequalities with unfeasible populist quick fixes, in which case neither the potential of *dirigiste* development nor the market efficiency of the free market strategy would be attainable. The other is that as the 'Lost Decade' prolongs, desperation generates a deeper sense of commitment to the larger society. In a sort of symbolic Bonfire of the Vanities, the élites temper their rent-seeking and tax avoidance and the masses their quick-fix populism in order to regain some developmental momentum. Such enoblement would greatly improve implementation of either of the strategies. But since the *dirigiste* development approach has the greater potential, why should we expect the enobled Latin American NICs to settle for the second-best small competitive open economy alternative?

NOTES

1. This paper updates David Felix, 'Reflections on Privatizing and Rolling Back the Latin American State', *CEPAL Review*, Santiago, Chile, April 1992.
2. This refers to the fact that the real tax on firms and households diminishes as the lag between assessment and payment and/or the rate of inflation increases. Obviously, if the nominal tax and the penalty interest rate are fully indexed, the Tanzi–Olivera effect is zero. Neither condition, however, has prevailed in Latin American countries.

3. The decline in purchasing power of existing private domestic money holdings resulting from inflationary emissions of new money to finance fiscal deficits serves as a 'tax' on the money holders. Shifting one's domestic money-holdings to foreign currency, for example, dollars, is a way of evading the 'inflation tax'. Complete evasion requires the foreign currency exchange rate to rise at least *pari passu* with the domestic price level.
4. See Pablo Gerchunoff *et al.*, *Las Privatizaciones en la Argentina*, Banco Interamericano de Desarrollo, Serie de Documentos de Trabajo 121, Washington, D.C., Marzo 1992, 175 pp.; and Alejandra Herrera, 'The Privatization of the Argentine Telephone System', *CEPAL Review*, No. 47, Santiago, Chile, April 1993, 149–61.
5. See statements by spokespersons for Goodyear Tire & Rubber and Procter & Gamble before the Joint Economic Committee, United States Congress, at its May 22 1990 hearings on the Hemispheric Free Trade Initiative.
6. A prime illustration is the opposition of Chile's free marketeers to a proposal that requires five major Chilean banks, bailed out in 1983, to start servicing their debts with the central bank. The bail-out terms had set the interest rate on the debt well below the market rate and did not penalize delinquency, so there has been little incentive for the rescued banks to service their debt. A recent audit of the Central Bank by Cooper Lybrand warns that the accumulating debt, already 10 per cent of GDP, will continue expanding faster than GDP, eroding Central Bank solvency. Since the rescued banks are judged incapable of fully servicing their debt from current earnings, the *Partido por la Democracia*, a member of the governing coalition, has proposed requiring that the banks regain solvency through additional injections of equity capital or be liquidated.

   Leading the attack on the proposal has been the *Instituto Libertad y Desarrollo*, a stronghold of Hayekian libertarianism and the major think tank of the Pinochetista wing of the Chilean élite. According to Carlos Caceres, its president, the proposal undermines the rights of the current shareholders and amounts to renationalizing the five banks. Caceres was the Treasury Minister who in January 1983 advised foreign banks that the government was taking over responsibility for servicing their loans to private Chilean firms. *Laissez-faire* anyone? For details see *El Diario*, Santiago, 30 April, 7, 8 May, 1991 and *El Mercurio*, Santiago, 9 May, 1991. The Cooper Lybrand report is published in the *Diario Oficial*, 24 January, 1991.
7. David Felix, 'Income Distribution and the Quality of Life in Latin America: Patterns, Trends and Policy Implications', *Latin American Research Review*, XVIII (2), 1983, 3–34.
8. See PREALC, *Informal Sector as in PREALC*, Working Paper No. 349, Santiago, August 1990, and *Employment and Equity: The Challenge of the 1990s*, Working Paper No. 354, Santiago, October 1990.
9. In John Williamson (ed.), *Latin American Adjustment: How Much has Happened?*, Washington, D.C., Institute for International Economics, April 1990, p. 337.
10. Demitris Papageorgiou, Michael Michaely and Armeane M. Chocksi (eds), *Liberalizing World Trade*, published for the World Bank by Basil Blackwell, London, 1991, 7 vols. In their summary volume of this collection of case studies of liberalization attempts, the editors conclude that sustaining a real devaluation was the salient *sine qua non* for successful liberalization.
11. For a detailed treatment of these summary observations see David Felix, 'Debt Crisis Adjustment in Latin America: Have the Hardships been Necessary?', in Robert Pollin and Gary Dymski (eds), *New Directions in Macroeconomics: Essays for Hyman P. Minsky*, University of Michigan Press, Fall, 1993.
12. Data from Table A-2 of David Felix, 'Suggestions for International Collaboration to Reduce Destabilizing Effects of International Capital Mobility on the LDCs', Washington University Department of Economics Working Paper No. 173, February 1993.
13. Based on data from 1991 as reported in David Felix, 'Debt Crisis Adjustment in Latin America', *op. cit.*, Tables 1 and 2.
14. In the perpetual inventory algorithm used to calculate the capital stocks, the assumption of fixed lives ensures that the average age of the capital items rises when the stock declines.

15. On the deindustrialization, see Patrico Meller, *La Apertura Chilena: Ensenanzas de Politica*, Documento de Trabajo 109, Washington, D.C., Banco Interamericano de Desarrollo, Marzo, 1992.
16. *The AMEX Bank Review*, **18**(1), 16 January 1991.
17. *Ibid.*
18. *Latin Finance*, No. 38, June 1992. The estimates vary considerably, depending on how the estimators value the heavily discounted bank debt paper which makes up the bulk of the payments under debt-equity swap privatizations.
19. Gerchunoff, *op. cit.*, Herrera, *op. cit.*
20. 'People are not involved,' the ambassador's wife says. 'And you must remember that anybody who has money is not an Argentine. Only people who don't have money are Argentines', V.S. Naipaul, *The Return of Eva Peron*, New York, Alfred A. Knopf, 1980, p. 108.
21. 'Now Even Freer Enterprise', *The Economist* London, January 15–21 1991, p. 38. 'US Takes Action on Corruption', *Latin American Weekly Report*, January 24 1991, p. 2.
22. *Latin American Regional Reports – Southern Cone*, July 1992.
23. David Felix and John P. Caskey, 'The Road to Default: An Assessment of Debt Crisis Management in Latin America', Table 1.8 in David Felix (ed.), *Debt and Transfiguration? Prospects for Latin America's Economic Revival*, Armonk, New York, M.E. Sharpe Inc., 1990.
24. See footnote 6 supra.
25. Mario Marcel, 'Privatizacion y Finanzas Publicas: El Caso de Chile, 1985–88', *Coleccion Estudios CIEPLAN*, No. 26, Santiago, Junio 1989, pp. 5–60.
26. This summarizes the data and assessment in Raul E. Saez, 'An Overview of Privatization in Chile: The Episodes, the Results and the Lessons', Santiago, January 1992, unpublished.
27. *Ibid.*, Tables 9–12.
28. According to data and estimates of Marcel, *op.cit.*
29. I give a more detailed treatment of many of the points briefly touched on in this section in David Felix, 'Import Substitution and Late Industrialization: Latin America and Asia Compared', *World Development*, **19**(9), 1989, 1455–69.
30. The factor price equalization theorem of static international trade theory has been used to make the case that free trade is an adequate substitute for international labour movements. President Salinas is currently trying to persuade US unions and other opponents of mass immigration from low-wage regions that a free trade pact with Mexico would curb the flow of Mexican migrants *al Norte*. For Mexico, however, the theorem as a welfare justification for free trade is a tattered fig leaf. Even the static conditions required for equalization of relative factor prices to be realized have been shown to be too onerous for the theorem to be taken seriously as a policy guide.
31. See Marcelo Diamand, 'La Estructura Desequilibrada y el Tipo de Cambio', *Desarrollo Economico*, Buenos Aires, April 1972. His special focus has been the 'Dutch Disease' as a deterrent to Argentine industrialization. See, for example, his 'Argentina's Pendulum: Until When?', in Jonathan Hartlyn and Samuel Morley (eds), *Latin American Political Economy: Financial Crisis and Political Change*, Boulder, Colo., Westview Press, 1986.
32. For example, the 1977 Banco de Mexico survey of household income and expenditure showed that around nine-tenths of private financial assets were held by the top 10 per cent of Mexican households. See Ifigenia Martinez Hernandez, *Algunos Efectos de la crisis en la Distribucion del Ingreso en Mexico*, Mexico, D.F., Instituto de Investigaciones Economicas, Universidad Nacional Autonoma de Mexico, 1989.
33. See Alice H. Amsden, *Asia's Next Giant: South Korea and Late Industrialization*, New York, Oxford University Press, 1989.
34. Andres Bianchi, Mitsuhiro Kagami and Oscar Munoz, *The Role of Government in Economic Development: A Comparison of Asia and Latin America*, Joint Research Programme Series No. 77, Tokyo, Institute of Developing Economies, 1989.
35. A path-dependent explanation of the superior performance of Asian over Latin American NICs is given in the *World Development* article cited in note 29.

6. Market Reform and the Changing Role of the State in Mexico: A Historical Perspective

Juan Carlos Moreno and Jaime Ros*

INTRODUCTION

This chapter looks at Mexico's current development problems from a historical perspective. It reviews long term development trends in the Mexican economy, and examines in particular some past episodes of radical shifts in development strategy and in the role of markets and the state. The shift of the last ten years is given particular attention. A major theme in the chapter is that, in the past, the real obstacles to economic development have often been misperceived. In contrast to the optimism which currently dominates perceptions of Mexico's economic prospects, we argue that the same may be happening at present.

The chapter is organized as follows. Section 1 reviews old and new debates on the long period of economic stagnation during the 19th century. Section 2 examines Mexico's modern economic growth from the *Porfiriato*, beginning in the late 19th century, to the oil boom of the late 1970s. Finally, section 3 focuses on the economic and policy adjustments to the external shocks of the 1980s and discusses the prospects of the Mexican economy under the current shift in development strategy.

THE 'ORIGINS OF BACKWARDNESS'[1]

During the colonial period, the economy of Mexico, then the New Spain, was closely organized around the extraction and exportation of precious metals, particularly silver. While most of the population (over three-quarters) lived in

*A former version of this paper was prepared for the Workshop on 'The State, Markets and Development', University of Notre Dame, 24–26 April 1992. The authors are indebted for comments to Amitava Dutt and Samuel Valenzuela. The views expressed in this paper are not necessarily those of ECLA with which the first author is associated.

108   *Empirical studies*

the rural areas, agricultural activity, especially for the market, was organized to serve the mining centres dispersed around the central and northern central regions of present Mexico as well as Mexico City, the kingdom's administrative capital. By the middle of the 18th century, the discovery of new and rich silver deposits, together with the introduction of explosives and other technological advances, created a boom in silver production which then reached the peak levels of the whole colonial era.[2] Economic activities closely linked to the mining sector benefited directly from the boom. The expansion of silver exports also made available imported raw materials and capital goods for the new industries which were being developed in Europe as a consequence of the industrial revolution. By the end of the century, small-scale manufacturing employed more workers and produced more output value than the mining sector itself (see Table 6.1). Textiles was the most important, but not the only, industrial activity benefiting from these conditions.

Table 6.1   GDP per capita and by sector, 1800–1910

	1800	1845	1860	1877	1895	1910
Per capita GDP at constant 1900 prices (index 1800=100)	100.0	78.4	70.9	85.0	128.8	190.2
% of GDP						
Agriculture[1]	44.4	48.1	42.1	42.2	38.2	33.7
Mining	8.2	6.2	9.7	10.4	6.3	8.4
Manufacturing	22.3	18.3	21.6	16.2	12.8	14.9
Construction	0.6	0.6	0.6	0.6	0.6	0.8
Transportation	2.5	2.5	2.5	2.5	3.3	2.7
Commerce	16.7	16.9	16.7	16.9	16.8	19.3
Government	4.2[2]	7.4	6.8	11.2	8.9	7.2
Other	1.1	—	—	—	13.1	12.9

[1] Includes livestock, forestry and fishing
[2] Does not include net fiscal remittances to Spanish treasury. Total government revenues, including these remittances, amounted to 7.8 per cent of colonial income.

Source: Coatsworth (1989) Tables 4 and 5

As a result of these trends, by the end of the 18th century Mexico was probably one of the most prosperous regions in the world. It was surely the wealthiest Spanish colony in America, with an economy whose productivity was possibly higher than that of Spain herself. Output per capita (in 1800) was around half that of the US, and Mexico's economy was less agricultural with an advanced mining industry and a significant manufacturing sector. The value of exports was similar to that of her northern neighbour, even though total output produced was around half (Coatsworth, 1978). Several of the conditions for rapid capitalist development were in place. The creation of an industrial labour force – that 'most difficult and protracted process' by which the umbilical cord connecting the population to land is broken (Gerschenkron, 1952) – although far from complete, was probably more advanced than in many European countries (especially in Central and Eastern Europe). The relatively high share of manufacturing in total output in 1800 (22.3 per cent, see Table 6.1[3]), also speaks about the presence of a critical mass of native entrepreneurs and more generally about a pattern of life that was probably not opposed to industrial values.

Mexico's Century of Decline (1780–1870)

Yet between 1800 and approximately 1860 – at the time when the US and other now developed economies were recording unprecedented rates of economic growth – total production fell by 5 per cent and per capita incomes declined by as much as 30 per cent. By 1877, Mexico's income per capita had fallen to around one tenth of that of the US, and has since then fluctuated between 10 and 15 per cent (Coatsworth, 1989; see also Table 6.1).

Whether this decline had already started in the later decades of the colonial period or not (see note 2), everybody agrees that independence did nothing to prevent the stagnation of the economy during the half century that followed it. Why didn't independence and the emergence of a national state provide greater stimuli to economic development?

Independence eliminated the fiscal burden on the gold and silver extracted from the colony. This had been a substantial burden – estimated by Coatsworth at 7.2 per cent of total output around 1800 – much higher, for example, than the burden of British colonialism on its North American colonies. Yet the end of Spanish rule also brought some unexpected costs for the mining sector that partly offset the removal of this burden. Not only were the direct effects of the independence wars on mining production highly disruptive, but they also involved the loss of low cost and guaranteed supplies of mercury (essential for processing low-grade ores) that Spain had provided from its large state-owned mine at Almaden. As a consequence of this disruption, silver production fell from 27 million pesos in 1812 to only 4.4 million in 1822, that is, to less than one-fifth, and the mining sector did not recover its pre-independence level of production until the 1860s (Cardenas, 1985). The depression of silver production had, in turn, other important consequences for the economy. Besides the contraction of all the activities linked to the mining sector, it implied a reduction in the volume of international trade and a decrease in the means of payment available in the domestic economy (Cardenas, 1985). The latter aggravated the consequences of capital flight brought about by the exodus of Spanish miners and merchants, and thus the general lack of financial capital which characterized this period up to the 1860s when the first commercial banks were founded.

The abolition of restrictions to foreign trade also turned out to be a mixed blessing. While generally regarded by economic historians as beneficial for the Mexican economy, the end of trade restrictions accelerated the diversion of Mexican foreign trade away from Spain and towards the emerging industrializing powers in the North Atlantic, a trend which had very harmful effects on domestic manufacturing and, therefore, on the major activity that could have compensated for the decline of the mining sector. Several studies have documented how exposure to US and British competition led to the collapse of the wool textile industry at the turn of the century and to the prolonged decline of cotton textiles throughout the first half of the 19th century. Trade opening towards the Atlantic economy and foreign competition – which in fact started in the period of *'comercio libre'* and *'comercio neutral'* introduced by the Bourbon reforms – also appears to have deepened the fragmentation of local markets and the cleavage between, on the one hand, a mining and agricultural north trading with the rest of the world and, on the other, a manufacturing centre and agricultural south plunged into economic depression (Thomson, 1986).

In addition, little progress was made in other areas. The colony had been one of the regions in the world with the sharpest social and regional disparities; a caste society, in fact, where access to employment as well as geographical and occupational mobility were restricted on the basis of ethnic distinctions, and where a number of institutional arrangements tended to increase, rather than reduce, the gap between the private and social benefits of economic activity. Although some changes did take place with independence,[4] many of these had little effect in a backward social and political order. The ultimate reason is probably the nature of the foundational act of the post-independence state: the fact that having begun and been defeated as a popular insurrection – feared by both the Spanish and Creole conservative élites – independence came eventually to Mexico through 'a virtual *coup d'état* by the colony's Creole élite, carried out largely to separate Mexico from the liberalizing process under way in the mother country' (Coatsworth, 1978).

This had several consequences. Institutional modernization was *de facto*, and sometimes *de jure*, slow. A new civil code was only produced in 1870 – almost 50 years after independence – and even then nothing replaced a repudiated commercial code. The mining colonial code remained almost intact until 1877. Modern banking and patent laws were non-existent. In spite of constitutional dispositions, taxes and restrictions on domestic trade remained.

The system of government preserved the arbitrary nature of political power in colonial times. Economic success or failure strictly depended on the relationship between enterprise and political authorities; or as Coatsworth (1978) puts it:

> Every enterprise, urban or rural, [was forced] to operate in a highly politicized manner, using kinship networks, political influence, and family prestige to gain privileged access to subsidized credit, to aid various stratagems for recruiting labor, to collect debts or enforce contracts, to evade taxes or circumvent the courts, and to defend or assert titles to land. ... The chief obstacle was the nature of the state itself, its operating principles, the basis for all its acts. Mexico's economic organization could not have been made more efficient without a revolution in the relationship between the state and economic activity (p. 94).

Most important, repeated efforts to preserve or recreate the arbitrary centralism of the colonial state plunged the country into a prolonged period of political instability and continuous struggle opposing the conservative and liberal factions.[5] Half a century of political, social and international wars annihilated the potentially beneficial effects of independence, while at the same time curtailing the resources needed for the state and the private sector to support the recovery of the mining sector and improve the transport infrastructure in a country where the lack of natural communications and the resulting high transport costs had highly adverse effects on the division of labour and regional specialization (Coatsworth, 1990).

In sum, while economic activity had remained 'state-centred', in the sense that 'every enterprise was forced to operate in a highly politicized manner', the state, compared to colonial times, had in fact been weakened and was unable to remove the obstacles to economic development resulting from the decline of mining activity, foreign competition, and the lack of transport infrastructure and financial capital. Economic and industrial stagnation followed, then, as a consequence of a persistent lack of markets and their fragmentation.

Liberal Misperceptions in the Mid-19th Century?

This list of obstacles to economic development in 19th century Mexico is equally significant for what it excludes. Recent revisionism by economic historians suggests, indeed, that two of the traditional culprits, the land tenure system and the economic power of the Church, were not in fact among the major causes of economic stagnation during this period.

The system of land tenure and agricultural production had been organized since the 17th century into large estates called 'haciendas'. While highly inequitable and, to this extent, socially and macroeconomically inefficient, the hacienda system was far from a semi-feudal organization, promoting waste and resource misallocation. Recent research has produced a new image of the hacienda as one of a capitalistic and technologically dynamic under-taking with an economic rationality comparable to that of a modern agricul-tural enterprise, and one which largely exploited its comparative advantages – economies of scale, and access to external credit and information on new technologies and distant markets (see, among others, Van Young, 1981 and 1986). A 'division of labour' had, in fact, been established through time between the hacienda and other forms of agricultural production – small landowners, tenant farmers or Indian villagers – by which each of them had specialized in those products and crops where they enjoyed a competitive advantage: cattle, sheep, wool, food grains, pulque, sugar and sisal in the haciendas, and fruits, tomatoes, chiles, silk, and small animals such as pigs and poultry in the villages and small-scale producers.

Similar revisionism applies to the Church as an economic institution. By the middle of the 19th century, the Church had become the country's single major landowner and an important lender in the emerging financial markets. With respect to its first role, recent studies suggest that Church haciendas were at least as well managed as private haciendas; and, in any case, after independence most of these estates were rented to private farmers and hacendados so that its efficiency did not depend on Church administration. On the other hand, the Church appropriated the tithe (*'diezmo'*), a 10 per cent tax on gross output (and charged mainly on agricultural and livestock pro-duction). As any other tax, the tithe reduced the profitability on agricultural production and probably discouraged it (although some authors have doubts about this[6]). More important, however, is the use to which these revenues were put. Far from financing wholly 'unproductive' expenditures, the Church invested a considerable portion of its revenues (including also private dona-tions and net income from its various properties) in loans to private entrepre-neurs with no legal or practical restrictions to prevent recipients from invest-ing in factories rather than haciendas or other activities. It did this by lending at below market interest rates – usually at a 6 per cent rate on the security on real property. Because it dominated the mortgage-lending market, this prob-ably had the effect, in turn, of bringing market interest rates down. As Coatsworth has put it, the Church 'performed like a modern development bank, charging taxpayers to subsidize the accumulation of private capital. ... Indeed, the Church probably raised the rate of investment above what it would have been had the tithe revenues remained in private hands'.

If the recent revisionism by economic historians is correct, then some of the main elements of the liberal economic programme – free trade, the privatization of corporate and public property, and the liberalization of the land market – were largely misdirected from a strictly (and admittedly narrow) economic development perspective. The first (free trade) probably gave further stimulus to the decline of local manufacturing – and to the 'ruralization' of the labour force – as the expansion of railways in the late 19th century sharply reduced the natural protection provided by traditionally high transport costs. The second, the privatization of corporate property, had the effect of destroying the major, and for a long time practically the only, banking institution in the economy; while the third, the liberalization of the land market, was to contribute to further land concentration and, eventually, to the social explosion of 1910.

The conservative faction was, of course, no better. Although some of its members, Lucas Alamán in particular, had the merit of pioneering the first, and short-lived, industrialization efforts in the 1830s – through industrial protection and the creation of the first public development bank (Banco de Avío) to finance the development of the textile industry[7] – the social and political forces that supported them tended to perpetuate the very arbitrary centralism of political power that had had such harmful effects on economic development since colonial times.

As a result, the coalition that could forge a developmental state did not emerge; and in its absence, some of the major obstacles to economic development remained in place. The politically liberal that could and were willing to carry out the country's political and social modernization were also furiously anti-statist in economic terms; while the only ones that favoured an economic modernization through an interventionist state were the politically conservative, strongly opposed to political and social modernization. It would take a social explosion and a popular revolution in the early 20th century to bring these two requirements for economic development into a less conflictive relationship.

MEXICO'S MODERN ECONOMIC GROWTH (1870–1980)

The *Porfiriato*: Political Stability and the Emergence of a Unified National Market

In 1877, when Porfirio Diaz seized power, 42 per cent of Mexico's GDP was generated by rural activities and only 16 per cent by manufacturing. Around 75 per cent of the population lived in rural areas and more than 70 per cent of those aged ten and above could not read or write. In the following two decades, a turnaround in Mexico's long-term decline was becoming evident. The barriers to economic recovery had been brought down by the transformation of the international economic environment and by domestic changes in

Mexico's political and economic structure that took place under the dictator-
ship of Porfirio Diaz, a 33-year period of political stability (1877–1910),
aptly named 'the *Porfiriato*' by Mexican historians.

Melding a liberal political background with conservative economic goals,
the *Porfiriato's* ideology is summarized in the positivist lemma of Order and
Progress. Order was considered a *sine qua non* for economic growth. The end
of the military and political struggles that had plagued Mexico since its
independence was seen as an essential pre-condition for business confidence
and the recovery of private investment. Strengthening of the central government was efficiently pursued, and combining the use of force and alliances
with relevant groups brought Diaz full hold of the political structure. In all
six presidential elections held between 1877 and 1910, he obtained at least 75
per cent of the vote.

Progress meant transforming Mexico into an industrialized nation by effectively addressing some of the traditional barriers to economic recovery,
such as the lack of transport infrastructure and financial capital. To foster the
expansion of the railway network, the state awarded concessions and financial incentives. Subsidies granted on railway construction amounted to 50 per
cent of their total cost. The expansion of the railway system – which expanded from 900 km to 19,000 km in the 1880s – had an enormous impact.
According to Coatsworth's estimates, it brought an 80 per cent reduction in
freight costs per kilometre from 1878 to 1910. This reduction, plus the one in
transportation time, amplified enormously the size of the market, brought
down local and regional trade barriers and intensified competition. This effect was reinforced by the significant increase in road travel safety that the
Diaz regime achieved.

Foreign investment was another key aspect of Diaz' development strategy,
and was actively sought after through various incentives. These inducements
and the profitable investment opportunities led to the inflow of foreign capital. From 1880, US capital flowed in, later followed by European investments
(Coatsworth, 1989). This flow increased continuously for the next 15 years,
and boomed in the first decade of the 1900s (King, 1970). More generally,
state policies were geared to promote private investment and guarantee the
best conditions for its operation. The legal framework for the conduct of
private business was soon transformed. In 1883 new legal codes for trade and
mining were adopted to improve conditions for foreign investment. Regional
tariffs on domestic trade were abolished. From the late 1880s, import tariffs
climbed continuously all along the *Porfiriato*, while at the same time exemptions on import duties for intermediate and capital goods were granted to
most manufacturing enterprises.

Accompanying these policy changes and responses was a more propitious
external economic environment. By 1870 the second industrial revolution in

the industrialized countries had spurred demand for minerals and other raw materials. In addition, there was a notable expansion of international investment to several less developed countries: between 1870 and 1900 this flow doubled the value of the outstanding capital stock held by foreign investors (Maddison, 1989). Combined with the end of political instability, the new environment helped to restore international creditworthiness. Having defaulted on its external debt on six different occasions between 1824 and 1880, in 1889 the Mexican government finally reached an agreement with foreign bankers on rescheduling Mexico's foreign debt. By the early 1890s, the country's access to international capital markets was restored and, from then until 1911, Mexico's external debt increased 300 per cent, mostly to finance public works in infrastructure.

What was the overall development outcome of this strategy? Economic growth and modernization was felt in many areas, reversing a century of decline, and from 1877 to 1910 Mexico's GDP increased by a multiple of 3.5 in real terms, achieving an annual average growth rate of 2.5 per cent in output per capita. Foreign investment meant access to world markets, and between the 1890s and 1910 Mexico's foreign trade as a share of GDP increased by more than ten percentage points, helping also to increase government funds, as taxes on foreign trade provided more than half of public revenues. The railroad boom benefited some old activities – such as mining[8] – and simultaneously helped in the creation of new activities whose production scales and capital intensity made them unprofitable in the absence of a unified national market.

Underlying this modernization was Mexico's first wave of large-scale industrialization. Through import substitution in textiles, beer, paper-making, cement and steel, manufacturing output increased at an average rate of 3.6 per cent per annum from 1877 to 1910 (Coatsworth, 1989; King (1970), however, quotes Solis (1970) who estimates manufacturing output rose at over 12 per cent per annum from 1877 to 1907). Manufacturing changed from being an artisans' activity, carried out in small handicraft firms, to a productive process done in large-scale plants. In fact, before 1890, the large-scale factory system had been present only in the cotton textile industry (Haber, 1989). This phase of industrialization, as Haber points out, was accompanied by changes in business management methods and industrial organization. Joint-stock corporations increasingly substituted family-managed enterprises giving origin to large, vertically integrated firms in a diverse array of manufacturing activities.

The size of the Mexican market was, nevertheless, rather small given modern technologies. This favoured high degrees of market concentration, as only oligopolies could survive, and concentration was strengthened by the lack of a modern banking system. Even then, dependence on foreign technol-

ogy designed for bigger markets led to a lack of exploitation of economies of
scale and high operation costs (Reynolds, 1970). Collusion among producers
probably inhibited efforts to innovate production methods and was often
aimed at manipulating the state and the market to hinder competition. These
problems were aggravated by a scarcity of skilled workers and, more generally, by a predominantly rural labour force whose working practices were still
very much alien to the proletariat. All these factors hindered labour productivity and, as a result, international competitiveness was weak: even though
wages in Mexico were less than half that of workers in Britain or New
England, costs of production in Mexico were 10 to 20 per cent higher (Haber,
1989).

The *Porfiriato*'s impact was not restrained to the industrial sphere. The
rural areas were also deeply transformed in their social and economic structure. Based on a diagnosis of the rural sector as unproductive, with most
agricultural output distributed through non-market channels, the Diaz administration pushed an accelerated redistribution of federal and communal land
to private development companies and wealthy individuals. In this process,
no attention was given to potential privatization revenues from the sale of
federal land (part of it being the previously large landholdings of the Church)[9];
rather, the aim was to extend private property in order to free idle resources
and favour its more efficient use. Privatization would promote large-scale
commercial cultivation. By 1890, 20 per cent of Mexico's total area was held
by less than 50 individuals or companies. By the early 1900s, 95 per cent of
all arable land was in the hands of 835 families (Manzanilla Schaffer, 1963).

By the early 1900s, this pattern of development started to show symptoms
of exhaustion. From 1903, real wages began to decrease in a systematic and
persistent way. Droughts in 1907 reduced output of food products, and furthermore increased their prices. By 1910, the cumulative decline in real
wages was 26 per cent relative to 1903. If hunger was not evident, poverty
was most common, especially in the rural areas.[10] At the same time, recourse
to force to repress labour and suppress political opposition became more
frequent and eventually unsuccessful. By 1910, the system's unequal distribution of benefits and access to power reached its limit. The emerging middle
classes excluded from political decisions, and the workers and peasants
marginalized from the benefits of economic growth, were successful in developing a triumphant coalition under the banners of political democracy,
agrarian reform and labour rights.

What had gone wrong? Clearly, the *Porfiriato*'s 'primary contradiction'
was in its results: the growing imbalance between rapid economic growth, on
the one hand, and the slow pace of political and social progress on the other.
Porfirio Diaz had set out to make of Mexico a modern industrial nation. But,
by 1910 only 28 per cent of Mexicans could read and write, and life expect-

ancy at birth was not above 37 years. With two-thirds of its population still living in rural areas, Mexico was still a fundamentally backward economy and, overall, a backward society.

There were also shortcomings in the design of the development strategy. Three of these turned out to be particularly relevant. First, rather than increasing labour mobility, the enclosure system implemented in the *Porfiriato* strengthened labour's links of dependency with the rural areas. Deprived of land plots, the great majority of the population was forced to work permanently as indebted labour in the haciendas. Thus, at the same time that the expansion of the railway system was creating a national market, huge contingents of the population were cut out from the possibility to enter it.

A second aspect concerns the sources of finance for development. The existing banking system was simply a source of short-term loans, at the most suitable to fit purely commercial needs. By 1897 no bank had legal authorization to give loans for a period longer than a year. By 1910, some banks were legally allowed to give such loans, but the great majority of them were provided for investments in real estate. Besides foreign investors, Mexico's first wave of industrialization was carried out by the merchant élite who financed it through the reinvestment of their accumulated profits.[11] At the end of the *Porfiriato*, Mexico still faced the urgent need to create banking institutions capable of financing its long-term investment needs.

The third is related to the role of the state in the quest for development in backward economies. For the *Porfiriato*'s élite, the role of the state, besides ensuring social peace, was to guarantee the best conditions for private investment without intervening directly in the productive sphere. Public investment never amounted to more than 5 per cent of total investment, and only 7 per cent of public expenditure was directed at capital formation purposes. While the emergence of a national market had broken through some of the barriers of stagnation, this limited role of the state proved insufficient to overcome the still enormous obstacles to economic development.

Revolution, the 1930s and the Emergence of a Developmental State

In 1910 the Pax Porfiriana drew to a dramatic close with the Mexican Revolution. Once more, the absence of social consensus became the fundamental obstacle for Mexico's development. The construction of a stable social pact would be fully achieved only three decades later.

The most violent stages of the Mexican Revolution ended with the adoption of a new Constitution in 1917. Political unrest continued for the next ten years – marked by the killings of important figures such as Zapata, Carranza and Obregon, and numerous uprisings – but the scale of armed struggle diminished significantly. The 1917 Constitution redefined the legal framework for land property and labour relations. It placed the nation over and above private property on matters regarding land, water and subsoil resources; established the right to form trade unions, a system of minimum wages, eight-hour workdays within a six-day workweek, and equal pay for equal work; and included an agrarian reform through the expropriation of large land holdings and its allocation to '*ejidos*', a land tenure system combining collective ownership with private exploitation of the land.

A fundamental move towards the consolidation of social peace and political stability was the creation of the Partido Nacional Revolucionario (PNR) in 1929.[12] Encompassing all relevant social forces of the Mexican Revolution, the PNR soon became a functional vehicle for political control and the only legitimate arena in which to settle political differences. Complete hegemony would be achieved during Cardenas' presidency (1936–40). Under the institutional framework established then, and still basically in place more than half a century later, the ruling president is the most powerful political force, with no relevant opposition in Congress or on the domestic scene. The official party – renamed Partido de la Revolución Mexicana (PRM) in 1938 and Partido Revolucionario Institucional (PRI) in 1946 – is the central instrument of corporatist control through a mixture of co-optation, negotiation and repression. This mixture has been most successful in retaining power control; the PRI has been acknowledged ample-margin victory in all presidential elections and, with very recent exceptions, in all state governor elections too.

By 1940, the government party had formed solid alliances with labour through the Confederacion de Trabajadores Mexicanos (CTM) and the Federacion de Sindicatos de Trabajadores al Servicio del Estado (FSTSE), and controlled peasants' organizations through the Confederacion Nacional Campesina (CNC). The private sector, although not formally included in the official party, was recognized and taken into account by the political system through a number of business organizations and chambers. In addition, by the 1940s the military had been professionalized, divested of its political role. The age of Caudillos was over, and Mexico's particular form of institutionalized authoritarian control had begun.

In the process of building a new stable social pact, Mexico's economic structure changed. The years of armed conflict brought production in certain areas to a standstill. Agricultural activities were, in general, most severely affected. Many intermediate and producer goods industries were shut down, given the disruption of the transport and communications network, but the manufacturing plant remained undamaged by the violent fight (FCE, 1963). Mining and oil, on the other hand, as well as a few manufacturing activities oriented to the production of army supplies, actually expanded their production and no large firm was destroyed in the Revolution. The first Mexican oil boom – which reached a production peak in the early 1920s – was carried out by British and American oil companies and, interestingly, actually began in the midst of the armed struggle. Besides the attractive profit opportunities provided by recent oil discoveries, a major factor was probably that contenders in the Revolution avoided harming industrial plants, machinery and equipment. Revolutionaries viewed large firms and businesses as important sources of finance, compulsory or voluntary (Haber, 1989). However, though productive capacity was not physically destroyed, it deteriorated massively as no investment or maintenance was undertaken except in a few areas. The collapse of the established social and legal order, the breakdown of the national market and the domestic monetary system, and the uncertainty this brought about, proved lethal for investment.

As soon as the most turbulent stages of the Revolution were over, manufacturing activity began to grow. Neither its productive nor its organizational structure had been changed by the Revolution. Its high concentration had even, perhaps, increased, and commanding oligopolistic positions were held by the same entrepreneurs as before. The cut-down of investment had lowered its productivity and competitiveness, intensifying its need of trade protection. In fact, in 1917, the First National Conference of Industrial Entrepreneurs – organized by the Ministry of Trade and Industry – agreed on the necessity of trade protection and the creation of a bank dedicated to financing industrial activities (FCE, 1963).

The Mexican economy had its own crash from 1926 to 1932. The impact of falling terms of trade and declining oil exports after the peak of the early 1920s was aggravated by a collapse in internal expenditure as the government actively pursued a balanced budget in conditions when its revenue dropped 33 per cent. Fiscal tightening was concentrated in current expenditure. While public employees were being dismissed and wages of government workers being lowered, public spending was maintained in refurbishing the railway and the highway system, two important capital-formation ventures. Whether intended or not, this pattern of response avoided further deterioration in the economy's productive potential. In 1930 a new tariff law was passed confirming trade protection.

The crash came as a blow on the mild recovery of investment that had begun in the early 1920s. However, with hindsight, the crash had an important positive element in that it convinced the government that rapid development would require a much more active economic role by the public sector. When Lazaro Cardenas was named the official party's presidential candidate, he put forward a Six-Year Plan (1934–40) in which, for the first time, the government explicitly presented a plan of actions for the next six years and committed itself to active development policies involving unprecedented investments in agriculture, industry and infrastructure, as well as in social development.

The process of consolidation of political power after the Revolution had been accompanied by an expansion in policy instruments available to the government.[13] With Cardenas, the public sector expanded further with several development or financial entities. Most important, the oil industry was nationalized and agrarian reform began to be implemented on a massive scale. With the commitment to long term development, fiscal restraint was abandoned. Fiscal policy became countercyclical and budget deficits were run to boost productive and social investment. Public expenditure was reoriented away from military and administrative spending. The highway system increased sevenfold, covering 9900 km by 1940. In addition, temporary flotation of the exchange rate led to a depreciation of the peso in real terms.

With the turnaround in the conduct of government policies and the extraordinary recovery in the terms of the trade of silver and oil (the country's main exports), Mexico resumed growth in 1933–34. The first new round of investment since the *Porfiriato* began in manufacturing and concentrated in new textile activities. Manufacturing became the most dynamic sector of the economy.

The Post-War Golden Age of Industrialization (1940–80)

In the process of achieving hegemony, the Mexican state arrived at a strong conviction that it should play an active role in investment and production if Mexico was to develop. By the late 1940s, it controlled fundamental resources and had increased the number of its policy instruments significantly. Whether it would succeed in launching a drive for growth on a permanent basis remained to be seen.

Not for long, however, as a complete overhaul of the economy and society was in its beginnings. For the next 40 years, Mexico's economy grew at a sustained pace of 6.4 per cent per annum in real terms and GDP per capita at 3.2 per cent per annum (see Table 6.2). The country was transformed from an agrarian one into an urban, semi-industrial society. From 1940 to 1980, the output share of manufacturing rose from 15.4 per cent to 24.9 per cent (see Table 6.3) and the share of the population living in urban areas soared from 35 per cent to 66 per cent at a time when the total population increased from 20 to 70 million people. Literacy rates nearly doubled, reaching 83 per cent in 1980. The average number of years of schooling of the adult population jumped from 2.6 to 7.1, and life expectancy at birth increased 24 years to 65 (see Table 6.4). Despite these improvements, the benefits of growth were far from being evenly distributed. By the end of this period, 20 per cent of the population accrued more than 50 per cent of total disposable income, while 58 per cent of Mexicans were still in poverty (less conservative estimates put this figure as high as 63 per cent (see Hernandez Laos, 1989)). Thus, at the

Table 6.2 GDP at constant prices, 1895–1980 (1970=100.0)

	1895	1910	1926	1932	1940	1955	1970	1976	1980
Total GDP	6.9	10.6	12.4	10.2	15.7	37.7	100.0	143.1	189.5
Agriculture*	17.3	21.8	20.9	21.1	26.2	59.3	100.0	117.1	139.9
Mining	4.4	10.9	24.1	15.4	21.1	38.1	100.0	141.9	244.8
Industry	2.1	4.4	6.1	4.6	9.9	28.1	100.0	148.7	200.7
(Manufacturing)	(2.4)	(4.9)	(6.2)	(4.5)	(10.4)	(28.4)	(100.0)	(147.8)	(199.3)
Services	7.6	11.5	12.9	10.5	16.2	38.2	100.0	145.9	191.8

* Includes livestock, forestry and fishing.

Source: Banco de México.

121

Table 6.3   Structure of GDP, 1895–1980 (per cent)

	1895	1910	1926	1932	1940	1955	1970	1970	1976	1980
			(based on 1960 prices)					(based on 1970 prices)		
Agriculture*	29.1	24.0	19.7	24.1	19.4	18.3	11.6	12.2	10.0	9.0
Mining	3.0	4.9	9.3	7.2	6.4	4.8	4.8	2.5	2.5	3.3
Industry	9.0	12.3	14.7	13.3	18.7	22.1	29.7	30.1	31.3	31.9
(Manufacturing)	(7.9)	(10.7)	(11.6)	(10.2)	(15.4)	(17.5)	(23.3)	(23.7)	(24.5)	(24.9)
Services	58.9	58.7	56.3	55.4	55.5	54.7	53.9	55.2	56.2	55.8
TOTAL	100.0	100.0	100.0	100.0	100.0	100.0	100.0	100.0	100.0	100.0

* Includes livestock, forestry and fishing.

Source: Banco de México.

Table 6.4 Population and social indicators (1895–1980)

Year	Total Population (Millions)	Rural Population (per cent)	Life expectancy at birth (years)	Literacy[1] (per cent)	Average Years of schooling[2]
1895	12.6	72	30	18[3]	NA
1910	15.1	NA	NA	28	NA
1930	16.5	66	37	38	NA
1940	19.7	65	41	46	2.6
1980	69.7	34	65	83	7.1

[1] Population age 10 or above
[2] Age 15 or above
[3] Age 6 or above
NA = Not available.

Sources: Maddison (1989) and INEGI.

123

end of Mexico's Golden Age, poverty and inequality were still major problems to be solved.

This long period of fast and sustained economic development can be broken down into three sections: the drive for industrialization from 1940 to the mid-1950s, from then until 1970 (the 'gem' of the Golden Age), and the 1970s, when the engine of growth began to run out of steam.

Growth with inflation: the first 15 years

From 1940 to 1955 Mexico's GDP grew at an average rate of 5.8 per cent per annum in real terms, and GDP per capita at 2.8 per cent. Manufacturing became the engine of growth, with rates of growth of production of 7.4 per cent per annum. The expansion of external demand in the first half of the 1940s and the Korean War in the early 1950s gave important impulse to manufacturing activity. But its sustained momentum was determined much more by domestic factors.

Public investment expanded systematically during the period (see Table 6.5), and was oriented to urban and industrial development. Additional incentives such as tax concessions were used to promote manufacturing activities. Investment in education and welfare held their share in federal expenditure. The industrialization drive also came hand in hand with a deepening of trade protection.[14] By 1947 protectionism had been officially adopted as a government intermediate objective (Mosk, 1950). Import substitution in consumer products advanced rapidly during these years. In 1940, consumer and capital goods each accounted for 30 per cent of total imports; by 1955 the consumer

Table 6.5   Investment rates and GDP growth, 1900–1980

Year	GDP (index 1910=100)	Total investment (% of GDP)	Public investment (% of GDP)
1900	73.1	10.1	0.5[1]
1910	100.0	10.1	0.4
1921	107.7	10.1	NA
1930	109.4	9.4	2.2
1940	148.6	9.3	3.5
1960	467.8	17.2	5.2
1980	1746.8	24.8	11.4

[1]   1895.
NA = Not available.

Sources: ECLAC and INEGI.

goods' share had been halved while that of capital goods had jumped to 40 per cent.

Agriculture as a whole recorded an impressive average growth of over 5.0 per cent per annum, but it evinced a dual structure. A gap, which widened in the 1950s, developed between commercial private farms in the north-western region and the *ejidos* of the central and southern regions. The former were oriented much more towards export markets and were the main beneficiaries from public investment in irrigation and roads. The latter continued to use traditional methods of cultivation and remained oriented towards the domestic market.

As manufacturing became the engine of growth, new and unforeseen problems appeared. After several years of trade surpluses, the foreign trade accounts began to register red figures. The strong expansion in economic activity led to higher imports, especially of capital and intermediate goods, over and above the availability of exports. The ensuing pressure on the foreign exchange market was at times worsened by short term capital outflows, triggering periodic balance-of-payments crises. Devaluation and increased trade protection were the usual responses. The new role of the state implied a restructuring and expansion of expenditures on its part, but no equivalent reforms had been made on the revenue side of the fiscal accounts. The inflation tax substituted for this during most of this first period.[15] With the financing reforms of the mid 1950s, the problem was solved through recourse to forced savings via the banking system reserve requirements. Later, it was through the increasing use of external finance.

Stabilizing development (1956–70)
The period from 1956 to 1970, commonly known as 'stabilizing development', is considered the Golden Age of Mexico's modern economic growth. During this era, GDP increased at an average rate of 6.8 per cent per annum, with an annual inflation rate of less than 4 per cent, and a fixed exchange rate against the US dollar which lasted for 22 years. Development policy continued to be centred on industrialization, with the state as an important agent. Macroeconomic stability was added as a major policy priority, and high inflation and exchange rate nominal depreciation were successfully avoided. The strategy was thus consistent with the drive for development implemented since 1940, but reflected greater concern for the observance of macroeconomic balances. Public expenditure managed to draw bigger shares of GDP, but its expansion was continuously subject to considerations on the evolution of the monetary base and its compatibility with predetermined targets.

Industrial protection was maintained, and even increased, as the share of imports subject to licences rose from 17.7 per cent in 1956 to 68.3 per cent in 1970 (Gil Diaz, 1984). Public investment, tax and credit facilities were also geared to stimulate industrial growth. In addition, prices of public utilities, in particular energy, were systematically less than fully adjusted to inflation.

Fostered by this environment, manufacturing expanded at annual rates of 8.9 per cent per annum with the dynamic domestic market as its major source of demand. Its profile was transformed as foreign investors, private entrepreneurs and, on some occasions, the government, switched the leading role in triggering successive waves of import substitution in the durable and intermediate goods sector, the motor vehicle and rubber industry, and simple machinery. By the end of the 'stabilization development' period, however, import substitution in the capital goods sector had yet to be accomplished.

The macroeconomic performance from 1940 to 1970 was undoubtedly impressive. The strategy on which it was based tackled important obstacles on the road to Mexico's development. However, it ignored or underestimated the magnitude of other obstacles. To the extent that the following administrations did not solve them, they could, and did, become painfully costly.

The first obstacle arose from the neglect of agriculture which, after 1965, faced serious difficulties in expanding production. Its rate of growth in the second half of the 1960s fell below the pace of demographic expansion. Among the factors explaining this decline were the dual character of the sector, the adverse trend in the prices of agricultural goods relative to manufacturing goods (as urban consumption was subsidized), and the continuous decline of its share in public investment after the 1950s. All these elements would contribute to an increase in poverty, a contraction of the potential domestic market, and a loss of social cohesion which led to emergent social instability.

Secondly, while trade protection proved a valuable instrument in promoting growth and import substitution in many sectors, there was no explicit policy, either from the private or the public sector, to strengthen over time the economy's export potential. Neither was it clear whether the policy as it stood could complete the most difficult phase of import substitution involving high-technology capital goods.

Finally, tax reforms systematically aborted, and public finances became increasingly dependent on external debt.[16] So too did the balance of payments, which became more and more vulnerable to short term capital flows, with their potentially destabilizing influence. As long as the Golden Age of world economic growth continued, misperceptions regarding the potential relevance of these issues could remain. Unfortunately, this Golden Age was coming to an end.

'Shared development' and the oil boom
The new Echeverria administration taking office in late 1970, had as a central point of its political platform the claim that the 'stabilizing development'

strategy had failed to address the fundamental problem of inequality. A new strategy of 'shared development' was thus proposed in which the benefits from economic growth would be more evenly distributed. In practice, however, the policies adopted would fail to fulfil these objectives.

As originally conceived, 'shared development' was going to achieve an improvement in the distribution of income by reorienting public investment and finance towards the agricultural sector, and reforming what was perceived to be an inequitable tax system. From 1970 to 1975, the share of agriculture in public investment increased while that of industry declined. In addition, government employment expanded by 70 per cent from 1970 to 1975. However, by 1972, private sector opposition had forced the government to abandon any ambitious plan of tax reform. Changes in this area were limited to an imposition of a 15 per cent tax on purchase of luxury goods and an increase of less than two percentage points in the excise tax rate. Real public sector prices continued to decline during 1970–73 (Clavijo, 1980). Their correction in 1974 left them only 7 per cent above their 1970 level. As changes in the structure of public revenue stalled, the burden of achieving a more equitable distribution of income was shifted to public expenditure. In five years, its share of GDP increased by more than ten percentage points.

Temporarily, the strategy did have the intended impact on the functional distribution of income. Gil Diaz (1987) shows that the share of labour in net national product went from 40 per cent in 1970 to 43 per cent in 1972–74, and reached 49 per cent in 1976. In addition, GDP achieved an average rate of growth of 6.1 per cent per annum. Unfortunately, these achievements were accompanied by the emergence of severe macroeconomic imbalances.

A number of reasons would account for this. On the external front, the collapse of the world's Golden Age had its toll on the Mexican economy. The first oil price shock found Mexico as a net importer of oil and, together with the decline in external demand, tightened the balance of payments constraints on growth. Moreover, the increase in domestic inflation rates to the 20 per cent range, the expansion of public investment, and a fixed exchange rate, tripled the trade deficit from 1970 to 1975. The model of industrialization also began to show some signs of exhaustion. Investment was carried out to modernize plants in old sectors already conquered by foreign competition, but failed both to increase exports significantly and to deepen import substitution in the capital goods sector. The limitations of capital goods manufacturing were evident, for example, in the fact that during 1974–75 they accounted for less than 8 per cent of manufacturing output, while at the same time they represented more than 50 per cent of total imports. As a share of GDP, overall exports declined, largely as a result of stagnating agricultural supplies and productivity. Manufacturing export coefficients increased but remained at low levels, and the share of imports in the domestic market started to climb as the investment process failed to diversify into new activities.

To the extent that tax reform was not addressed, public revenues lagged behind. The fiscal deficit climbed from 2.5 per cent of GDP to 9.9 per cent between 1971 and 1976, and was increasingly covered through monetary expansion and external debt (which increased at an average annual rate of 40 per cent from 1973 to 1976[17]). In addition, private enterprise did not find a fertile ground in the 'shared development' rhetoric, and soon the economy's expansion was being driven exclusively by public spending. Eventually, the situation worsened significantly as a result of capital flight. Notwithstanding the increase in import controls and tariffs, balance of payments pressures forced the government to depreciate by nearly 100 per cent in 1976, thus abandoning the exchange rate parity that had remained fixed for more than 20 years.

Despite the severity of the 1976 crisis, in a year or so the economy's prospects were fully turned around with the announcement of Mexico's vast oil resources. Their exploitation and sale in the international market would bring a swift and strong recovery. The trade deficit was under control again, averaging 1.5 per cent as a share of GDP. The term profile of foreign debt was restructured and, for a while, new indebtedness did not grow in a noticeable way. An ambitious industrialization plan was launched on the assumption of a sustained long-term increase in the price of oil. Manufacturing investment soared, boosted by public and private entrepreneurship, and GDP reached rates of 8 to 9 per cent per annum from 1978 to 1981. A major tax reform was also carried out in this period, and these changes reduced some of the inequities of the Mexican tax system.[18]

However, with the benefit of hindsight, some signs were already worrying by the late 1970s. The inflation rate had reached a plateau of around 18 per cent and did not seem to climb down. Interest payments were increasing as nominal rates in the international credit markets floated upwards in an unprecedented way. Few investments were directed to the export sector, although two exceptions are worth noting: the motor-vehicle industry – where a new generation of plants was being built with state-of-the-art technology, explicitly designed to compete in the world markets – and the petrochemicals sector, where the public sector was investing heavily.

The whole strategy had been based on: (1) the premise of a long-term foreign exchange and fiscal abundance from oil exports – and the 1979–80 oil price hike had only confirmed expectations that the era of high real oil prices had come to stay; and (2) the notion that the external debt problem was over, given the low real interest rates that had so far prevailed. Thus when in 1981 the oil market started to crumble and foreign interest rates drastically jumped upwards, both of these shocks were taken to be transitory, and thus to be dealt with by additional external finance. Short-term external indebtedness was accelerated in an effort to sustain economic expansion. The increase in foreign indebtedness in 1981 was equivalent to 10 per cent of GDP and, by the end of that year, the current account deficit reached 12.5 million dollars, half of it due to interest payments, while capital flight was soaring. Indeed, the whole international economic environment that made the oil boom possible had been tragically misperceived (by the government, foreign banks and international financial institutions alike) and when this became clear Mexico suddenly became a highly indebted country, that is, an over-indebted borrower given the new levels of interest rates and export revenues with which the old debt had to be serviced. In 1982, the oil boom was over.

THE SHIFT IN THE MARKET–STATE BALANCE IN THE 1980s

As is well known, the Mexican economy was subject to two major external shocks during the 1980s: the 1982 debt crisis which increased debt service and curtailed new external finance, and the 1986 oil price shock which dramatically cut off a major part of the country's main source of foreign exchange and fiscal revenues. These external shocks created imbalances in both the balance of payments and the fiscal accounts.

The strategies adopted to restore domestic and external balance and the adjustments that followed can be briefly summarized as follows. In the wake of the 1982 debt crisis, a very orthodox, stabilization-first strategy was adopted, with the aim of rapidly restoring price and balance-of-payments stability. This was to be followed by a gradualist approach to structural adjustment which would promote an incremental process of resource reallocation in a stable and growth-oriented macroeconomic framework. This 'high growth–slow structural adjustment strategy' – which prevailed as a policy stance during 1984 and part of 1985 – was soon to be abandoned in favour of a path of increasing radicalization of market reform measures which, contrary to conventional wisdom and advice, took place within the highly adverse macroeconomic environment created by the 1986 oil price shock. At the same time, and after the failure of successive orthodox attempts at inflation control, macroeconomic policy shifted in late 1987 to a rather heterodox approach to stabilization – the 'Economic Solidarity Pact' – aiming at rapid disinflation through the combination of wage and price controls, an exchange rate freeze, and tight fiscal and monetary policy. From then, market reform measures, especially in the areas of trade policy and privatization, underwent a radical acceleration.

By the early 1990s the foreign exchange and fiscal gaps that were opened by the debt crisis and the oil shock had been closed. But the legacy of these external shocks – the collapse of public and private investments in the wake of the debt crisis and the loss of foreign exchange and fiscal revenues after the 1986 oil shock – has been harsh. Together with the stagnation of productive activity and the contraction of the population real incomes that followed, they adversely affected the economy's growth potential by reducing the domestic savings rate and producing an ageing of the capital stock and lower overall economic efficiency.[19] With low investment and domestic savings rates compared to the past, Mexico's economic growth in the early 1990s was half of what it was during the oil boom. On present trends (around 3 per cent per annum), it would remain significantly below the long-term rate of the post-war period (6.5 per cent per annum), let alone the growth rates of the oil boom period. Despite a foreign savings rate well above historical levels, the economy invests today a lower proportion of its output than at any time in the two decades before 1980, and thus expands its productive capacity at a slower pace than in the past. The economy, in sum, emerges weaker, rather than stronger, from the years of crisis and adjustment.

At the same time, a 'great transformation' has taken place in between, if we may appropriate Polanyi's expression for events of a different scale. The massive reform process has involved a number of major reforms in the trade and industrial policy regime, a large-scale privatization of state-owned enterprises, and massive deregulation of foreign investment flows and domestic economic activities. This has occurred with a view to giving a larger economic role to the private sector and greater scope to market forces, and to accelerating integration into the international economy.

Market Reforms, Economic Efficiency and Productivity Growth

Are market reforms likely to affect significantly the economy's productivity growth rate and external competitiveness so that, despite lower rates of accumulation, the economy may recover some of the growth potential lost during the crisis?

Some policy reforms – especially those affecting the domestic regulatory framework – were long overdue (as exemplified most strikingly by the regulations in road transportation) and, overall, were clearly desirable on both efficiency and equity grounds.[20] Their adverse impacts have been rather limited or even absent, and the benefits of regulatory changes in many areas have by and large exceeded the costs. These have not been, however, the most radical reforms, nor those from which the greater benefits were to be expected. In what follows we focus on the most important of these reforms – trade and investment liberalization, privatization and state reform – and on a preliminary evaluation of their effects.

The case for greater selectivity in state participation in the economy and, indeed, for state disengagement in a number of productive activities, has been based on macroeconomic grounds: a government rationed in credit markets, pressing social needs to be met, and a private sector with ample financial resources abroad ready to be invested in previously state-dominated activities which do not have a high social priority.[21] The case is certainly extremely powerful. But this is so for macroeconomic reasons related to the special conditions of the 1980s. This particular argument has less significance for the long-term growth potential of the economy, beyond the promise (which so far largely remains just that) of a considerable expansion in human capital investment that the huge privatization revenues make possible.

There is also, of course, the more traditional microeconomic case for privatization based on the notion that a greater participation of the private sector will bring about improvements in the overall efficiency of investment. If the latter is a positive function of the share of private investment in overall investment, then part, if not all, of the fall in the overall rate of accumulation could be compensated by the shift in the composition of investment. And as shown in Table 6.6, there has indeed been a dramatic shift in the composition of investment during the 1980s: from 56 per cent in 1980–81, the share of the private sector in total fixed investment rose to 77 per cent ten years later.

The first point to be made in addressing this issue is to recognize that the efficiency of overall investment does not depend only on its private/public sector composition, but also on the rate of investment itself, which affects investment efficiency through its consequences on the age distribution and the structure of the capital stock (residential/non-residential, net investment/depreciation). Now, as clearly shown also in Table 6.6, the shift in the private/public composition of investment was a result of the absolute decline in the rate of public investment, rather than of an absolute increase in private investment: the latter, as a fraction of GDP, was in the early 1990s at approximately the same levels as ten years earlier (14 to 15 per cent of GDP). If its share in overall investment increased, this was only because of the collapse of public investment rates from around 11.5 per cent to 4.5 per cent. Unless the productivity of public investment was actually negative – and nobody to our knowledge has argued this – the efficiency losses resulting from the absolute fall in the overall rate of investment are bound to outweigh any efficiency gains brought about by the shift in its composition. The rise in the capital–output ratio since 1982 (see Table 6.6) is fully consistent with this conclusion.

In addition, the relationship between the efficiency and the composition of overall investment is surely more complex than generally assumed. It is likely to have the shape of a Laffer curve, as shown in Figure 6.1, with low efficiency levels being consistent with both too high and too low shares of

Table 6.6 Investment and savings rates, 1980–91

	1980	1981	1982	1983	1984	1985	1986	1987	1988	1989	1990-p	1991-p
In % of GDP (at constant 1980 pesos)												
Fixed investment	24.8	26.5	22.2	16.6	17.0	17.9	16.4	16.0	16.8	17.3	18.8	20.0
Residential	7.7	7.8	7.8	6.7	6.9	7.1	6.7	7.0	7.3	7.5	NA	NA
Business and infrastructure	17.1	18.7	14.4	9.9	10.1	10.8	9.7	9.0	9.5	9.8	—	—
Net investment	16.2	17.9	12.7	5.0	6.2	7.4	4.8	4.6	6.3	6.9	—	—
Depreciation	8.6	8.6	9.5	11.6	10.8	10.5	11.6	11.4	10.5	10.4	—	—
Private	14.1	14.4	11.9	10.4	10.7	11.7	10.9	11.5	12.4	13.1	14.3	15.7
Public	10.7	12.1	10.3	6.2	6.3	6.2	5.5	4.5	4.4	4.2	4.5	4.3
In % of nominal GDP												
Domestic savings	22.2	21.4	22.4	24.7	22.5	22.4	17.8	22.3	20.1	20.7	17.7	17.6
Public savings	7.1	2.1	4.7	7.0	6.3	5.8	4.1	7.0	1.4	2.7	6.6	7.0
External	4.1	3.2	5.0	6.2	5.5	4.4	0.5	1.6	-0.2	0.0	1.3	0.8
Domestic	3.0	-1.1	-0.3	0.8	0.8	1.4	3.6	5.4	1.6	2.7	5.3	6.2
Private savings	15.1	19.3	17.7	17.7	16.2	16.6	13.7	15.3	18.7	18.0	11.1	10.6
Private disposable income	80.2	83.7	79.3	78.6	79.3	81.1	81.8	80.6	87.5	85.0	79.4	78.9
Average propensity to consume	0.832	0.787	0.835	0.807	0.817	0.818	0.866	0.848	0.799	0.794	0.871	0.871
Inflation tax	2.0	1.9	5.5	3.1	2.1	2.2	3.2	3.6	1.4	0.6	1.0	0.5

Real private income per capita (index 1980=100)	100.0	109.4	97.1	87.8	87.5	89.3	78.5	79.2	82.1	85.7	80.5	81.8
Capital–output ratio[1]	2.6	2.6	2.9	3.1	3.2	3.2	3.4	3.5	3.6	3.6	NA	NA
Capital–output ratio (non-residential)[1]	1.5	1.5	1.7	1.8	1.8	1.9	2.0	2.0	2.0	2.0	—	—
Average age capital stock[1]	10.9	10.7	10.8	11.1	11.5	11.7	12.0	12.3	12.6	12.9	—	—

[1] Refers to gross capital stock
NA = Not available.

Source: Banco de México, Indicadores Económicos; Presidencia de la República, Criterios Generales de Política Económica; and Hofman (1991).

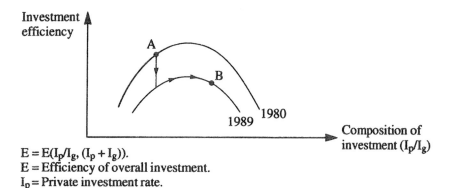

$$E = E(I_p/I_g, (I_p + I_g)).$$
$E = $ Efficiency of overall investment.
$I_p = $ Private investment rate.
$I_g = $ Public investment rate.

Figure 6.1   Relation between efficiency and the composition of investment

public investment. This is so because public investment itself, as much recent empirical research suggests, affects the productivity of private investment, and thus at low levels of public investment further reductions can bring about losses rather than gains in overall efficiency. Given the sharp contraction of public investments during the 1980s, and the fact that the microeconomic efficiency gains and performance improvements of the newly privatized enterprises are yet to be seen in most cases, the question arises as to whether the economy moved to the wrong side of the Laffer-type curve. Such a result is illustrated in Figure 6.1: starting from point A (the pre-crisis level and composition of investment), the fall in public investment had two consequences: it shifted the curve downwards (through its adverse effect on the overall investment rate) and also brought about an excessive movement along the curve (through its perverse effect on the composition of investment). In such circumstances, an increase in public investment in areas with high social returns and high positive externalities for the productivity of private investment is the best way of addressing the problem of investment efficiency.

The results of trade policy reform are also controversial. Let us look first at the static efficiency gains expected by classical trade theory.[22] One of the striking features of the Mexican transition towards a liberalized trade regime is the smoothness of the microeconomic processes of resource reallocation. The absence of massive reallocation processes is revealed by the fact that current trends in the trade *pattern* and industrial *structure* are largely an extrapolation of the past. Beyond a few exceptions – the growing export shares of the wood industry and, since 1985, of textiles and apparel – the 1980s have witnessed an extrapolation of past trends in the trade and industrial patterns marked by the increasing importance of heavy intermediates, consumer durables and capital goods. Since 1985, the first year of radical trade reform, these trends have continued unabated[23] and, in the case of consumer durables and capital goods, have, if anything, accelerated.

The counterpart of this smoothness and of the lack of reversal in the direction of structural change in manufacturing is, however, that the classic efficiency gains expected from trade liberalization cannot possibly be very important. For those expecting a large, painful but greatly beneficial reallocation of resources in favour of traditional exportable goods, labour- and natural resource-intensive, the experience with trade liberalization to date should have been, in fact, greatly disappointing. In our view, two major factors explain these developments. First, and perhaps paradoxically, the adjustment to the debt crisis and declining terms of trade in the 1980s forced macroeconomic policy to provide unprecedented levels of 'exchange rate protection'. This facilitated the adjustment of industrial firms to a more open economy and prevented job losses which, up to 1987–88, were largely the result of the contraction of industrial demand rather than of import penetration. The second is simply Mexico's successful import-substitution experience in the past and the advanced stage that intra-industry (and intra-firm) processes of specialization and trade had already reached by 1980, precisely in those capital-intensive, large-scale manufacturing industries which have been responsible for most of the export boom of the decade. The industrial policy reforms of the late 1970s, especially in the automobile industry, gave further impulse to those processes (see note 25). The incentives provided later by a very attractive exchange rate and by the mid-1980s' trade reforms fell thus on an already fertile ground. The outstanding export performance of Mexico's manufacturing in the 1980s is thus, to a large degree, a legacy of the import-substitution period and highlights in a very real sense its success: it led, indeed, to an irreversible change in the economy's structure of comparative advantages.

What can be said now about the dynamic effects of trade liberalization on productivity performance?[24] In the economy as a whole, labour productivity has stagnated since the early 1980s (compared to a historical trend growth of the order of 3.5 per cent per annum), and this applies to the periods both before and after the 1985 trade reform. At the same time, growth in manufacturing productivity shows a recovery in the post-trade liberalization period since 1985 compared to the first half of the decade. Although difficult to disentangle from other effects, including those of privatizations, industrial policy[25] and a declining real exchange rate since 1988, the contribution of trade liberalization to productivity growth appears to have been positive in a number of manufacturing industries. In those sectors producing capital goods and heavy intermediates, it has facilitated a greater degree of intra-industry (and intra-firm) specialization in foreign trade, as suggested by the rapid and

simultaneous expansion of both exports and imports in some of these industries. In some light manufacturing industries – such as food processing and
segments of the textile industry – it has shaken out less efficient local producers or forced them to modernize, as conveyed by the fact that the recovery of
productivity growth has taken place here in the midst of a slowdown of
output growth partly explained by the high rates of import penetration in
these sectors. However, the benefits of import penetration, in terms of productivity performance, become much more doubtful when we look at other
manufacturing sectors. In the experience of the wood industry and other
manufacturing, which show also a rapid displacement of local producers
resulting from increased exposure to foreign competition, the result of import
penetration has been a worsening of both output and productivity performance whether compared to historical trends or to the period immediately
preceding trade liberalization.[26]

The surge in imports that followed the 1987–88 acceleration of the trade-
liberalization programme had other impacts of doubtful value. Recent import
trends – by which imports at current dollars have been growing at an annual
rate of over 30 per cent since 1988 – have left the country's current account
balance in a very vulnerable position. Combined with the export slowdown in
recent years, it has led to a declining trade surplus which turned later into a
widening deficit. These developments are also partly explained by the real
appreciation of the peso in recent years, the decline of the domestic savings rate
throughout the decade, and the recent recovery of aggregate demand and
private investment. But the fact that the import boom appears to be clearly
linked to the trade liberalization measures of late 1987 provides a strong
indication that trade liberalization since 1987 has contributed to the worsening
of the trade-off between growth and the current account of the balance of
payments that is so characteristic of recent years. By tightening foreign exchange constraints, its overall effects on medium-term economic growth could
thus turn out to be negative. In the longer term, these macroeconomic effects
become more uncertain, to the extent that the initially dominant and negative
effects on import functions could be gradually offset by a spurt of productivity
growth and a change in the structure of investment and productive capacity
towards exportable goods, with its positive sequel on export functions.

In any case, it seems very unlikely that the Mexican economy will be able
to resume and sustain its historical rates of growth unless substantial capital
inflows, well above historical levels, can permanently finance a current account deficit that by now appears to be in the range of 6–7 per cent of the
gross domestic product. If the efficiency and productivity growth effects of
market reforms are unlikely to make up for the loss of growth potential
during the 1980s, what about their effects on external capital inflows and the
prospects for increasing the rate of accumulation by these means? Can the

shift in the market-state balance bring about a permanently higher flow of external savings, significantly greater than historical rates, that would allow an increase in the rate of accumulation, despite the sharp decline of the domestic savings rate?

The impact of recent economic reforms on business confidence and capital inflows has clearly been positive, as witnessed by the spectacular amounts of portfolio investment and capital repatriation in recent years. There is, however, little ground for optimism. Those capital inflows of a more permanent nature – such as direct foreign investments – still appear to be of a secondary order of magnitude in the total. Moreover, reform has recently reached its climax, or at least its symbolic peak, with the reform of the land tenure system and the current negotiations for a Free Trade Agreement with the United States and Canada (which are now entering their final stage). Privatization entered its final phase in 1992, with the sale of the remaining banks and the insurance company, as well as parts of the operations of CONASUPO – the food distribution company – and of SIDERMEX – the largest steel producer. This means that a substantial fraction of recent capital inflows is likely to disappear in the near future, in particular those inflows related to privatization revenues.

State Reform and the Tasks of Development Policy

The other side of market reform is the retreat of the state and its restructuring. By shrinking in size, the chances improve that it will be able to do a better job in its priority tasks. Or so the argument goes. Some recent trends in the revenue and transfers sides of fiscal accounts are certainly encouraging: the efficiency of tax collection has improved, the tax base has expanded, several inequitable subsidies have been eliminated, and the inflation tax has practically disappeared. But many other changes on the expenditure side have been far less fortunate. Overall, Mexico's fiscal adjustment has not encouraged a greater internal efficiency of the public sector, despite, or perhaps because of, its massive character. Especially before 1985, fiscal adjustment was, by and large, achieved through deep cuts in public investment and the real salaries of public employees, hardly a useful means to improve the efficiency of the state and its bureaucracy. On the other hand, and despite some positive recent trends in social spending, state disengagement has not served its main stated purpose: the expansion of social infrastructure. The main contribution of privatization revenues has been to support (very effectively, no doubt) recent stabilization efforts by temporarily compensating for the fall in the inflation tax and strengthening the capital account of the balance of payments through the financial assets that the private sector had to bring back home to purchase the public enterprises on sale.

The state is smaller, but not necessarily more efficient. The implications of this are more important than generally acknowledged because the priority tasks of the state, social policy in particular, are today far more formidable than in the past. This is so for several reasons. There is, first, the accumulated backlog of unmet social needs from the 1980s. Secondly, some social disparities are likely to be exacerbated in the future in the absence of strong social and regional policies. This, of course, will depend very much on the long term effects of current strategies on economic growth; but holding this factor constant, there are at least two ways in which the present development pattern will have this effect: state retreat from agriculture and the reform of the land tenure system may bring private capital and prosperity to some rural areas, but may also inadvertently tend to impoverish large masses of rural workers in a similar way that agricultural modernization under the *Porfiriato* did on purpose and on a much more massive scale. The benefits of a greater integration with the international economy, and with the US in particular, are also likely to be very unevenly distributed within the country. Just as in the late 18th century the 'opening of North Atlantic trade' exacerbated the 'fragmentation of regional markets', there will be a tendency towards a deepening of regional disparities, especially between a prosperous north increasingly integrated with the US economy and a poor and backward south plunged into agricultural stagnation.

Finally, and no less fundamentally, by abandoning, without effective replacement, the trade and industrial policy instruments that have worked successfully in the past, current development strategy encourages the exploitation of present rather than potential comparative advantages. The basic task of development policy – the task of changing and enhancing the present endowment of resources and, over time, shifting the pattern of comparative advantages towards higher value-added, technology-intensive activities – falls now fully, in the absence of industrial policy, upon social policies. A proportionate response to this challenge could actually make things better than otherwise (that is, than, say, under an active industrial policy with little social policy), but our point is that the challenge itself is much bigger and the response remains to be seen. A less than proportionate response would lead to freezing the present stage of development – of getting stuck in the relatively unskilled and low-pay tasks of the production processes of capital-intensive industries. This is a far from desirable prospect for a country that needs to grow fast and rapidly to increase the living standards of its nearly 90 million people.

Concluding Comments

All this leads us to a final and most important aspect of the overall reform process, on which we can only raise the relevant questions. Does the change mentioned in entrepreneurial attitudes and behaviour reflect a temporary euphoria of financial markets or, rather, a long-lasting revival of animal spirits which in the future could turn out to be seen as the major positive outcome of the reform process? This question is, in fact, part of a broader issue regarding the consequences of the shift in the market-state balance and the change in ideological climate. Is this change in ideology a sign that, after having reduced economic backwardness by state-sponsored industrialization, use of a different set of ideas becomes more suitable in the new stage, a shift that is the natural companion of the transition from Gerschenkronian to Schumpeterian entrepreneurship? Or is it still the case that 'to break through the barriers of stagnation in a backward country, to ignite the imaginations of men, and to place their energies in the service of economic development, a stronger medicine is needed than the promise of better allocation of resources...' (Gerschenkron, 1952)? Dealing with these questions falls outside the scope of this chapter, and of the wisdom of its authors. But on their answers depends not only the size of the macroeconomic adjustment problem that lies ahead on Mexico's medium-term horizon, but also its longer-term prospects for rapid economic development.

What we can say, however, is that the origin of the adjustment problems and the new problems created by the adjustment process are not being adequately perceived in current development policy. First, the notion that the crisis was brought about by the exhaustion of past development strategies should not be taken for granted, even though we would be very far from defending every single aspect of past development strategies. Secondly, the solution to the new obstacles – the deterioration of the growth potential as a result of decreased investment efficiency and domestic savings – may require more and better, rather than less, state participation in the economy. As we have tried to show, the source of these new problems has to be found in part in the retreat of the state, in such areas as the provision of social services and public investment. But as a result of the shift in ideological climate, very little attention is being given to these problems and to what government policy can do about them while, at the same time, too much is expected from the efficiency gains of market reforms. Is it the case that, just as a century and a half ago, the real obstacles to economic development are being misperceived?

NOTES

1. The title of this section is borrowed from John Coatsworth's (1990) book of essays on Mexico's economic history in the 18th and 19th centuries, on which, as the reader will notice, this section heavily relies.
2. The role of the 'economic liberalization' reforms of the Bourbon monarchs in the second half of the century, and the duration of the mining boom itself, are subject to controversy. The conventional view (which sees the Bourbon reforms as supportive of the economic expansion of the period and the mining boom as extending until the end of the colonial period in the early 19th century) is presented, among others, in Florescano and Gil Sánchez (1976) and Cardenas (1985). Coatsworth, in contrast, dates the beginning of economic decline and the end of the mining boom in the 1780s, well before the independence wars (1810–1821). In this view, increasing costs as a result of inflation and falling market prices for silver output produced the decline in mining production (Coatsworth, 1989).
3. The manufacturing employment share, according to INEGI (1985), was 10 per cent in 1790.
4. Ethnic distinctions in the access to employment, justice and in fiscal treatment – which, among other things, had severely restricted capital and labour mobility – were formally abolished; many corporate privileges, including most of the guilds, were eliminated, while corporate property rights were limited to the Church and the Indian communities and town councils. The number of royal monopolies on the production and distribution of many commodities was reduced and their activities regulated; efforts were also made to modernize the judiciary and revise archaic judicial codes .
5. In the 55 years between independence and the *Porfiriato*, the presidency changed hands 75 times (Haber, 1989). The most disastrous consequence of the prolonged civil strife was the loss to the US of half of the national territory in the mid-19th century. Fifty years after the 1848 Treaty which ended the US–Mexico war, and also after the beginning of the California 'Gold Rush', the mineral output alone of the lost territories exceeded Mexico's total GNP (Coatsworth, 1978).
6. See, in particular, Garcia Alba (1974) and Coatsworth (1978). The reason is that the effect of the tithe in pushing labour and capital out of private agriculture was probably very small because the Church itself, and the Indian villages, produced a major portion of the country's farm products and livestock. And the net effect on GNP was, in any case, probably positive since differences in productivity between private agriculture and the rest of the economy suggest that non-agricultural activities were already more productive than agriculture.
7. Another figure worth mentioning is Estevan de Antuñano, a creole industrialist, whose very many pamphlets best articulated the case for protectionism and industrialization.
8. Mining would most likely have remained abandoned without the railway expansion as neither the necessary capital inputs for its development nor the commercialization of mineral products would have been profitable.
9. As noted by Reynolds (1970): 'As a result the government supported what amounted to an enclosure movement, in which federal land and peasant communal holdings, as well as other private properties with clouded titles, were redistributed to land development companies and to individuals successful in gaining favor with the administration' (p. 136).
10. As noted by Haber (1989), the extent of poverty was such that the increase in the price of corn due to any bad harvest would reduce workers' consumption of manufactures by enough to provoke a crisis in the cotton garment industry.
11. For accounts of finance, banking and industry during the *Porfiriato*, see Haber (1989) and Batiz and Canudas (1980).
12. For detailed accounts of the creation of the PNR and its role in long-term political stability, see Newell and Rubio (1984).
13. The Bank of Mexico was established in 1925, and started to operate as a central bank in the early 1930s as a response to the Depression. By then, the Public Agricultural Credit

Bank had been established, and the creation of other banks followed. In 1933, the Budget Ministry created the National Finance Entity, which was soon to become Nacional Financiera, the first fully fledged development bank and the financial pivot for industrial and other long-term investment.

14. At the time of the War, in 1942, Mexico and the US signed a reciprocal free trade agreement committing both sides to freezing tariffs on various products. A year later, however, the agreement was cancelled and Mexico proceeded to raise trade tariffs and, for the first time, in 1944, imposed licence requirements (King, 1970) .

15. Inflation averaged 18 per cent per annum from 1940 to 1955 as measured by the wholesale price index in Mexico City, fluctuating within a wide range.

16. By 1972, the debt–GDP ratio and the debt-service–exports ratio had both reached 18 per cent (compared to 1 per cent in 1946). While these magnitudes did not yet imply a serious macroeconomic imbalance, they reflect the dynamic evolution of foreign indebtedness during the period.

17. The belief that development, especially social development, could be accelerated while sacrificing fiscal discipline was rightly criticized by orthodox economists at the time. See Solis (1977) for a forceful statement.

18. An adjustment for inflation was introduced in personal income taxation. A value-added tax and a new corporate income tax were established. The tax base broadened as loopholes were closed, and the whole administrative and compliance process was simplified. The one to five minimum wage bracket went from contributing 58 per cent of labour income tax collections in 1978, to 28 per cent in 1981; whereas the highest wage bracket 'more than 15 minimum wages' went from 8 per cent to 25 per cent of the total. For a detailed description, see Gil Diaz (1987).

19. For a detailed analysis, see Ros (1993).

20. For an analysis of reforms in the domestic regulatory framework, see Ros (1991). For an international comparison of policy reform in these areas, see Williamson (1990).

21. Under such conditions, a clear comparative advantage argument can be made for privatization, even if public enterprises had absolute efficiency advantages over private firms, for society as a whole would clearly gain from a reallocation of public investments from areas where social and private returns do not differ greatly to activities yielding a higher social/private returns differential.

22. For a detailed discussion of resource reallocation processes see Ros (1992) and, in particular, Moreno (1988) for an analysis of the most important aspect of these processes, the restructuring of the automobile industry and its role in the 1980s manufacturing export boom.

23. The declining share of heavy intermediates between 1985 and 1989 is largely due to the falling share of petrochemicals, whose export boom was concentrated in the first half of the decade as the large expansion of productive capacity undertaken during the oil boom found no outlet in the domestic market. The share of heavy intermediates in 1989 was, nevertheless, well above 1980 levels.

24. For a more detailed analysis, see Ros (1992 and 1993).

25. For example, in the case of the auto industry, one of the star performers in the recent productivity growth recovery, the improvement appears to be associated with its special policy regime and the international developments in this sector since the late 1970s. In particular, the export-oriented investments of the late 1970s and early 1980s, following the 1977 reform of the automotive decree, must have made a significant contribution to the technical modernization of the industry, whose effects were only fully felt well into the 1980s as the new plants created by these investments came into operation and rapidly expanded their share in the industry's output (see Moreno, 1988). In the basic metals sector, the industry's rationalization has probably been determined by a government programme with precisely that goal, and which included the shutdown and privatization of many public enterprises in a sector where the latter have traditionally shown a relatively high share of the industry's output (29.5 per cent compared to 7.2 per cent, on average, for manufacturing) .

26. This mixed picture is not fundamentally altered when we look at the evidence on total factor productivity growth (TFP). For the economy as a whole there has also been here a clear deceleration with respect to historical trends. Nor is the performance of TFP in manufacturing much more encouraging, despite some claims to the contrary. On the subject, see Hernandez Laos (1990), Kessel and Samaniego (1991), Moreno (1992), Ros (1993) and Tybout and Westbrook (1992).

REFERENCES

Batiz, J.A. and Canudas, E. (1980), 'Aspectos Financieros y Monetarios (1880–1910)', in Ciro Cardoso (ed.), *México en el Siglo XIX (1821–1910)*. *Historia Económica y de la Estructura Social*, México, D.F.: Editorial Nueva Imagen.

Cardenas, E. (1985), 'Algunas Cuestiones Sobre la Depresión Mexicana del Siglo XIX', *Revista Latinoamericana de Historia Económica y Social*, **3**.

Clavijo, F. (1980), 'Reflexiones en torno a la Inflación Mexicana', *El Trimestre Económico*, **47**(188), October–December.

Coatsworth, J. (1978), 'Obstacles to Economic Growth in Nineteenth-Century Mexico', *American Historical Review*, **83**(1), February, 80–100.

Coatsworth, J. (1989), 'The Decline of the Mexican Economy, 1800–1860', in R. Liehr (ed.), *América Latina en la Epoca de Simón Bolivar*, Berlin: Colloquium Verlag.

Coatsworth, J. (1990), *Los Orígenes del Atraso. Nueve Ensayos de Historia Económica de México en los Siglos XVIII y XIX*, Mexico, D.F.: Alianza Editorial Mexicana.

FCE (1963), *Mexico 50 Años de Revolución*, México, D.F.: Fondo de Cultura Económica.

Florescano, E. and Gil Sánchez, I. (1976), 'La Época de las Reformas Borbónicas y el Crecimiento Económico', in D.C. Villegas (comp.), *Historia General de México*, México: El Colegio de México, tomo 1.

Garcia Alba, P. (1974), 'Los Liberales y los Bienes del Clero', El Colegio de México, manuscript.

Gerschenkron, A. (1952), 'Economic Backwardness in Historical Perspective', in B. Hoselitz (ed.), *The Progress of Underdeveloped Countries*, Chicago: University of Chicago Press.

Gil Diaz, F. (1984), 'Mexico's Path from Stability to Inflation', in A. Harberger (ed.), *World Economic Growth*, San Francisco: Institute for Contemporary Studies.

Gil Diaz, F. (1987), 'Some Lessons from Mexico's Tax Reform', in D. Newberry and N. Stern (eds), *The Theory of Taxation for Developing Countries*, Oxford: Oxford University Press.

Haber, S. (1989), *Industry and Underdevelopment: The Industrialization of Mexico, 1890–1940*, Stanford: Stanford University Press.

Hernandez Laos, E. (1989), 'Efectos del Crecimiento Economico y la Distribucion del Ingreso Sobre la Pobreza y la Pobreza Extrema en México (1960–1988)', México, D.F.: Universidad Autonoma Metropolitana (mimeo).

Hernandez Laos, E. (1990), 'Política de Desarrollo Industrial y Evolución de la Productividad Total de los Factores en la Industria Manufacturera Mexicana', informe presentado al Fondo de Estudios Ricardo J. Zevada, México, D.F.: Universidad Autónoma Metropolitana.

INEGI (1985), *Estadísticas Históricas de México*, México, D.F.: Instituto Nacional de Estadística, Geografía e Informática.

Kessel, G. and Samaniego, R. (1991), 'Apertura Comercial, Productividad y Desarrollo Tecnológico. El caso de México', Reporte final elaborado para el Banco Interamericano de Desarrollo Washington D. C., México, D.F.: Instituto Tecnológico Autónomo de México.

King, T. (1970), *Mexico: Industrialization and Trade Policies Since 1940*, Oxford: Oxford University Press.

Maddison, A. (1989), *The World Economy in the 20th Century*, Paris: Development Centre of the Organisation for Economic Co-operation and Development.

Manzanilla Schaffer, V. (1963), 'Reforma Agraria en México', in FCE, *Mexico: 50 Años de Revolución*, México, D.F.: Fondo de Cultura Económica.

Moreno, J.C. (1988), *The Motor-Vehicle Industry in Mexico in the Eighties*, Geneva: ILO.

Moreno, J.C. (1992), 'Multifactor Productivity Growth in Mexico: Some Notes on Recent Research', University of Notre Dame, manuscript.

Mosk, S. (1950), *Industrial Revolution in Mexico*, Berkeley: University of California Press.

Newell, R. and Rubio, L. (1984), *Mexico's Dilemma: The Political Origins of the Economic Crisis*, Boulder and London: Westview Press.

Reynolds, C. (1970), *The Mexican Economy: Twentieth-Century Structure and Growth*, New Haven: Yale University Press.

Ros, J. (1991), 'The Effects of Government Policies on the Incentives to Invest, Enterprise Behaviour and Employment: A Study of Mexico's Economic Reform in the Eighties', Working Paper. no. 53, World Employment Programme Research, Geneva: ILO.

Ros, J. (1992), 'Mexico's Trade and Industrialization Experience Since 1960: A Reconsideration of Past Policies and Assessment of Current Reforms', Helsinki: World Institute for Development Economics Research (WIDER, Helsinki).

Ros, J. (1993), 'Trade Liberalization with Real Appreciation and Slow Growth: Sustainability Issues in Mexico's Trade Policy Reform', Helsinki: World Institute for Development Economics Research.

Solis, L. (1970), *La Realidad Económica Mexicana: Retrovisión y Perspectivas*, México, D.F.: Siglo XXI Editores.

Solis, L. (1977), *A Monetary Will-O' the Wisp: Pursuit of Equity through Deficit Spending*, Geneva: ILO.

Thomson, G. (1986), 'The Cotton Textile Industry in Puebla during the Eighteenth and Early Nineteenth Centuries', in N. Jacobsen and H.J. Puhle (eds), *The Economies of Mexico and Peru during the Late Colonial Period, 1760–1810*, Berlin: Colloquium Verlag.

Tybout, J. and Westbrook, D. (1992), 'Trade Liberalization and the Structure of Production in Mexican Industries', Working Paper no. 92–03, April 1992, Department of Economics, Georgetown University.

Van Young, E. (1981), *Hacienda and Market in Eighteenth Century Mexico: The Rural Economy of the Guadalajara Region, 1675–1820*, Berkeley: University of California Press.

Van Young, E. (1986), 'The Age of Paradoxes: Mexican Agriculture at the End of the Colonial period, 1750–1810', in N. Jacobsen and H.J. Puhle (eds), *The Economies of Mexico and Peru during the Late Colonial Period, 1760–1810*, Berlin: Colloquium Verlag.

Williamson, J. (1990), *Latin American Adjustment: How Much Has Happened?*, Washington, D.C.: Institute for International Economics.

7. The Public–Private Interface: Brazil's Business–Government Relations in Historical Perspective, 1950–1990

Helen Shapiro*

INTRODUCTION

After waging a successful campaign against the Brazilian state, Fernando Collor de Mello was inaugurated on 1 March 1990 as Brazil's first democratically elected president in 30 years. Although he had been governor of the small northern state of Alagoas, he was an outsider to the political mainstream and his political party was simply a vehicle for his presidential ambitions. He ran against the federal government and politicians in Brasília, presenting himself as a champion of the 'shirtless ones' and the 'hunter of the maharajahs', or those who lived like royalty on the public payroll. Indeed, he blamed the entire legacy of Brazilian state intervention for bringing the country to the edge of the abyss. In his view, the intricate system of incentives and subsidies was purely clientelistic in nature, involving the distribution of favours to privileged sectors and firms. Rather than promoting growth, industrial policies had fostered a protected, inefficient and cartelized industrial sector while bankrupting the state.

This type of attack on the efficacy of state intervention is not unique to Brazil. Collor is only one of many world leaders who have promoted economic restructuring programmes that involve liberalizing trade and markets and privatizing state-owned firms. Nevertheless, the coincidence of liberalization policies across the globe has obscured the fact that Brazil's interventionist policies, and the intricate web of business–government interactions they spawned, were once credited with bringing about the economic 'miracle' of 1968–73 and sustaining high growth rates throughout the 1970s.

* The author would like to thank members of the Business History Seminar at the Harvard Business School, where an early version of this chapter was presented, Ben Schneider and Bill Lazonick for their helpful comments, and participants in the workshop on 'The State, Markets and Development', Kellogg Institute for International Studies, University of Notre Dame, 25–26 April, 1992.

Average annual growth rates averaged over 7 per cent from 1940 to 1980, and real per capita income increased fivefold, from $490 to $2 450 in 1989 prices (Carneiro and Werneck, 1993, p. 415). Brazil was the Third World success story, often characterized as a Gerschenkronian late-comer. Along with the East Asian tigers, its economic performance generated the category of 'newly industrializing country', or NIC. Nothing of consequence in either the economic or political realm occurred without state participation, and most accounts of Brazil's rapid growth gave primary credit to the state as a source of capital, bureaucratic administrator and builder of effective alliances between state-owned enterprises, multinationals and domestic firms.

In contrast, the 1980s and early 1990s were marked by economic stagnation. The government and the business community were at loggerheads, blaming each other for Brazil's stagflation, low investment rates and technology gap. The state had lost the fiscal and administrative capacity to shape economic development and, therefore, the confidence of the private sector.

This chapter will explore why the set of economic policies and institutional arrangements that emerged in the 1950s and, by many criteria, worked effectively throughout the 1960s and 1970s, has not been able to respond successfully to the development challenges of the 1980s and beyond. It will show how the import-substitution model in which state intervention and planning were critical for reducing investor uncertainty, eliminating bottlenecks and allocating resources, became less sustainable as a result of an intractable fiscal crisis. It will argue that explanations for Brazil's post-war development cannot be reduced to a set of macroeconomic and trade policies, but must include the institutional environment they fostered.

The inefficacy of technocratic solutions to Brazil's current impasse is the logical corollary to this institutional perspective. This chapter will argue that it is precisely Brazil's institutional specificity that has made implementing a standard IMF adjustment programme so difficult and Brazil's inflation so impervious to the traditional levers of fiscal and monetary policy. It will show how economic actors have been successful at evading the intent of government policy. The Collor government's experience demonstrates that economic restructuring and moving beyond the import-substitution paradigm are not simply technocratic problems of reducing trade barriers, but involve institutional change and the creation of new forms of interaction between the state and the private sector. Indeed, the chapter goes so far as to suggest that the Brazilian road to macrostabilization and structural adjustment is more arduous, and the degree of resistance greater, than elsewhere in Latin America due to the relative success of the country's institutional innovations in surmounting structural constraints.

The chapter provides a selective overview of Brazil's development model since the 1950s, with special emphasis on fiscal and regulatory regimes, industrial policies and business–government relations. It begins by describing the emergence of the modern developmentalist state in the 1950s and the adoption of an import-substitution industrialization programme supported by foreign capital. It then covers the military governments from 1964–85, during which time, despite their initial rhetoric to the contrary, the state grew in size and scope. It analyses the turbulent years of the 1980s that witnessed the return to democracy and economic stagnation combined with ever-higher inflation. It briefly compares the experience with import substitution in the auto industry in the 1950s with that in computers in the 1980s to highlight the difficulties of applying a similar set of policies to industries of different technological bases. It concludes with some lessons from Collor's first year in office and their implications for the future.

Given that the crisis in Brazil remains unresolved, this chapter is necessarily speculative in nature. Yet there appears to be enough evidence dating from the early 1980s to support the proposition that the crisis is not simply conjunctural or cyclic in nature, that its roots are historic and that economic recovery will require much more than fine-tuning. Although Collor himself was discovered to have fleeced the country and to have practised extortion, for which he was impeached in December 1992, state and institutional reform continues to dominate the Brazilian public policy debate.

THE TRIUMPH OF DEVELOPMENTALISM

President Juscelino Kubitschek (1956–61) took office amidst a polarized élite and military. Under the campaign slogan of '50 years [of development] in 5', he unified those sectors associated with international capital and mobilized urban masses into a populist alliance. By welcoming multinational firms and limiting the state's responsibilities to the co-ordination and subsidization of private capital and to investment in infrastructure, he differed from the previous 'developmental' president, Getulio Vargas (1930–45 and 1951–54), whose industrial policies envisioned a larger role for public enterprise.

Nevertheless, Kubitschek drew heavily upon Vargas's state-building legacy. He benefited from Vargas's civil service reform which set a precedent of insulating an élite technical corps from a federal bureaucracy rendered ineffective by patronage.[1] He made ample use of the Bank for National Economic Development (BNDE) which was established in 1952 to provide loans and technical expertise.[2] Kubitschek also maintained Vargas's network of state-owned enterprises in steel, oil, mining and electricity.

Kubitschek's development goals were encapsulated in a five-year Target Plan that set out to eliminate bottlenecks in the economy. Targeted areas for public investment included electricity, oil refining, shipping, railroads and road construction. Targets were also established for motor vehicle and tractor production as well as for capital goods production, which remained the province of private capital. An array of incentives was provided to foreign firms to heighten the attraction of Brazil's potentially large and protected domestic market, and to deepen the import-substitution process that had been gaining momentum since the 1930s.

Financing arrangements for the Target Plan were not as clearly defined as the production targets. While the state was assuming greater responsibility for development, it remained fiscally weak. Its capacity to tap resources directly through taxation was limited and its revenues came primarily from indirect taxes.

The executive branch, the agent of the industrialization drive, was not hegemonic within the state apparatus and lacked full autonomy over the resources that were at public disposal. As president, Kubitschek was able to unite nominally different sectors and classes around an ideology of 'national developmentalism' but the industrial élite was by no means in firm control. Both corporatist and clientelist tactics were used to consolidate political support. Interest groups and political parties were organized through the state and dependent upon it. While Kubitschek tried to insulate the technical planning agencies within the executive branch, Congress and the political parties maintained control over the budget and the traditional bureaucracy. This became the recipe for maintaining political support and stability, particularly with respect to labour and the rural oligarchy, the latter still over-represented in Congress.[3] The Target Plan had been 'legislated' through executive decree and much of the executive's revenues came in the form of 'earmarked funds', the allocation of which was predetermined.[4]

These attributes of the Brazilian state had direct consequences on the nature of its intervention. In general, the lack of direct access to resources caused the state to resort to indirect financing methods. Because of the scarcity of foreign exchange and the executive branch's control over foreign exchange instruments, commercial policy played a developmental role in Brazil. Brazil could not afford the luxury of an unregulated transfer mechanism when private and social costs of foreign exchange were not closely aligned. Moreover, the economic and political power of the export sector precluded the use of direct export taxes. The second-best alternative was relied upon, that is, a differential exchange rate on imports and exports to transfer resources from agriculture to industry. Favourable exchange rates for industrial inputs were the most common form of subsidy to the industrial sector.[5]

The state also resorted to inflationary finance. Albert Hirschman suggested that Brazil's capacity to use inflation as an alternative institutional mechanism to capture savings qualified it as a Gerschenkronian late-comer, since it had resolved what Gerschenkron defined as the fundamental constraint to development: the extraction of savings and their allocation to the industrial sector. Hirschman went further, arguing in a Keynesian fashion that savings and investment decisions were interdependent in less developed countries, and that savings would respond when investment opportunities presented themselves in the course of development; inflation, therefore, would be self-liquidating.[6] As is generally the case, an increasingly rapid inflation rate was necessary to maintain a real transfer of resources. Furthermore, while inflation provided a short-run solution, it produced collateral effects and did not address the long-run fiscal problems of the state.

Kubitschek also relied on foreign savings and encouraged foreign direct investment, particularly in consumer durables. With few exceptions, Vargas had planned for public enterprise to serve as the growth pole for private investment. What was to be the exception for Vargas became the prototype of the Target Plan. Indeed, many of the technocrats from the Vargas era concluded that they had no alternative but to rely heavily on foreign capital. Although precedents for state enterprises had been established in steel, mining and oil, they had emerged under particular conditions that were unlikely to be repeated.[7] Moreover, prospects for multilateral or bilateral assistance from foreign governments or agencies were bleak.[8]

Technocrats were given an unprecedented degree of authority to implement the Plan. The primary institutional innovation accompanying the Target Plan was the creation of executive groups that were formed for each key sector. Each group united representatives of all the agencies involved in defining and implementing a particular target. The purpose of joining the directors in a single unit was to streamline decision-making and insulate the Plan's administration from clientelistic pressures. Armed with the power of executive decree, Kubitschek and his executive groups could implement programmes independent of the fragmented, policy-making bureaucracy.

The executive groups reduced uncertainty with respect to the investment environment and the potential for arbitrary treatment. They provided the private sector with privileged access to the bureaucracies and assistance with getting the necessary approval for foreign investment, import licences and BNDE credit. They paired up foreign firms with domestic suppliers, which was often the only way for these firms to meet domestic content requirements. By targeting the development of sectors and their supplying industries, the executive groups also guaranteed minimum economies of scope to individual firms.[9]

Brazil made great strides during the Kubitschek years. The economy grew at annual rates of 8.1 per cent in the period 1956–61. The targets for infrastructural projects were completed. In 1955–62, public sector expenditure as a share of GDP increased from 20 per cent to 27 per cent (Bacha,

1977, p. 57). The public sector's contribution to total capital formation increased from 26 per cent in the 1953–56 period to 37 per cent during the 1957–61 period covered by the Target Plan. When state-owned enterprises are included, the share rises to 48 per cent (Economic Commission on Latin America, 1964, p. 178). These public projects also provided enormous stimulus to the domestic capital goods industry.

The Kubitschek administration established a number of important precedents. First, voices for traditional economic liberalism were all but silenced as short-run price stability was sacrificed for growth. Technocrats had a green light to ignore short-run static efficiency criteria in the pursuit of '50 years in 5'. Secondly, in the absence of fundamental reform with respect to the state's administrative and fiscal capacities, the executive branch became adept at relying on second-best policy instruments and parallel regulatory mechanisms to finance and oversee industrialization. Thirdly, the state assumed the role of mediator between foreign and domestic capital. Overall, the state took on a co-ordinating and supportive role to private firms and 'the Target Plan ...gave final shape to a process whereby...the private sector had gradually delegated to the Government the powers and instruments through which to achieve industrial complementarity' (Economic Commission on Latin America, 1964, p. 160).

The Plan's costs exceeded the state's fiscal resources. In addition to financing public works projects, the state also bore the brunt of subsidizing the users of public sector services and products such as steel and energy, whose prices failed to keep up with inflation. A tariff reform completed in 1961 made exchange rates more uniform and benefited exports, but cost the government one-fifth of its tax revenues. The government also had to acquire surplus coffee stocks during the bumper crop years of 1958–60. A coffee export tax was insufficient to cover these purchases, and the government resorted to large-scale monetary expansion. The federal budget deficit rose from 1 per cent to 5 per cent of GDP in 1955–62 (Bacha, 1977, p. 57). Inflation accelerated from 23 per cent to 33 per cent in 1956–61. Kubitschek faced balance-of-payments problems in 1958, when coffee revenues fell off drastically and short-term foreign credits became due, but he broke off negotiations with the IMF in 1959 rather than implement an austerity programme.

The economic problems did not diminish for either of Kubitschek's successors, Janio Quadros (1961–62) or João Goulart (1962–64). The slow growth, high inflation years of 1963 and 1964 were also accompanied by rising political turmoil, and democratic politics would soon disappear from the Brazilian landscape for the next 20 years.

THE MILITARY AUTHORITARIAN STATE

After staging a violent coup in April 1964, the military came to power, and appointed generals served as president until 1985. Despite initial rhetoric to the contrary, the Brazilian generals did not demonstrate the liberalization fervour of their Argentine or Chilean partners in crime. They were not inclined to dismantle the state apparatus or to sell state-owned enterprises, many of which they had lobbied for in the name of national security and development.[10] They adopted Brazil's statist tradition and remade it in their own image, but left the crucial economic and planning ministries under the control of civilian technocrats.

Several key policy decisions taken during the first years of military rule are important to emphasize. After a three-year flirtation with orthodox stabilization policy, Brazilian technocrats embraced the structuralist argument that the most effective way to counter inflationary expectations was through economic growth. The tight monetary and fiscal policies introduced in 1964 were based on the assumption that excess demand was driving the annual inflation rate of 88 per cent. Despite real wage cuts, a steep drop in industrial output and a reduction in the cash deficit from 5 per cent of GDP in 1963 to 1.1 per cent in 1966, inflation remained stuck at over 30 per cent and growth was sluggish.

In 1967 a new military president took office with an economic team which concluded that supply rigidities rather than excess demand were driving Brazilian inflation. In their view, a concentrated industrial sector granted firms market power and allowed them to respond to falling demand by marking up prices. To the extent that higher interest rates and public prices were passed along in higher prices, tight monetary policies only fuelled the inflationary spiral. The trade-off between price and output declines appeared to be very steep in the short run, a cost the military government was unwilling to pay.[11] Releasing the monetary brake did in fact generate a supply response, and the economy took off in what has become known as the Brazilian 'miracle'. From 1967 to 1974, annual growth rates surpassed 10 per cent, led by the manufacturing sector. Inflation settled in the low 20 per cent range and the cash deficit shrank to 3 per cent of GDP by 1971.

The astounding growth rates seemed to provide additional proof that Brazil was indeed 'unique' and could defy traditional economic trade-offs. The experience also created a strong bias against IMF-style austerity programmes as generations of Brazilian economists and policy-makers, including those opposed to the military regime, concluded that sacrificing growth for price stability was neither effective nor necessary. Economic growth also lent credence to the military's vision of *grandeza*, or superpower status worthy of Brazil's size and potential. It provided the military governments with a source of legitimacy, particularly in the eyes of the growing middle class on whose consumption of consumer durables the 'miracle' was based. The Brazilian private sector, after suffering bankruptcies as a result of the credit crunch, was also pleased.

Choosing this growth strategy meant that collateral economic instruments had to be devised to accommodate inflation. The most important was widespread indexation, which adjusted nominal values for past inflation to ensure that relative prices would still be a useful guide for resource allocation. 'Monetary correction' was originally introduced in 1964 to guarantee a real return on government bonds and to allow for non-inflationary deficit financing. It was extended to other financial instruments as a way to direct savings into long-run assets, as well as to mortgages, rentals and fixed assets. A special indexing calculus was devised for wages and, in 1968, regular mini-devaluations of the cruzeiro were introduced.

Indexation did help to neutralize distortions caused by inflation, but it did nothing to reduce inflation as it acted as a powerful feedback mechanism. Moreover, since the timing and magnitude of adjustments were determined largely by government discretion, indexation became a potent instrument of public policy. It proved to be an ingenious strategy for allocating resources as the government saw fit, and for establishing a high level of tolerance of inflation among certain sectors of society.

The federal government's fiscal base was restored. A tax reform made the central government less reliant on taxing foreign trade as its main source of revenue. The federal government was also strengthened *vis à vis* individual states in terms of access to resources.

Other structural reforms strengthened the state's fiscal capacity as well as its administrative reach, even if unintentionally. The weight of state-owned enterprises in the economy increased substantially. From 1968 to 1974, state control of the total net worth of the 100 largest firms increased from 60 per cent to 75 per cent. In terms of investment capital, the participation grew from 37 per cent to 45 per cent. The top 20 firms in terms of net worth were state-owned, including six in energy, four in transportation and one in chemicals. Given their weight, these firms had a large impact on final prices as primary buyers or sellers of key inputs. In addition these enterprises became self-financed by moving from marginal – or below marginal – cost pricing to average cost pricing, no longer subsidizing users to the same extent (Mendonça de Barros and Graham, 1978, p. 8).

A reformed stock market was supposed to serve as an alternative source of corporate financing for the private sector. In practice, however, trade became dominated by a handful of state-owned enterprises. With their monopolistic or oligopolistic rents and the perception of the federal government as their guarantor, the stocks of these firms were correctly identified as low-risk, high-return investments for minority shareholders. As Mendonça de Barros and Graham put it, 'Thus, what began as an institutional reform to promote the low cost capitalization of private sector growth has in effect become a vehicle for public enterprise capital expansion' (1978, p. 10). The state's overall control over domestic savings increased as various compulsory taxes were instituted to fund housing and other state-controlled banks and funds.

RELATIONS WITH THE PRIVATE INDUSTRIAL SECTOR

A variety of agencies was set up to implement the federal government's new regulatory authority. In 1969 the Council of Industrial Development (CDI) was created to license investment and to co-ordinate the lending activities of the BNDE, the procurement and partnership policies of the large state-owned enterprises and the Council on Tariff Administration (CPA), which could give tariff exemptions for imported inputs. The Foreign Trade Bureau of the Bank of Brazil (CACEX) had to approve import licences. The Interministerial Price Council (CPI) had to approve any price increase for most businesses.

Although state approval was required for virtually every important strategic decision a firm made, the military regime maintained the support of the private sector. Unprecedented growth rates and looser credit helped mitigate any negative reaction to the visible hand. Growth was especially robust in the consumer durable sector, which was helped along by new consumer credit mechanisms. (For example, from 1968 to 1974, motor vehicle demand sustained average annual growth rates of 22 per cent.) Wage indexation was also skewed in capital's favour; real wages fell by 20 per cent from 1964–66 and nominal wages continued to trail inflation. Even if price controls, combined with taxes, allowed the state to extract rents from the private sector, growth compensated for reductions in unit profits;[12] moreover, price increases were granted on a cost-plus basis.

In addition the state as entrepreneur generated demand for the private sector. Although state-owned firms bought a greater share of their inputs from abroad as the foreign exchange constraint loosened along with the 'nationalism' from the 1950s, growth expanded the absolute amount of their purchases. State-owned firms also forced their multinational partners to take on domestic firms as the third leg of tripod arrangements in vast petrochemical projects. Finally, trade liberalization was asymmetric; the protectionist regime was maintained as the exchange rate became less discriminatory towards exports.

These new agencies changed the way in which the private sector related to the state. Agencies such as the CDI became direct points of contact and negotiation between the state and individual firms; there was no need to go through business or class associations. Since the bureaucracy itself was fragmented, horizontal links developed that cut through the bureaucracy and the private sector and connected segments of state-owned enterprises or state agencies to multinationals and their Brazilian affiliates. These 'bureaucratic rings', as Fernando Henrique Cardoso labelled them, became stronger than traditional class or interest-group associations and brought politics within the state itself (Cardoso, 1975, p. 182). The expression and negotiation of private interests would become particularly intense in the mid-1970s with the Second National Development Plan.

THE FIRST OIL SHOCK, EXPANDED IMPORT SUBSTITUTION AND FOREIGN DEBT

Brazil was particularly vulnerable to the oil shock of September 1973, when oil prices quadrupled. The economy was heavily dependent on oil and imported 80 per cent of its needs. Rather than adjust to the oil shock through contraction of the domestic economy, the technocrats decided to maintain the accelerated growth strategy that previously had served them so well. Growth was also critical to President Ernesto Geisel's plan to liberalize Brazilian politics. However, the underlying conditions of the mid-1960s that fostered the 'miracle' had changed. The 'miracle' had benefited from the availability of significant excess capacity; by 1974, rates of capacity utilization were at all-time highs. Sustaining growth would require higher investment rates, but financing them with domestic savings would contradict the incentives offered to spur the demand of consumer durables. In addition, Brazil had benefited from improving terms of trade that reduced its borrowing needs. The oil shock and slower growth in world trade would change these external conditions.

The military responded to the tightening foreign exchange constraint by approving an ambitious industrialization plan in December 1974. The Second National Development Plan aimed to deepen the import-substitution process in basic inputs such as petrochemicals and capital goods, as well as hydroelectric power and mining. It relied on the state's vast array of regulatory instruments, incentives and purchasing power to direct private investors into top priority sectors.

Tighter domestic procurement and domestic content targets were required of investment projects to win CDI approval and to gain access to fiscal incentives and credit. State-owned enterprises were required to purchase local inputs, as were foreign firms in joint ventures. With massive public investment projects in energy, electricity and transport, this demand was vast. These policies also favoured Brazilian over foreign capital, especially in large-scale projects, reflecting the military's view of national security and the demands of the private sector. Quantitative restrictions on imports, which had begun to take a back seat to tariffs during the 'miracle' years, were reintroduced with a vengeance. If a nationally produced substitute existed, an import licence was hard to come by.

But as its fiscal responsibilities were increasing, the state sector's share of aggregate income was shrinking as a result of these increased transfers to the private sector and a falling tax burden. The private sector, hit with stringent price controls in the government's attempt to limit inflation, not only resisted tax increases, but demanded and received increased credit subsidies as additional compensation. Furthermore, as Albert Fishlow has pointed out, in contrast to the 1950s phase of import substitution, there was no export boom to tax. To the contrary, exports were being heavily subsidized to compensate for the anti-export bias of the protectionist regime (Fishlow, 1989, p. 112).

Despite these financial difficulties, the Brazilian military presidents were once again determined to reconcile the contradictory goals of adjustment and growth, but this time through increased capital inflows. Foreign debt allowed Brazil not only to cover its increased oil bills, but to sustain high investment rates and dampen inflationary pressures through cheap imports and finance. Moreover, since foreign banks preferred public over private borrowers, debt was consciously used as means by which public enterprises could subsidize the private sector through reduced prices on publicly provided goods and services.

At the decade's end it appeared that Brazil had again done the impossible and that heterodoxy had triumphed. While most countries were growing at sluggish rates, Brazil continued to grow at an average annual rate of 7 per cent from 1974–78. The auto industry, producing over a million vehicles a year, became the eighth largest in the Western world. The domestic intermediate and capital goods sectors prospered. Between 1975 and 1980, the ratio of imports to domestic production of rolled steel and high-density polyethylene fell from 0.3 to virtually zero. For 'made to order' capital goods, the ratio fell from 0.7 to 0.5 (Fishlow, 1989, p. 94). The drop in manufacturing's import propensity was accompanied by export growth due to export promotion and real exchange rate devaluation. Annual inflation jumped to 40 per cent in 1974 and stayed at that level throughout the decade. On the political front, the military was allowing more open federal and state elections, and a universal political amnesty was declared in 1979.

The foundation underneath *grandeza* was shaky, however. As its debt burden mounted, the state was considerably weakened and the economy as a whole more vulnerable to external shocks. The burden of adjustment would fall disproportionally on the public, not the private, sector, which was no longer a source of net savings in the economy.[13]

Brazil, the largest oil importer and debtor in the Third World, was subject to a double external shock in 1979: a second oil shock and record-breaking interest rates. After a brief interlude of contractionary policy, Delfim Neto, considered the architect of the economic 'miracle', was brought back as finance minister. His return was greeted with enthusiasm by the business community, as it signified a return to growth policies. Once again, rather than adjust through reducing aggregate demand, he tried to increase domestic supply. This strategy also satisfied the wishes of the newly appointed military president, João Figueiredo, who assumed that economic growth would smooth the ongoing political transition. This time, however, the economic results were disastrous, not miraculous, and forced Delfim to adopt orthodox policies in November 1980. His about-face drove the economy into recession and GNP fell by 2 per cent in 1981. The last time GNP had fallen was in 1942; 90 per cent of Brazilians had never lived through an economic contraction. Apparently even Brazil could not escape the inevitable.

CONSTRAINTS THAT BIND: THE STAGNANT EIGHTIES

Forty years of continuous growth came to an abrupt halt in the 1980s. From 1981 to 1989, average annual growth rates fell to 2.3 per cent, and 1981 and 1983 registered significant declines (Carneiro and Werneck, 1993, p. 415). Led by exports, growth resumed in 1984. Brazil's economic contraction was not as severe or lengthy as some of its Latin American counterparts, and no serious fiscal reform or adjustment took place. Inflation, which picked up in 1983, was maintained at high rates due to inertia (caused in part by indexation) and a growing fiscal deficit after 1985. After 1987 macroeconomic instability led to stagnant industrial activity and falling rates of investment. Nevertheless, mechanisms such as widespread indexation, worsening income distribution and the ongoing transfer of resources from the state allowed the private sector to survive and even thrive in some years. As a result there was no powerful constituency behind a reform programme. Weak political leadership in the context of redemocratization worked against it as well. Brazil's institutional framework and economic autarky were both a blessing and a curse in that they could postpone the need for adjustment, but not for ever. Three phenomena from the 1980s are important to emphasize: the transfer of resources from the state to the private sector; the quick-fix attempt at stabilization with the Cruzado Plan; and the inefficacy of 1950s-style import-substitution policies for the industries of the 1980s.

Resource Transfer

Brazil's economic performance in the 1980s was shaped by the need to send as much as 5 per cent of annual GDP abroad to service the foreign debt. This caused a serious fiscal problem for the state, which held the lion's share of the debt and had to generate domestic funds to purchase foreign exchange from the private sector. This was done through monetary expansion and rising internal debt. Inflation accelerated, further aggravating public finances.

The high real interest rates required to fund the internal debt resulted in a massive resource transfer to the wealthy. High returns on government bonds, and indexing more generally, may have reduced the degree of capital flight that might have occurred in their absence. While these financial profits maintained the profitability of many firms, ever-higher rates of interest were required to fund the debt. By 1989 interest payments on the government's domestic debt came to 9.5 per cent of the GDP, while those on the external debt came to only 2.8 per cent.

Firms in cartelized industries were able to sustain themselves by marking up prices faster than inflation. Exports, heavily subsidized, also served as a 'vent for surplus' when the domestic market contracted. Demand in some sectors was sustained by worsening income distribution. Middle and upper classes profited from investing in the financial markets and from having privileged access to fixed rate mortgages and the like. With domestic demand sluggish and financial profits easily accessible, very little investment was made in plant and equipment.

There was no industrial policy to speak of during the 1980s. Economic policy-making was reduced to short-term crisis management. However, the myriad of incentive systems was still in place, lacking co-ordination. As policy became more *ad hoc* and decentralized, there was no check on the private sector and its agency contacts. For example, CACEX controlled import licensing, but the requirements were arbitrary and other agencies also had the power to ban or admit imported items. This decentralization of authority meant that if a firm was unsuccessful with one agency, it might do better in the next. There were a number of special import schemes under which a firm could apply for tariff exemptions. According to Fritsch and Franco, nearly two-thirds of Brazilian imports in 1985 benefited from tariff reductions or exemptions (Fritsch and Franco, forthcoming).

Ironically, an insulated technical bureaucracy that originally was created to protect economic policy-making from clientelistic pressure, had become captive to private interests as a weakened central government could provide no countervailing pressure or co-ordination. The mark of being a good businessperson was knowing whom to call and having the right government contacts in key agencies. Insulation meant that these agencies had no public accountability, particularly under a military regime. Brazilians spoke of the *de facto* 'privatization' of the state. Over the decade an estimated 3–4 per cent of GDP was transferred to the private sector each year in the form of government expenditures or revenue foregone (Carneiro and Werneck, 1993, p. 422).

The Cruzado Plan

The Cruzado Plan of February 1986 is important in this context because of its impact on inflationary expectations. The Plan was an emergency measure to attack the 'inertial' component of Brazilian inflation by freezing prices, wages and exchange rates, and by constraining fiscal expenditure. A new currency, the cruzado, sliced three zeros from the face value of the old currency, the cruzeiro. With few exceptions, official indexation schemes were abolished. The minimum wage was raised by 15 per cent and all workers received an immediate 8 per cent bonus. If annual inflation was to hit 20 per cent, wage adjustments were guaranteed. The Plan's architects promised to bring 'zero inflation' to Brazil and the president became a popular hero.

A consumption boom ensued, fuelled by wage increases and, after a few months, by expectations that the freeze would not hold. Shortages appeared throughout 1986 as a result of hoarding and factories operating at near full capacity. In late 1986, a Cruzado-Two Plan was needed to realign key prices. Inflation revived, the wage trigger was set in motion and the deficit grew as a result of uncontrolled government spending. In February 1987 a unilateral moratorium was declared on foreign debt payments. By mid-year inflation hit an annual rate of over 1 000 per cent and formal indexation was gradually reintroduced.[14]

In the popular mind, the Cruzado Plan set a precedent that a quick, painless solution to inflation was possible and desirable. Politicians saw an easy way to become popular. The private sector learned to raise prices as quickly as possible after an increase in public sector prices, a sure sign of an imminent price freeze. Overall the plan had two contradictory legacies. On the one hand it raised public scepticism about the government's ability to carry through a successful shock programme. On the other hand, the idea that Brazil's inflation was partly inertial in character made some think that a 'quick fix' really was possible.

Industrial Policy

The only major industrial policy initiative of the late 1970s and 1980s was an informatics policy, whose aim was to establish a domestic computer and information processing industry. A brief comparison with Brazil's experience with the auto industry, the high-tech industry of the 1950s, indicates that not only were macroeconomic policy and the fiscal demands on the state no longer sustainable, but that the model of industrial development upon which past import substitution in consumer durables and heavy industry had been based was no longer effective.

As with previous import-substitution programmes, the informatics policy closed the domestic market to computer imports. As was the case for the automotive sector, an argument could be made that Brazil's market reserve was a legitimate strategy in the face of a foreign, oligopolistic industry reaping technological rents. Given the centrality of technological change to the computer industry, and scepticism about whether foreign firms in other sectors had transferred technology along with production to Brazil, the policy restricted foreign ownership and the licensing of foreign technology.

However, it is precisely the rapid pace of technological change and diffusion that complicated import substitution into this sector. The nature of competition in the industry has been such that the monopoly held by a firm over technology and differentiated products is temporary and relatively short term. As a result of imitation and competition, the benefits of decreasing costs have been transferred largely to consumers via lower prices and the pace of diffusion has accelerated (Flamm, 1987). Despite the Schumpeterian rents accruing to the firms, therefore, on a macroeconomic level these private returns have been swamped by social gains. Users have been the primary beneficiaries of cost-reducing technical change. Due to these particular characteristics of the microelectronics sector, the relevant policy choice may not have been between domestic manufacture versus importation, but between domestic production and use.

Furthermore, in contrast to consumer durables such as automobiles, the sector provided both final and intermediate goods. The ramifications of a technological gap for the industrial sector as a whole were therefore more widespread, as was opposition to the plan. Brazil had previously import-substituted into basic industrial inputs such as steel. However, many of those products were characterized by relatively stable technology. Relatively high-tech industrial inputs such as petrochemicals had been financed by the state directly or in association with foreign capital.

Computer technology changes rapidly and the R&D requirements are huge. More importantly, microelectronics are not simply production inputs, but change the production process itself and/or the nature of the final good. Historically, higher cost was the major problem associated with the domestic production of previously imported industrial inputs. Generally this problem was often rectified directly through subsidies to the industrial producer. However, financial subsidies alone cannot compensate for inputs which are technologically backward.

The import-substitution process in automobiles was initially a success because its linkage effects were not more dispersed throughout the industrial sector. Since cars were not productive inputs, their high prices did not then inflate the cost structure of dependent industries. Final consumers paid for the initial subsidies and inefficiencies, and transferred resources to the state. The state's administrative and fiscal capacities were less strained, as fewer sectors clamoured for their own compensatory subsidies. Clearly, the micro-electronics sector's elevated cost structure and technological lag take on additional significance for those industries that have successfully penetrated foreign markets.

Leaving the financial constraint aside, the industrial policy framework may be ill-suited for the tasks of the future. It was set up for multinational-centred projects or for large-scale projects in which the state was the major player, using investment incentives and local content requirements as the key policy instruments. As Ben Schneider has pointed out, the pressing tasks of modernizing the technological base and the agricultural sector, as well as resolving social disparities, imply working with dispersed private actors rather than a select few (1987, p. 223). Moreover, market protection and high domestic content levels have meant that many products are unique to Brazil, even those produced by multinationals, making integration and technological upgrading more difficult as well.

THE COLLOR PLAN

When Fernando Collor took office in March 1990, the country was on the verge of hyper-inflation. Even Brazil's highly indexed economy could not accommodate monthly inflation rates of 80 per cent. The social fabric was beginning to fray seriously and the federal government was literally broke. Financial transfers to the private sector, which had formed the basis of business–government relations, were unsustainable. The network of agencies that administered industrial policies was rendered ineffective.

Following in the footsteps of his predecessors, Collor promised that his antidote to inflation was going to be painless and to take effect within the first 100 days of his administration. He pledged to 'kill the tiger of inflation with a single bullet' – the most radical economic stabilization plan in Brazil's history. The plan involved a currency reform and a 30-day price freeze. Wage and price indexation was abolished, except for overdue tax receipts. The most radical move was an 18-month freeze on amounts greater than the cruzado equivalent of $1 000 dollars in savings accounts and $500 in 'overnight' accounts, which had paid interest daily. These accounts were to be repaid with interest in a new currency, the cruzeiro, at the end of the 18-

month period. The freeze reduced the money in circulation by two-thirds and represented a moratorium on interest payments on the internal government debt that the overnight accounts had funded. It was one of the biggest liquidity squeezes in history, reducing the money in circulation by an estimated $115 billion.

Structural reforms were introduced to reduce the size and financial obligations of the state and to place greater reliance on unimpeded market forces and the private sector. Brazilian policy-makers' decision to shrink the state was motivated primarily by pragmatic rather than ideological concerns. On the one hand the state was broke and could no longer finance its domestic debt. On the other hand, it was seen as hopelessly clientelistic, catering only to special interests.

Proposed reforms included an administrative reform to reduce the number of ministries and public employees, and targets for reducing the public payroll overall. Approximately one-third of the approximately 188 state-owned enterprises were to be privatized, and the protectionist trade regime was to be gradually dismantled; the average tariff on manufactured goods was to be reduced from 80 per cent to 20 per cent by 1995. Most fiscal subsidies to the private sector were eliminated, including those for export. Administrative points of contact between the private sector and the state were abolished, including agencies involved with industrial policy and price control. The state's role in the economy was to stabilize the economy and provide a favourable investment climate. Private capital was to be the main agent in the production process.

By October 1991, one-and-a-half years after the Collor Plan was first introduced (followed by Collor Plan II in February 1990), the monthly inflation rate was again hovering at around 20 per cent, interest rates were at record highs and the economy was in deep recession. The worst economic performance since the Brazilian Institute of Geography and Statistics started calculating growth rates in the 1940s was registered in 1990; GDP fell by 4.6 per cent. Little progress had been made on structural reforms and no state-owned enterprise had been privatized. Debt negotiations had not yet produced a comprehensive agreement with the IMF or private banks. One minister of the economy had been sacrificed, the second was on shaky ground, and Collor, who still had over three more years in office, was already being portrayed as a lame duck president.

The Collor government displayed frustration and bewilderment in the face of this predicament. Ibrahim Eris, the first president of the central bank and an author of the original Collor Plan, best captured the typical response when he said, 'That which failed was not the economic plan but the world' (*Gazeta Mercantil*, 27 November 1990). It is true that profligate spending by state governors, constitutional constraints on firing public employees and unanticipated leakages of blocked cruzados into the system, all helped to undermine the Plan's efficacy, as did the brief oil shock caused by the Iraqi invasion of Kuwait.

Nevertheless, the domestic mishaps could have been anticipated, particularly the leakages. With financial skills well-honed after years of high inflation, savvy Brazilians were quick to take advantage of the Plan's loopholes. The government allowed companies to withdraw funds to pay old bills and back-taxes. Many were quick to come up with back-dated invoices. A secondary market in blocked currency developed. Blocked funds could also be used for local taxes and charitable contributions. Municipal governments and charities had a field day, even if they did not keep the entire windfall. An estimated one-third to one-half of the frozen assets leaked back into the money supply in the first few months of the Plan.

This failure to take Brazilian reality into account was indicative of the economic team's technocratic approach. The Plan was flawed for not considering the feasibility of implementation and for assuming that even if implemented, it would have succeeded. By focusing only on macroeconomic levers, reducing the size of the state and threatening to open the economy, Collor's team ignored the legacy of 40 years of state tutelage in terms of industrial structure and expectations. This 'institutional memory' could not be so easily erased. It would serve to undermine stabilization attempts and make macroeconomic stabilization inextricably linked to industrial and trade policies.

Collor did not overcome the private sector's scepticism, accumulated from past attempts at stabilization.[15] The economic team's rhetoric also reinforced private sector suspicions. As prices continued to rise in the face of high interest rates and deepening recession, government spokespeople blamed the cartelized industrial sector for sabotaging the stabilization process.

Cut off from state support and left to its own devices, the private sector responded to high interest rates and weakening demand as it always had: by raising prices. It sought out remaining points of influence within the government and ways to protect itself against interest costs as the number of bankruptcies soared. Firms interpreted the increase in public prices in the autumn of 1990 as a sign of an imminent price freeze, despite government protestations to the contrary. When a temporary price freeze was in fact decreed under Collor Plan II, not even the mayor of São Paulo was willing to abide by it. Moreover, by dismantling the various price control agencies, the federal government had lost the capacity to administer any price controls properly. The credibility of the stabilization plan was slipping fast, especially as the federal government seemed to be cutting its deficit with temporary measures such as not paying its bills or giving public workers rises; no fiscal reform was on the horizon, fuelling inflationary expectations. The actions of the private sector, which did not believe that tight monetary policy would work, and preferred inflation to recession, helped to guarantee that the trade-off between recession and falling prices would be very high.

The government's weapon to break oligopolistic price behaviour was import competition. Yet in the Brazilian context, opening the economy to imports in itself is not sufficient to break cartels and reduce prices in the short run. There are various non-tariff barriers to trade, such as other taxes, freight and insurance charges, and so on. Moreover, as a 1990 World Bank study concluded, the previous incentive regime gave established firms cost advantages which helped them consolidate their market position.

In addition many firms were unwilling to change their purchasing practices in the short run. In the absence of a foreign debt agreement, they worried about a future shortage of foreign exchange. With vivid memories of the central bank cracking down on access to foreign exchange in times of crisis, many were hesitant to begin foreign sourcing only to face retaliation by domestic suppliers if forced to return to the domestic market. Importers of finished consumer durables would need to set up sales networks and service centres, thereby slowing down the process until a minimum amount of sales could be guaranteed. Therefore, in the short run, tariff reduction led to increased imports of luxury items and consumer goods, rather than components and complicated consumer durables. The official response that a flexible exchange rate would resolve any foreign exchange constraint was unconvincing.

The Collor administration also viewed opening as a way to force firms to modernize. It was unrealistic to expect firms to invest under conditions of domestic recession and high interest rates. Moreover, investment had always been accompanied by government support, and evidence indicates that, rather than crowding out, public investment crowds private investment in through complementarities. Needless to say, public investment was not forthcoming. Instead of offering positive investment incentives, the government only threatened to raise the costs of not investing through import liberalization. After years of autarky, the industrial sector would be exposed to import competition at its weakest moment – after a decade of low investment rates and low capacity utilization.

In the medium run, therefore, the only direct instrument at the government's disposal was the interest rate. Surprisingly, an economic team steeped in Brazilian history and structuralist economics miscalculated how the domestic private sector would respond. It also expected that subsidiaries of multinational corporations would tap their parent companies for cash in the face of domestic liquidity constraints, and that, in general, they would respond quickly to the opportunities provided by economic opening. Most of these subsidiaries were self-financing, however, and their parent companies were unwilling to invest in the domestic market for the same reasons as the domestic private sector. By overestimating Brazil's importance in a changing world, the government demonstrated an insularity similar to that of the protected private sector, as well as an inability to get beyond the history of *grandeza*. Fortunately for Brazil, most multinational firms do not treat their past investments as simply sunk costs and will not pull out so quickly. In this respect, early import-substitution policies were successful (Shapiro, 1993b).

An alternative approach to relying on tight monetary policy would have been for the government to take some steps towards breaking the prisoner's dilemma of the inflationary spiral by attempting to form a social pact. Neither the private sector nor labour were in a position to take on this task. The private sector in particular was adrift; after years of state tutelage and relying on 'bureaucratic rings', its industry associations were weak and had no alternative projects. While it is unclear whether the political and institutional conditions exist for a social pact to work in Brazil, without the state as a mediator, industry and labour will continue to try to protect themselves.

It is understandable why the Collor government wanted to do away with the old regime of business–government relations, but it put nothing in its place. Civil society floundered while the Collor government looked on in silence from Brasília. It is not evident that the current government of Itamar Franco, Collor's successor, has a better alternative.

CLOSING COMMENTS

Brazilian governments devised ingenious ways to get around the economy's underlying fiscal and foreign exchange constraints. Import substitution was facilitated by the country's large domestic market, and industrialization was financed to varying degrees by inflation, export taxes, foreign direct investment and debt. The financing strategy became unsustainable for domestic and external reasons, and the business–government relations that developed around this strategy became obsolete.

It will be difficult not only to find new ways to fund the state but to change these institutional structures. Stabilization and structural adjustment cannot be separated. Business was conducted successfully for many years based on an autarkic economy with an import share of only 5–6 per cent. Due to this success, and Brazil's ability to maintain the basic elements of the strategy even through years of adversity, no strong constituency formed behind liberalization. While most agree that there is now no alternative, no one knows what to put in the place of previous practice.

This general argument is akin to that of others who have approached development from an institutional perspective, such as Gerschenkron (1968) and, more recently, Elbaum and Lazonick (1986) on the United Kingdom. Unlike the countries studied by these economists, however, Brazil still retains the profile of a 'less developed country', so it is not only a question of decline but of abbreviated success.

Furthermore, despite all its institutional innovation, the country never fully resolved the problem of the state's fiscal weakness. Mancur Olson (1982) claimed that Latin America's stunted growth was the result of too much instability rather than the fossilized structures responsible for poor economic performance elsewhere. It can be argued, however, that despite superficial regime changes, countries such as Brazil have suffered from too much stability in their underlying classes and institutional structures. The maintenance of extremely concentrated wealth and decision making, the lack of an agrarian reform and the disproportional representation of rural, north-eastern interests in the political process have, in effect, blocked any attempt to expand the state's tax base and have kept it fiscally weak. As Albert Fishlow (1990) and Luiz Carlos Bresser Pereira (1993) have pointed out, what has differentiated the East Asian NICs from Brazil is not only their outward orientation, but the fiscal authority of the state.

Brazil's recent experience raises a larger and more fundamental issue of the state's role in the economy. In development economics, the operating assumption of imperfect markets has been replaced by the presumed inevitability of imperfect states. Even if markets are imperfect, it is asserted that state intervention only makes things worse. This new wave of neoclassical criticism has correctly pointed to development economics' implicit assumption that the state has unlimited capacity to intervene as its biggest weakness. Early 'developmentalists' simply expanded the scope of market failure to provide a rationale for enlarging the scope of intervention, but stopped short of explicitly considering the state's political and institutional capacity to meet its prescribed role. However, in contrast to the new literature's criticism of the state, an idealized market is posited in its stead.

Brazilian policy-makers today seem to arrive at a market solution from a starting point that is essentially pragmatic rather than ideological. The defence of a non-interventionist industrial policy is based not on the proposition that state intervention is inherently inefficient, but on the conclusion that it is necessary due to fiscal constraints. However, if one's point of departure is pragmatism and necessity, one cannot then assume that the market will 'work' and that the private sector will pick up the pieces. The notion that market forces alone can resolve the problems facing Brazilian industry is just as voluntaristic as the earlier expectations of the state, and is based on assumptions for which there is no theoretical or empirical justification.

We have learned that market failure arguments are not sufficient to justify state intervention and that constraints on the state are real. Nevertheless, it is ill-advised to create unrealistic expectations about the capacity of the Brazilian market and private sector. Moreover, it is important to reconsider why the import-substitution strategy was chosen in the first place and what problems it was expected to address. It is by virtue of its earlier success that new problems, requiring different institutional responses, have emerged. The appropriate lesson from studying the dynamics of states and markets is not how to choose between one or the other, but how to define policy so that they can most effectively interact. It is important to understand the economic and political conditions under which state intervention can succeed, and how they vary across sector and over time.

In Brazil, private firms' past behaviour was shaped by the incentives they faced. In order to induce the desired behaviour on the part of the private sector, the appropriate incentives must be designed and enough time must pass to ensure credibility. There is an inherent contradiction between tough criticism of the private sector and the expectation that it will take over functions previously carried out by the state. In any event, no matter what one's evaluation is of the Brazilian private sector, it is the only one there is.

A review of the Brazilian experience also shows the danger in indiscriminately lumping countries such as Brazil with the countries of Eastern Europe in terms of the nature of the adjustment tasks they face. The critical issue is not the creation of a private sector, but the public–private interface, which is really at the heart of development in countries such as Brazil where private, rather than state-owned, firms are the principal conveyors of state policy.

NOTES

1. For more on bureaucratic insulation, see Geddes (1986) and Nunes and Geddes (1987).
2. The BNDE was one of the few projects recommended by a Joint Brazil–United States Commission that came to fruition. The formation of this Commission was a provision to the 1950 Act of International Development, which elaborated development projects and defined a leading role for public investment. One-third of the BNDE's original capital was provided by the World Bank. The Eisenhower administration that took office in 1953 placed greater emphasis on private capital flows rather than multilateral or public initiatives for less developed country development.
3. In this regard, Brazil differs from Japan where, according to Chalmers Johnson, 'there was no pretense that the diet did anything more than rubber-stamp the bureaucracy's budget' (Johnson, 1982, p. 10).
4. Specific taxes on items such as fuel, petroleum imports, railway fares and electricity, which had designated purposes, amounted to 22 per cent of total federal receipts in 1957. These funds remained outside of the federal budget and Congressional control.
5. Extracting rents from the export sector by creating a wedge in foreign exchange markets is not a viable long-run strategy, as exporters eventually do recognize the resource transfer. However, it may be highly effective in the short run. This is particularly so if the export product has a long growing cycle and cannot be easily redirected towards the domestic market, as was the case with Brazilian coffee. It was not the case for Argentine

beef, however, which presented different economic and political challenges for industrial and trade policy in that country.

6. See Hirschman (1968). Latin American structuralists joined Hirschman in arguing that inflation in an economy plagued with bottlenecks was a necessary evil. It is worth noting that inflation was not available as a financing mechanism in Mexico, which followed a 'stabilized development' strategy until the 1970s.

7. In the 1940s, multinational firms were uninterested in investing in heavy industry and Vargas was adept at playing off the Axis and Allied powers against each other to generate resources. See Draibe (1985, p. 128) and Martins (1976).

8. The potential veto power of the IMF and the World Bank on the one hand, and the difficulty in generating internal resources on the other, made state-led development projects appear less viable. In protest over Vargas's restrictions on profit remittances and returns to capital in 1952, the World Bank withheld financing. With the exception of one loan in 1958, no World Bank assistance was offered to Brazil from 1955 to 1965 (Malan *et al.*, 1980, p. 35). After Brazil broke off negotiations with the IMF in 1958, all credit lines with international agencies were cut until 1960 (Sochaczewski, 1980, p. 183).

9. For more on executive groups, see Geddes (1986), Lafer (1970) and Lessa (1964). For the executive group for the automotive industry, see Shapiro (1993a, b).

10. Baer (1969) cites military pressure as the most important factor behind the establishment of the National Steel Company in the 1940s. The military was also a powerful lobby behind the programme to manufacture motor vehicles in the 1950s, which was originally based on a state-owned enterprise but was quickly dominated by transnational firms.

11. Orthodox economic policies failed as a result of poor implementation and a misdiagnosis of the roots of inflation, especially with respect to wages and deficits. For further discussion, see Fishlow (1973) and Taylor (1981).

12. The subsidies granted to industries such as the auto industry in the 1950s were not pure subsidies in that the state regained the revenue that was sacrificed in the 1960s in the form of increased tax revenue. Because firms were not allowed simply to pass along these taxes as higher profits, the state proved itself capable of extracting rents from the private sector rather than consumers. For a full account of this resource transfer, see Shapiro (1993a).

13. Nevertheless, this period saw a political backlash from the private sector against 'statization' of the economy. State-owned enterprises accounted for an average of 5.4 per cent of product by 1974–78, up from 4 per cent in 1970–73; their share of investment jumped from 17 per cent to 23 per cent in the same period. Partly reflecting its growing strength, the private sector was increasingly offended at the state's heavy intervention and the 'statization' issue became part of a general campaign by an important segment of Brazil's entrepreneurs against the military regime.

14. The notion that much of Brazilian inflation was inertial in character was correct. Due in part to indexation, prices reflected past inflation even in the face of falling demand. For an account of the Cruzado Plan's failure, see Shapiro and Oliveira (1987).

15. Mexico's experience after private banks were nationalized in 1981 confirms the difficulty in winning back the confidence of the private sector after it has been lost. President Miguel de la Madrid's efforts to undo the damage caused by his predecessor in this respect were noteworthy.

BIBLIOGRAPHY

Abranches, S. (1978), 'The Divided Leviathan: State and Economic Policy Formation in Authoritarian Brazil', PhD dissertation, Cornell University.

Bacha, E. (1977), 'Issues and Evidence on Recent Brazilian Growth', *World Development*, 5(1–2), January–February, 47–67.

Baer, W. (1969), *The Development of the Brazilian Steel Industry*, Nashville: Vanderbilt University Press.

Baer, W. (1973), 'The Brazilian Boom 1968–72: An Explanation and Interpretation', *World Development*, 1(8), August, 1–15.
Baer, W. and Kerstenetzky, I. (1964), 'Import Substitution and Industrialization in Brazil', *American Economic Review*, 54(3), May, 411–25.
Baer, W. *et al.* (1973), 'The Changing Role of the State in the Brazilian Economy', *World Development*, 1(11), November, 23–34.
Barzelay, M. (1986), *The Politicized Market Economy: Alcohol in Brazil's Energy Strategy*, Berkeley: University of California Press.
Bergsman, J. (1970), *Brazil: Industrialization and Trade Policies*, London: Oxford University Press.
Bresser Pereira, L.C. (1993), 'Economic Reforms and Economic Growth: Efficiency and Politics', in L.C. Bresser Pereira, J.M. Maravall and A. Przeworski, *Economic Reforms in New Democracies: A Social Democratic Approach*, Cambridge: Cambridge University Press.
Cardoso, F.H. (1975), *Autoritarismo e Democratização*, Rio de Janeiro: Paz e Terra.
Cardoso, F.H. and Faletto, E. (1979), *Dependency and Development in Latin America*, Berkeley: University of California Press.
Carneiro, D. and Werneck, R.L.F. (1993), 'Brazil: Medium-Term Development Issues', in L. Taylor (ed.), *The Rocky Road to Reform: Adjustment, Income Distribution, and Growth in the Developing World*, Cambridge: MIT Press.
Draibe, S. (1985), *Rumos e Metamorfoses: Estado e Industrialização no Brasil 1930/1960*, Rio de Janeiro: Paz e Terra.
Dye, D.R. and Silva, C.E. de Souza C. (1979), 'A Perspective on the Brazilian State', *Latin American Research Review*, 14(1), 81–98.
Elbaum, B. and Lazonick, W. (eds) (1986), *The Decline of the British Economy*, Oxford: Oxford University Press.
Evans, P. (1979), *Dependent Development: The Alliance of Multinational, State, and Local Capital in Brazil*, Princeton: Princeton University Press.
Fishlow, A. (1973), 'Some Reflections on Post-1964 Brazilian Economic Policy', in A. Stepan (ed.), *Authoritarian Brazil*, New Haven: Yale University Press.
Fishlow, A. (1974), 'Indexing Brazilian Style: Inflation Without Tears', Washington: *Brookings Papers on Economic Activity*, 1.
Fishlow, A. (1989), 'A Tale of Two Presidents: The Political Economy of Crisis Management', in A. Stepan (ed.), *Democratizing Brazil*, New York and Oxford: Oxford University Press.
Fishlow, A. (1990), 'The Latin American State', *The Journal of Economic Perspectives*, 4 (3), Summer, 61–74.
Flamm, K. (1987), *Targeting the Computer*, Washington, D.C.: The Brookings Institution.
Fritsch, W. (1990), 'A Política Industrial de Nôvo Governo', manuscript.
Fritsch, W. and Franco, G.H.B. (forthcoming), 'Import Compression, Productivity Slowdown, and Manufactured Export Dynamism: Brazil, 1975–1990', in G.K. Helleiner (ed.), *Trade and Industrialization in Turbulent Times*, Oxford: Oxford University Press.
Geddes, B. (1986), 'The Insulation of Economic Decision Makers in the Brazilian Bureaucracy, 1930–1964', paper presented at the XIII Congress of the Latin American Studies Association, Boston, October.
Gerschenkron, A. (1968), *Economic Backwardness in Historical Perspective*, Cambridge: Harvard University Press.

Hirschman, A. (1968), 'The Political Economy of Import-Substituting Industrialization in Latin America', *Quarterly Journal of Economics* **82**, 1–32.

Johnson, C. (1982), *Miti and the Japanese Miracle*, Palo Alto: Stanford University Press.

Lafer, C. (1970), 'The Planning Process and the Political System in Brazil: A Study of Kubitschek's Target Plan 1956–1961', PhD dissertation, Cornell University.

Leopoldi, M.A.P. (1984), 'Industrial Associations and Politics in Contemporary Brazil', PhD dissertation, Oxford University.

Lessa, C. (1964), *Fifteen Years of Economic Policy in Brazil*, **IX**(2), December, Economic Commission on Latin America.

Malan, P.S. *et al.* (1980), *Política Econômica Externa e Industrialização no Brasil 1939–52*, Rio de Janeiro: IPEA.

Martins, L. (1976), *Pouvoir et Développement Économique: Formation et Evolution des Structures Politiques au Brésil*, Paris: Editions Anthropos.

Mendonça de Barros, J.R. and Graham, D. (1978), 'The Brazilian Economic Miracle Revisited: Private and Public Sector Initiative in a Market Economy', *Latin American Research Review*, **13**(2), 5–38.

Nunes, Edson de Oliveira, and Geddes, B. (1987), 'Dilemmas of State-Led Modernization in Brazil', in J. Wirth, E. Nunes and T. Bogenschild (eds), *State and Society in Brazil*, Boulder: Westview Press.

Olson, M. (1982), *The Rise and Decline of Nations*, New Haven: Yale University Press.

Schneider, B.R. (1987), 'Framing the State: Economic Policy and Political Representation in Post-Authoritarian Brazil', in J. Wirth, E. Nunes and T. Bogenschild (eds), *State and Society in Brazil*, Boulder: Westview Press.

Schneider, B.R. (1991), *Politics Within the State: Elite Bureaucrats and Industrial Policy in Authoritarian Brazil*, Pittsburgh: University of Pittsburgh Press.

Shapiro, H. (1991), 'Determinants of Firm Entry into the Brazilian Automobile Manufacturing Industry, 1956–1968', *Business History Review*, **65**(4), Winter, 876–947.

Shapiro, H. (1993a), *Engines of Growth: The State and Transnational Auto Companies in Brazil*, Cambridge: Cambridge University Press.

Shapiro, H. (1993b), 'Automobiles: From Import Substitution to Export Promotion in Brazil and Mexico', in D. Yoffie (ed.), *Beyond Free Trade Firms, Governments and Global Competition*, Boston: Harvard Business School Press.

Shapiro, H. and Oliveira Filho, G. (1987), 'Brazil: Stabilization Shock', *NACLA Report on the Americas*, **21** (2), March/April.

Shapiro, H. and Taylor, L. (1990), 'The State and Industrial Strategy', *World Development*, **18** (6), June.

Sochaczewski, A. C. (1980), 'Financial and Economic Development of Brazil, 1952–1968', PhD Dissertation, University of London.

Taylor, L. (1981), 'IS/LM in the Tropics', in W.R. Cline, and S. Weintraub (eds), *Economic Stabilization in Developing Countries*, Washington, D.C.: The Brookings Institution.

Werneck, R.L.F. (1986), 'Poupança Estatal, Dívida Externa e Crise Financeira do Setor Público', *Pesquisa e Planejamento Econômico*, **16**(3), December.

World Bank (1990), 'Industrial Regulatory Policy and Investment Incentives in Brazil', Report No. 7843-BR, March 15.

8. Market Miracle and State Stagnation? The Development Experience of South Korea and India Compared

Amitava Krishna Dutt and Kwan S. Kim*

INTRODUCTION

South Korea (henceforth: Korea) and India present a sharp contrast in economic performance in the post-World War II era. India, listed as among the 25 poorest countries in the world by the World Bank, in many respects epitomizes the problems which beset and characterize a typical developing economy. As measured by levels of production, capital wealth and human capital accumulation, India has not made the progress necessary to meet its own development goals. In contrast, Korea, which up to well into the 1960s was a backward economy based on subsistence agriculture with all of the difficulties facing a typical developing country of today, is at present the world's 12th-largest trading nation, and is on the threshold of joining the ranks of industrialized, developed nations.

It is often claimed that this difference in performance is explained by Korea's heavy reliance on markets and India's *dirigiste* shackles (Lal, 1988b); the experiences of these two countries are thus often cited to extol the virtues of free markets and the faults of state intervention.[1] The purpose of this chapter is to compare the recent development experiences of India and Korea to contribute to this debate on the role of state versus markets in development, in the light of specific country experiences, and to the more general discussion of why the newly industrialized countries performed so much better than other less developed economies.

It may be argued that while, in general, differences between their histories and structures make all cross-country comparisons difficult, the comparison between our two countries is especially treacherous, which is perhaps why it

* An earlier draft of this paper was presented at a conference on 'The State, Markets and Development' at the University of Notre Dame, April 1992. We are grateful to Anindya Datta and Jong-Il You for helpful comments.

has not already been thoroughly and systematically attempted.[2] The problems here have to do with the great difference in the size of the two countries – India with about 850 million people, and Korea with just over 42 million people – and with the special geo-political situation of Korea. While we recognize the great importance of these and other differences between the two countries, we still believe that there is much to be learnt from a careful comparison of their experiences which takes into account their differences in an explicit manner, but also does not lose sight of their similarities (a colonial past, low levels of development in both countries until the 1960s, and the fact that they are both in Asia). While it would be foolish to expect to understand fully from our comparative analysis the reasons for Korea's miracle and India's stagnation, we can expect our analysis to shed some light on several important debates in development economics, such as those concerning states and markets, and inward and outward orientations.[3]

The rest of this chapter proceeds as follows. The next section provides a summary account of some key facts regarding the development experiences of Korea and India. The two subsequent sections provide perspectives on the development experiences in Korea and India, respectively, stressing the roles of history, value systems, narrowly-economic determinants of development experience, and the state and its relationship to civil society. These sections do not follow a common framework, the discussion on each country reflecting and emphasizing its own patterns of change or continuity. Because the Korean experience is characterized by drastic political and policy changes, these changes are emphasized in our discussion. For India, on the other hand, we stress the essential continuity of policies and the role of the major constraints on development. The task of comparing the main features of experiences of the two countries, especially on the role of the state and markets, is left to the penultimate section and the final section concludes.

COMPARATIVE DEVELOPMENT PERFORMANCE

Table 8.1 compares basic indicators in social and economic development for the two countries. In 1989, India's GDP was about 1.5 times South Korea's, but India had a population close to 20 times that of Korea. Thus, expressed in the per capita term, the average income in Korea ($4 400) was about 13 times the average in India ($340). The difference in the distribution of income is also striking. Income is considered as more evenly distributed in Korea; according to a UNDP estimate, the average Gini coefficient in Korea over the period between 1970 and 1985 is 0.36, compared to 0.42 in India. Korea's development strategy seems to have worked well, probably, until recently, resulting not only in rapid growth but also in gradual eradication of absolute

Table 8.1   Basic socio-economic indicators for South Korea and India

	Korea	India
Population (millions – mid-1989)	42.4	832.5
Annual growth rate (%)		
1965–80	2.0	2.1
1980–89	1.2	1.7
Areas (1000 sq. kilometres)	99	3288
GNP per capita		
Dollars 1989	4400	340
Average annual growth rate	7.0	1.8
1965–89 (%)		
Gross domestic investment as %	28.8	20.8
of GNP (1965–89)		
Structure of production (%)		
Agriculture		
1965	38	44
1989	10	30
Industry		
1965	25	22
1989	44	29
Services		
1965	37	34
1989	46	41
Merchandise trade		
Current account balance		
(millions of dollars – 1989)[1]	5,008	–8,038
Exports – annual growth rate		
1965–80	27.2	3.0
1980–89	13.8	5.8
Imports–annual growth rate		
1965–80	15.2	1.2
1980–89	10.4	3.5
Debt service–exports ratio		
1980	19.7	9.1
1989	11.4	26.4
Gini coefficient (1970–85)*	0.36	0.42
Infant mortality (per 1000 births–1989)	23	30
Life Expectancy (years)	70	59
Adult Literacy rate (1985)*	95	44
Mean years of school (above age 25–1989)	6.6	2.2

[1]   Before official transfers.
*   UNDP: *Human Development Report 1991.*

Source: World Bank: *World Development Report 1991.*

poverty: the nation's unemployment rate is currently around 3 per cent and the incidence of absolute poverty is estimated at 5 per cent of the nation's population.[4] As for India, in 1977–78 40 per cent of the rural population and 39 per cent of the urban population were considered as poor, with a head count of over 250 million in total (Bardhan, 1984, pp. 2–3).

The differences in per capita GDP are also reflected by those in human development indicators. For example, life expectancy in India is 59 years, compared with 70 years in Korea; the infant mortality rate in Korea is far less than that in India; and the average years of school and adult literacy rate in Korea are more than twice those in India in the same year. Thus, by standard socio-economic measures, India's performance relative to Korea has been poorer.

The past performance in economic development has indeed been uneven in the two countries. During the period between 1965 and 1989, India's GDP at constant prices grew at an average annual rate of 1.8 per cent, compared to the corresponding average of 7.0 per cent for Korea. Population in India grew at an annual rate of 2.1 per cent between 1965 and 1980, and at a rate of 1.7 per cent between 1980 and 1989. The corresponding rates for Korea were 2.0 per cent and 1.2 per cent during the respective period. The slower growth in per capita income for India is partly attributed to its higher population growth.

Despite its slower GDP growth, India has achieved marked progress in industrial development in the post-war era. For the industrial sector, the annual growth rate of 6.8 per cent between 1950–51 and 1964–65 fell to 4.2 per cent between 1965–66 and 1980–81, rising to 6.9 per cent throughout the 1980s. Except during the period of stagnation after the mid-1960s, the performance has been better than the pre-independence period, as total manufacturing grew at 4.7 per cent in 1900–13 and at 3.3 per cent in 1919–39 (Lal, 1988a, p. 192). In the agricultural sector, value-added grew at a somewhat slower rate of 2.4 to 2.5 per cent per annum during the period of 1965–66 and 1980–81. In the 1980s, however, the growth rate in agriculture averaged 2.9 per cent. By 1989, agriculture as a share of total GDP declined to 30 per cent from 44 per cent in 1965, while the share of industry rose to 29 per cent from 22 per cent over the same period.

In the case of Korea, rapid economic growth brought with it a drastic transformation in Korea's industrial structure; primary activities which accounted for as much as 40 per cent of total economic activities in 1962–64 declined to 18.3 per cent by 1980, while manufacturing and mining rose from 18.1 to 30 per cent. The share of industry rose rapidly from 25 per cent of total GDP in 1965 to 44 per cent in 1989, while agriculture's share dropped from 38 per cent to 10 per cent over the same period.

Korea's economic development has been led by export expansion. From 1965 to 1980, the average rate of export growth was about 27.2 per cent a year, followed by a reduced growth rate of 13.8 per cent during the 1980s. The nation's annual export value soared from a modest $55 million in 1962 to a massive $27 billion by 1982. Whereas the ratio of exports to GNP was a pitiful 1 per cent or so in the 1950s, it rose to 30 per cent and more in the late 1970s. Exports, considered as the country's 'engine of growth', became something of a cliché in government and business circles, with its overall contribution to real GNP growth estimated at about 45 per cent for the 1962– 82 period and around 60 per cent for the 1970s (Kim, 1991, pp. 20–23). Imports also kept growing at quite a considerable pace. They attained an average growth of 15.2 per cent from 1965 to 1980, and 10.4 per cent during the 1980s. It was not easy for Korea to hold imports down since the bulk of them were fuel, raw materials and intermediate goods that went into the production of its exports.

In contrast to Korea's export orientation, India's trade policy, given its potentially large domestic market, has basically centred on import substitution. Between 1965 and 1980, exports at constant prices grew at 3.0 per cent. During the 1980s, however, the growth rate in India's exports has risen to 5.8 per cent. In terms of the share of exports in GNP, it doubled from 4 per cent in 1965 to 8 per cent in 1989. Indian export efforts have been more recent in origin, and its past export expansion has not played an important role in development.

THE STATE AND MARKETS: THE KOREAN EXPERIENCE

In this section we review, by way of a background to the ensuing discussions on the role of the state, the process of Korea's economic development from a historical perspective. The discussion then turns to the recent historical evolution in the relationship between the state and civil society, and to the implications of the supremacy of the Korean state for economic development.

Development from a Historical Perspective

The colonial legacy
The transition from a feudal agrarian economy to a modern industrial state in Korea began under Japanese colonial rule from the early 20th century until 1945. Japan was a late comer in a global struggle for colonization. Its ultimate interest in the contiguous colonies such as Korea and Manchuria was to integrate them closely with the metropolis and to use the conquered territories as a basis to supply human and physical resources as a basis for resisting the West.

Japan's ultimate intention to make Korea a perpetual part of the metropolis prompted heavy investment in administrative infrastructure, railroads, ports, communications and other physical facilities. The colony was used as the location for industry by drawing on indigenous labour and raw materials. To facilitate the process of industrialization, the colonial administration exercised a strict control over the economy, relying on a triad state apparatus made up of *zaibatsu* conglomerates, the central bank and administrative bureaucracy. As Landes (1965) points out, the colonial state stepped in to fill in the role of an absent or incipient, but not yet developed, entrepreneurial class in the colony. Japan's efforts to assimilate the colony were made easier by the fact that Koreans and Japanese are ethnically and culturally similar.

The colonial rule was harsh, but nonetheless contributed to the building of a basic physical infrastructure, laying down the basis for industrial development (Kim, 1973).[5] More significantly, it provided a model of highly-articulated, disciplined colonial bureaucracy, later to be adopted by Koreans for state-directed development. The colonial industrial organization is another legacy to post-war Korea. The Japanese introduced a model of *zaibatsu* conglomerates. The Koreans in the post-war period fostered their version of conglomerates, called *jaebol*, a close replica of the *zaibatsu* system. The corporate system is organized on the principle of an extended family, with an emphasis on loyalty, hierarchy and paternalistic authority.

Liberation from Japan in 1945 crippled the Korean economy, as it had been closely integrated to the metropole Japan. The subsequent separation of the north from the south further disabled the economy: heavy industries, electrical power resources and mineral deposits were mostly located in the northern part of the country, whereas industries in the south were mainly food processing and light consumption goods. The fragile industrial infrastructure left in the south was soon destroyed during the Korean War (1950–53), this time almost entirely. The south had to industrialize out of the ruins left in the wake of the War.

Inward orientation, 1953–60

The years between 1953 and 1960 mark the period of reconstruction under an import-substitution regime. Policy emphasis was on import substitution of non-durable consumer and intermediate goods behind a protective wall of tariffs and quotas. The domestic currency was maintained persistently at an overvalued rate, which thwarted the export potential of the economy. Thus, exports remained negligible throughout the period, on average amounting to less than 1 per cent of GNP. Imports, on the other hand, which were mostly financed by US grants-in aid, accounted for more than 10 per cent of GNP. Any kind of systematic, longer-run commitments on the part of the state towards sustained development were conspicuously absent.

The Korean economy in the 1950s possessed all the characteristics of an extremely poor Third World country. In 1953, its per capita GNP was about $130 in 1970 dollar prices. About 46 per cent of its GNP was generated by the agricultural sector, with manufacturing contributing only 6 per cent of GNP. The average annual growth rate of GNP during the period was 4 per cent. In 1961 nearly two-thirds of the working population were engaged in agriculture.

Outward orientation 1961–79
The military coup in 1961 was a turning point in Korean development. This is the beginning of the era during which the state pursued systematic, aggressive, outward-oriented policies to achieve rapid economic growth. Initially, the government decided to intensify its promotion of import substitution. However, the inflow of US aid, which peaked in 1957, had already started its irreversible decline. The government had to turn to such alternative sources of foreign exchange as foreign loans and export expansion, along with fiscal and interest rate reforms to mobilize domestic savings.[6] Besides, markets for most import-substitutable products were already saturated in Korea by the early 1960s. The shift towards export expansion was a timely and logical move.

During the period of outward orientation, sustained state intervention in major economic activities became the rule rather than the exception. Three features of development strategy are worth noting. The first is the practice of targeting 'strategic' sectors and firms for special support; the second is the neomercantilistic trade policy of maximizing exports while minimizing imports; and the third concerns the state's agricultural policy.

The Korean government slipped into the practice later known as 'targeting industry and product'. The targeting system was introduced as the government began to select 'strategic' industries for support over a series of five-year development plans. With the notable exception of the first five-year plan (1962–66) when infrastructure development was emphasized, the dynamic sequencing in industrial development was designed to reflect the changing patterns of comparative advantage for Korea. The state support started with labour-intensive industries, moving on to capital- and skill-intensive sectors in the subsequent plans.[7] The choice of 'strategic' industries has varied over time, ranging from sophisticated electronics to heavy and chemical sectors, iron and steel, shipbuilding and automobiles. Rather than channelling funds and adopting projects on an *ad hoc* basis as opportunities might arise, systematic efforts were made to adapt to the technological changes taking place in the industry world-wide, to reflect scale economies and inter-industrial linkages, and to direct the economy along the desired path as perceived by the planners.[8]

The second feature of strategy concerns trade policy. Korea's outward-oriented policy was an eclectic one, in that, while exports have been emphasized, protection of selective domestic industries for import substitution – in particular, intermediate and capital goods sectors – has been given no less importance. The vertical integration of production structure was intended to lessen the economy's dependence on imports, while the longer-run strategy has been to establish a viable industrial structure that can prove adaptable to the shifting comparative advantages in international markets. Thus, in the case of Korea, import substitution and export promotion proceeded together, possibly with some time-lags.[9] Its experience in outward orientation must not be interpreted as an example of trade liberalization in the neoclassical sense.

The final feature of strategy relates to rural development. Korean agriculture, despite its importance in the economy, has for most of the time been subordinated to the goal of industrialization. Park's technocrats were much more concerned with industrialization than with agricultural development, although Korea was already in substantial food deficit. Park's strategy was to mobilize resources for activities that accelerate the pace of industrialization. Thus, to ensure lower industrial wages through cheap imported food, the state denied to agriculture the protection awarded industry, and allowed imports of food grains. The consequent rural sector's adverse terms of trade ensured a continual flow of labour to urban industry. Throughout the 1960s, the rural sector remained, relative to the urban area, impoverished.

In the early 1970s rural political instability became a threat to the state. The political leadership saw the promotion of farming interests as a viable route to retaining political power.[10] To put brakes on the rapid deterioration in the rural economy, the Park government, along with providing extension services through the rural-oriented New Village Movement *(Saemaul)*, initiated a massive rice procurement programme at prices several times the world market price to support farm incomes. As a result, the first half of the 1970s saw substantial improvements in rural living standards. In the case of Korea, the success with industry facilitated agricultural development through reallocation to it of industrial surpluses. The rising incomes also made possible improved health standards, high levels of educational attainment, and access to basic services. Thus, social and rural development in Korea depended on the pace of industrial development.

The policies to force growth with equity by supporting declining agriculture, on the other hand, proved economically costly. From the early 1970s onwards, the government has found itself committed to heavy subsidies on fertilizer and to the difference between the prices it paid to farmers for rice and barley and the lower prices at which it sold to consumers. The financial cost of supporting agriculture adds to the economic cost to the nation of protecting agriculture against competing imports. The labour-intensive small farm sector, once functional to industrial development, has now become a hindrance.

The results of these efforts were predictable. Korea achieved a significant level of import substitution behind heavy protective tariffs in such products as cement, fertilizer, refined petroleum, textile yarn and fabrics, which in due course emerged as a new generation of exportable goods. Also, export promotional policies gathered momentum over time. Taking advantage of a favourable trade environment in the 1960s and privileged access to US offshore procurements during the Vietnam War, the government resorted to an all-out effort for exports. Exports rose dramatically: over the period of 1962–79, Korea's real exports grew at the average annual rate of 33.7 per cent. The growth performance was also spectacular: the average growth rate in real GNP during the 1965–79 period was 9.7 per cent; real per capita income showed an 18-fold increase to $1,481 in 1980 from $87 in 1962. Rapid economic growth brought with it a drastic transformation in Korea's industrial structure; primary activities, which accounted for 40 per cent of the total economic activities in 1962–64, had declined to 18.3 per cent by 1980, while manufacturing and mining rose from 18.1 to 30 per cent.

Towards the late 1970s, the overall income distribution deteriorated as the government drastically reduced farm subsidies and continued with anti-labour policies while sheltering the interests of industrial capitalists. Pro-*Jaebol* policies, in particular, contributed particularly to the widening of intra-industry income gaps. Moreover, as fiscal policies tended to concentrate on industrial infrastructure development, ignoring social areas, the incidence of poverty became more acute in urban areas and on economically disadvantaged groups such as the elderly, disabled and female-headed households. Regional disparities have, in addition, emerged as a political polemic, resulting from the regional proclivities of economic policy-makers. Government concerns with social welfare and income inequality have been of relatively recent origin in the 1980s.[11]

Balance and liberalization, 1981 to the present

By the late 1970s, however, it became clear that the state's implementation machinery was working too effectively. The state bureaucracy's excessive zeal to surpass targets, and consequent excessive interference in market functions, gradually built into serious distortions and imbalances in the economy. Private companies blindly followed the government's lead without paying much attention to the underlying economic ills characteristic of inflation, and distortions and rent-seeking activities in the economy; too many production units were crowded into too few strategic sectors, resulting in too much capacity too quickly. Some of these sectors did not really possess a comparative advantage, revealing distortions in the allocation of resources. Wage suppression and pro-business policy also aggravated income distribution.[12]

Coming to the late 1970s, a series of economic set-backs took place, including a crop failure and the impacts of the second oil shock and the global recession. These provoked a decline in real GNP in 1980 (for the first time since 1953) and high inflation. The economic crisis was confounded with a series of political crises epitomized by the anti-government Kwangju uprising in 1980. The military regime led by Chun Doo Hwan intervened to repress the strong societal reaction, consolidating an authoritarian rule, and set to the task of economic stabilization.

The Chun regime initiated a two-pronged economic policy of adopting a macroeconomic stabilization, while aiming at a longer-term balanced growth and liberalization through restructuring of the economy. The self-imposed stabilization programmes included aggregate demand control through restrictive monetary policy, elimination of subsidies, reduction in government expenditure, and realignment of real exchange rate on a floating basis.

As regards programmes for structural adjustment, excessive aspects of the command structure were gradually being discarded in favour of more initiatives from the private sector, and businessmen were urged to pay more heed to market signals and profits. A gradual and cautiously scheduled import liberalization programme was introduced, reflecting a recognition of the importance of market forces in an already complex and highly sophisticated economy. The new programme also included denationalization of the banking system, and elimination of cartel arrangements and price-fixing, and a better balance between small- and large-scale firms. For this, with the help of timely Japanese loans and aid,[13] the state initiated the sectoral reorganization on the principle of one *jaebol* for each industrial sector.

Chun's structural adjustment policies abetted the performance of the economy. Stabilization measures succeeded in bringing down inflation and, partly helped by the recovering world markets beginning in 1983, the Korean economy was on its way to expansion, registering an average of 9.5 per cent growth in GNP between 1983 and 1987.

The step-down of one term president Chun in 1987 was followed by a wave of labour and student unrest. The subsequent years of rapid democratization under Roh saw a general weakening of the macroeconomic performance of the economy. Wage increases began to outstrip productivity gains by wide margins, thereby fuelling inflation and sharply eroding export competitiveness. As inflation continued to accelerate and imports rose rapidly under ongoing trade liberalization, the nation's trade balance, which reached a surplus of $14 billion in 1988, has worsened in the last two years. Korea has been going through a critical period of transition from an authoritarian rule to political liberalization, and at the same time from excessive statism to economic liberalization.

The political transition to a democracy has been creating a new environ-ment in which economic policy-makers must now work. Externally, Roh's government was committed to internationalizing the Korean economy by opening domestic markets to foreign trade and investment. The state's role in industrial development was limited to assisting in the continued development of technology and human capital. Internally, a wider participation in political decisions forced the state to pay close attention to social welfare and equity. The government faced the challenge of striking a proper balance between growth and equity. As a result, government spending gave greater priority to meeting basic needs; operating more public assistance programmes, includ-ing low income housing, for those especially disadvantaged.[14] Political liber-alization and active participation of civil society began to have a salutary impact on social services. On the other hand, the prospect of high growth policies was held in check. The economic growth rate, in fact, slowed down considerably from 12 per cent a year in 1986 to 1988, to 7 per cent in 1990 to 1991. A GNP growth rate of 7–8 per cent was targeted in the sixth five-year plan (1987–92).

The State and Civil Society: the Case of Korea

Korea's success in rapid industrialization is, to a large extent, attributable to a strong state regime capable of energetically executing plans and strategies. The questions that need to be answered are: where has the primacy of the state derived from? What has been the extent of state control? How autono-mous has the Korean state been in relation to various groups of civil society? And how has the state elicited the compliance of the private sector? This section focuses on the origin and evolution of statism in Korea, and the relationships of the state to civil society in historical and cultural perspective.

The emergence of a Weberian state
The rise of a Weberian, modern state in Korea can be traced to Japanese colonial rule. Upon colonizing the country, the colonial state promptly swept away the traditional feudalistic order, replacing it with a bureaucratic, cen-tralized state apparatus. The modernization of the colony was to be facilitated by sweeping changes from above. The consolidation of a new political order was followed by the introduction of new capitalist social relationships in industry, in which a tripartite alliance of the colonial state's bureaucracy, central banking, and *zaibatsu* conglomerates dominated, while in pre-capital-ist agriculture the state introduced landlord–tenant relationships to exploit exportable surplus grains from Korea.

The colonial mode of production influenced the indigenous class structure. While tenancy in agriculture pauperized indigenous farmers, turning them

into urban proletarians in industry dominated by Japanese capital, there also
emerged a new class of indigenous capitalists, mainly in trade and small-
scale industry, and a significant number of indigenous landlords. The emerging, propertied class tended to rely on the colonial state apparatus in sharing
surpluses as a way to retain its wealth and privilege. In the case of agriculture, rural society continued to retain the feudalistic land-tenure system serving the interests of the colonial state, which turned into a factor contributing
to the peasant uprisings immediately after Korea's liberation from Japan.

In post-liberation Korea, the land reforms initiated by the US military
regime, which redistributed land to the tillers and outlawed tenancy, virtually
eliminated the land-owning class as a contending political force. The few
indigenous industrial capitalists remaining in the wake of Japanese with-
drawal from Korea were a disorganized, weakened economic force. The
policy-makers in liberated Korea could act autonomously, free from the
interference and demands of élite classes.

In terms of dealing with non-élite classes, a geopolitical dimension was
contributing to the enhancement of state authority in the post-liberation era.
The US security interest in Korea during the rapidly evolving Cold War years
prompted the build-up of a strong, anti-communist state apparatus backed up
by the national police in a revived form of the colonial police. The tragic
experience of the Korean War and the continued threat of renewed war by
North Korea reinforced the authoritarian rule of Syngman Rhee with strong
backing from the military forces. While the post-liberation state in Korea
formally professed a resemblance to Western democracy with free elections
and civil liberty, the state's coercive apparatus was used to suppress civil
rights and political oppositions in the name of national security. The state, in
particular, enforced an anti-labour policy, as organized labour was seen as a
left-leaning disruptive social force.

Thus, the state apparatus inherited by post-colonial Korea was in a position to subordinate all the indigenous classes with the inheritance of a military–administrative apparatus. No particular social groups or forces could
dare to challenge the state authority. The Korean state was in a position
directly to appropriate a large part of economic surplus, deploying it in
bureaucratically directed activities.

After the end of the Korean War a number of family-based industrial
conglomerates, *jaebol,* began to emerge as the new economic élites. As a
result of extensive damage inflicted by the War, the Korean economy depended heavily on consumer goods imports, which were mostly financed by
US aid. The Rhee regime's plan was to encourage the development of domestic manufacture to replace gradually consumer goods imports. As the regime's import substitution-based industrialization plan was based on a heavy
reliance on foreign aid and imports, windfall profits could be had through

privileged access to foreign exchange and import licences. The corrupt Rhee regime prompted the rise of new economic élites by expediting accumulation in selected enterprises. Because of the close relationship between the state and selected private capital, the effects of government measures for industrial development were largely concentrated on the emerging *jaebol*.

The emergence of new capitalists did not detract from the state's exercising its autonomy. Under the Rhee regime, private capital was created and supported to serve as the instrument of the state. This resulted in the formation of a close relationship with the state in sharing the fruits of rent-seeking activities involving mainly commercial deals. What prompted the demise of the particular capitalist social relationships in the 1950s was the indignation of the populace directed against the rent-seekers under commercial capitalism, and the inability of commercial capital to provide for the needs of the people. Despite some advances made in import substitution to replace potential imports, the impact fell far short of paving the way towards a self-sustained economy; the economy under an inefficient and corrupt administrative infrastructure remained a stagnant, dependent one, with import dependence rising in many manufacturing sectors and most significantly in agriculture.

Statism during the export-led phase

The economic and moral crisis engendered by an inept and corrupt regime made it easier for Park Chung Hee's military faction to legitimize the coup in 1961 in the name of national security and economic survival. After coming to power, Park's immediate task was to institutionalize an authoritarian and interventionist rule in carrying out a kind of economic revolution from above. The military coup was organized by a previously isolated section of the state apparatus with no linkages to particular social groups. The coup came under the revolutionary mandate to eliminate rent-seeking activities and to restore national security and economic prosperity. There were no countervailing forces to check the huge military institution. The military regime was soon able to institutionalize an authoritarian rule.

Learning from Japanese experience in the Meiji Restoration (*Ishin*), Park saw sweeping changes from above as the only way to facilitate the modernization of Korea. Under the pretext of national 'revitalization' (*yushin*), the Constitution was amended to consolidate the dominance of the executive under one-party rule. After amassing sweeping powers for the presidency, the Park regime set itself to the task of designing and implementing strategies for accumulating industrial capital. Park saw rapid industrialization as the way to modernize the nation. A system of meritocratic bureaucracy backed by military muscle was ushered in to implement policies to develop a modern manufacturing industry. The political system envisioned as ideal to carry out such a strategy was one wherein the policy-makers, based on the coalition of competent bureaucracy, business and the military, were autonomous in decision-making with no interference from non-capitalist classes.[15] The elimination of leftist forces, which continued throughout the 1950s after the Korean War, freed the government from the need to pursue populist policies, making it easier for the state to consolidate and narrow down the range of debates on policy alternatives. The period of the Park regime witnessed the rebirth of a kind of Japanese colonial rule of militarized control, decisive economic planning, and all-out mobilization of resources for industrial development (Henderson, 1988).

The state's strategy for accumulation of industrial capital has had far-reaching consequences for class structure in Korean society. One particular class viewed by the state as a potential threat to the success of economic growth has been industrial labour. The success of export-oriented industrialization required mobilization of cheap and disciplined labour. The military regime played a critical role in shaping the form of labour movements, and also that of the labour process, through intervening within the factory or through ruling capital–labour relations.

Historically, Korea's trade unions, created by the state to support the anti-communist struggle against left-wing labour movements, have often acted like its agency. Workers have until recently been denied the right to organize unions that might foster class consciousness. Industrial unions are typically organized at the enterprise level. Collective bargaining is carried out at the enterprise level. This internal company unionism precluded the possibility of unions forming a united front on common economic and social interests, thereby diminishing their influence on national policies.

The politics of labour demobilization continued throughout the 1970s. When the average real wage rate rose in response to tight labour market conditions developed in the early 1970s, Korea was threatened with a deterioration in the competitive edge of its labour-intensive exports. The government quickly enacted a series of measures to restrain wage increases by curtailing the power of trade unions.[16] As a result, real wages fell behind the rise in labour productivity which, for instance, increased almost 50 per cent faster between 1967 and 1978.[17] The slower growth in relative wages reflected labour's declining share in output;[18] labour's share in manufacturing value-added declined from 36.6 per cent in 1958 to 23.0 per cent by 1975.

While repressing labour movements, the state reorganized the capitalist class. At the time of the advent of the military regime, the old bourgeoisie, discredited with the downfall of Rhee, was on the verge of extinction. When Park decided to pursue a capitalist strategy for industrialization, he needed to enlist business support. The previous industrialists were given the opportunity to collaborate with the state while creating new business interests. The business sector was not, however, allowed to become autonomous in relation to the state.

The nurturing of big businesses was seen as an imperative for the development of heavy industry in Korea. Economic logic favoured large-scale production, as a minimum scale in plant size would be required for efficiency of production in such heavy sectors as automobiles, steel and shipbuilding. The *jaebol* must compete in international markets with the large-scale foreign multinationals. The size of the firm is also an important factor to consider in joint ventures with foreign partners, since there would be the risk that the latter could dominate and control the domestic counterparts.[19]

As a result, the breadth and speed in the rise of the *jaebol* have been unprecedented in Korea's history of enterprise. There were some 50 major conglomerates, with each unit composed of half a dozen to 50 member firms that were horizontally and vertically integrated in the industrial structure.[20] Between 1973 and 1978, the annual rate of growth in value-added contributed by the ten largest conglomerates was as high as 30 per cent. In terms of the share of their contribution to GDP, they accounted for 14 per cent in 1973, rising to 23.4 per cent by 1978 (Kim, 1991, pp. 36-7). The top 46 firms, taken together, accounted for 31.8 per cent of GDP in 1973, which rose to 43 per cent over the same period. These measures clearly show the extent of progress in industrial concentration during the military regime.[21]

To elicit compliance from private capital, the state resorted to a strictly enforced system of 'carrots and sticks'. Incentives were offered to those who complied with the directions of the state. The most important instrument was the allocation of bank credit and of access to foreign capital. Businesses in Korea critically depended on bank credits, as over two-thirds of the cash flow of manufacturing firms came from borrowing from financial institutions controlled by the state. The debt–equity ratio in the private sector typically ranged from four to six, and the industrial capitalists were put in a weak bargaining position in dealing with the state.

Within the public sector, which included state-run enterprises, heavy pressures were exerted on the bureaucrats, frequently by imposing output targets, to execute their jobs well . The forms of intervention ranged from a 'friendly' telephone call from the president's office, to the allocation of bank loans. One influential administrative institution is the tax authorities. They have sanctioned non-compliant enterprises by inspecting their returns more strictly. The state also controlled prices to subsidize export- and targeted-sector activities through reductions in imported input prices or through increases in monopolistic prices for profits. The 'carrots and sticks' system worked well for Korea; industrial capitalists soon realized that compliance with government directions would be the only way to survive and prosper.

In sum, the Korean state during the export-led phase was free from the constraints of civil society and could direct the economy to pursue the national goals in ways perceived and formulated by technocratic bureaucrats. Given the geopolitical constraint to remain a capitalist system, the state guided the form and pace of capital accumulation by cajoling or forcing the collaboration from private capital. The state thus ruled over the interests of capitalists without allowing the possibility of the latter's dominating over the former. State involvement turned out to be most extensive and substantial during the export-led phase of Korean development.

Statism in the context of structural adjustment

The decade of the 1980s began with political and economic crises. The assassination of President Park in 1979 was followed by a brief move towards civilian constitutionalism, which ended with the Kwangju riot where the army suppressed an incipient pro-democracy rebellion with considerable force, resulting in hundreds of casualties. Economically, as already discussed, Korea was severely affected by the global economic downturn during the late 1970s and early 1980s. Precipitated by the social unrest and a crop failure in 1980, the economy was plunged into stagnation for the first time since 1961. The general-turned-president, Chun Doo Hwan, elected for a single seven-year term, decided to oversee the continuation of the Park regime.

State intervention under the Chun regime revolved around two major themes of macroeconomic stabilization and balanced growth in the context of economic liberalization at a piecemeal pace. As far as the basic character of the state was concerned, it was still close to a bureaucratic authoritarian state as described by O'Donnell. The control of the state continued to remain comprehensive, technocratic and often repressive. The goals of the state were to be attained at all costs – social and economic. When the market system worked in the desired way, it was to be left alone; when it couldn't, state intervention to direct it in the desired way was considered legitimate. Class structure was to be reformulated to suit the needs of the state.

Thus despite the urgency for economic liberalization and decentralization, the subordinate relationship of business to the state remained unchanged under the Chun regime. Although alarming trends of industrial concentration set in,[22] the government continued to work with big businesses. Large firms with scale economies could be counted on to complete more successfully crucial projects for national development. Funds flowed more readily into larger companies, since they were generally in a better position to outbid smaller firms in government-financed projects.

The impressive economic growth combined with low inflation rates during the Chun regime was indeed attained at the expense of workers and farmers. To maintain export competitiveness, the state pursued a thorough repression of labour, outlawing strikes and unions,[23] and reduced farm subsidies while attempting to liberalize agricultural imports. Chun's government initially evinced greater interest in promoting balanced growth with equity. In reality, the reforms for equitable development had been incremental in changes. There were no drastic structural reforms in the political economy. At the same time, Chun's structural adjustment policies relied on the effective working of state bureaucracy. The capacity of the state to formulate and execute strategies under the Chun regime is not very different from that under the Park regime. The state continued to influence class formation. While differences between the two regimes exist in the choice of economic strategy, the character and structure of the state remains essentially the same.

The deepening of industrialization in Korea gradually weakened the state's strength and autonomy in relation to various groups of its political economy. As the economy grew in size and complexity, state intervention became more costly, economically and politically. As the number of labourers increased and the *jaebol* became economically more powerful, they became increasingly vocal about the negative aspects of the centralized role of the state. The labourers and the previously very acquiescent farmers have become most outspoken in their demands for a larger share of the benefits of economic growth.

The state in the transition to democracy
The year 1987 when Chun stepped down from the presidency became a turning-point in Korea's political life. The crisis of state authority had already erupted in 1985 when the opposition parties gained more strength in the February parliamentary election. The ensuing presidential election, as a result of splits among the opposition party candidates, restored the former military general Roh as president of the sixth republic. Roh's government faced a National Assembly dominated by the opposition parties,[24] which made agreement on policy issues difficult.

Certainly, the recent political reforms have led to political liberalization and the widening of the power base, but not democratization. The genuine democratic institutions that could hold the government accountable for its actions and offer an alternative set of policies to the voters did not emerge. Pluralism was legalized, but a viable alternative opposition force did not surface. The post-1987 period continued to witness in Korea a rigid, but not a very strong, state. There has, however, been a significant reduction of state autonomy from civil society; the government is now more prone to pressure from influential interest groups. A transition from 'hard' to 'soft' authoritarianism appears to have been taking place.

Statism embedded in East Asian culture

The preceding discussion has related the primacy of the Korean state to historical factors. We have argued that state authority in Korea has not been derived from linkages to a particular civilian base of support. The state has, on the contrary, determined the formation of class structure, creating alliances with particular classes as it sees necessary.

The emergence in Korea of a 'hard state' – a dominant state strongly committed to economic development – cannot, however, be viewed as a simple historical accident. The question remains: why has statism, despite its many potential pitfalls, worked in East Asia? In accounting for the legitimacy of state authority, one must go beyond the historical process in the development of state capitalism in East Asia. The primacy of the state has a long history in East Asia, embedded in its culture and tradition throughout the entire phase of modernization.

The centuries-old Confucian ideology in Asian societies, which inculcates the virtue of authority emanating from a vertical social order, legitimizes state intervention. Civil servants are accorded highest status in the social hierarchy. Under the Confucian civil service system in Korea, meritocratic examinations have traditionally been used to recruit the best minds into the state bureaucracy. As the state under Park gained almost absolute autonomy from civil society, a meritocratic recruitment system via élite academia was reinforced to build a competent bureaucratic organization for facilitating the process of industrial transformation.

Under the Confucian system of hierarchy, business is expected to serve the rulers of the state, and non-élite classes to respect the guidance of élites.[25] Thus, the concept of a horizontal social order, as exemplified in Adam Smith's 'invisible hand', would be utterly at odds with Confucian ethics which values 'the wisdom and moral ethics of the supreme ruler and ruling élite' (Luedde-Neurath, 1988, p. 98). This lingering influence of traditional culture has made bureaucratic authoritarian rule easier and more acceptable to the populace in East Asia. Of course, in the case of Korea, the linguistic and cultural homogeneity in a territorially compact nation facilitates the formation of a centralized polity.

Efficacy of state authority

The selective but vigorous promotion of infant industries and the upgrading of the country's competitive advantage by articulate industrial policies, all this through the concerted efforts for resource mobilization, were the key elements of state activism in Korea. The question to address here is whether these state actions have benefited the economy. Given the complexity of the developmental process, it would be impossible to measure the consequences of state intervention. Neither is it possible to appraise the counterfactual case in which Korea had followed a non-interventionist strategy. Thus, the most one can conclude from the available data is that rapid economic growth in Korea has taken place under a strong interventionist state which is dedicated to economic development.

The particular contribution of state intervention is more discernible, however, when the judgement involves the efficacy of implementation. A major characteristic of bureaucratic organization under Park was centralization of economic policy formulation and implementation by the Economic Planning Board. The Board, staffed by well-trained, competent technocrats and headed by a deputy prime minister who is directly accountable to the president, is an all-powerful agency in the economic arena. It had the ultimate power to plan and execute economic policies by co-ordinating the activities of economic ministers through control of the budgetary process. Centralism was viewed as necessary to facilitate speed and flexibility in decision-making and implementation.

If the effectiveness of state intervention is judged on the basis of how closely the targeted goals have been achieved, the Korean case can be seen as a success. The Korean planners in the earlier period were known to have a tendency to set output targets in over-ambitious, quantitative terms. Despite this practice, actual performance exceeded planned targets by substantial margins in all the five-year plan periods except during the fourth plan period. Throughout the period covering the initial three consecutive five-year plans (1962–76), the economy grew by 9.2 per cent per annum, while the targeted growth rate in real GNP averaged out at 7.5 per cent.[26] Only during the fourth plan period (1977–81) did the actual growth rate fall short of the targeted one. During this period, the economy encountered unusually adverse shocks – both external and internal in origin.

The polemic surrounding the Korean state

The polemic surrounding the role of the state in Korean development is not whether or not the state has intervened in the economy. By now, that the Korean state has been dominant and active is widely accepted. The issue of contention seems to be concerned with the quality of intervention. A number of neoclassical economists have argued that Korea pursued neutral, market-oriented trade policies (Frank et. al., 1975; Westphal, 1978 and 1990; Krueger, 1979; Balassa, 1982; Little 1982). Export promotional measures during the rapid growth phase neutralized the bias against exports from the prior policies of import substitution. The policy neutrality is seen as coming close to a free trade regime in the sense that the resulting resource allocation is consistent with comparative advantage, and one that would theoretically be obtained under free trade.[27] In this context, Korea and Taiwan have often been quoted as cases of rapid growth attained by 'getting the prices right'.

To attribute the high growth during the export-oriented phase to the working of 'correct' pricing is, however, an unhelpful over-simplification of the
Korean experience. There are fundamental flaws in the argument. First of all,
the assertion that the Korean state's intervention was 'neutral' is questionable
on empirical grounds. While Westphal's study (1990, p. 44) concludes that
'the most important incentive apart from the exchange rate was the virtual
free trade regime, which accounted for more than two-thirds of total export
incentives in 1968', this argument is contradicted by Nam (1981, p. 205),
who shows that Korean export sales, on average, received greater incentives
than domestic sales. In particular, the effective protection in agriculture alone
averaged more than 70 per cent during the growth phase. This fact alone
should make the whole argument of a free trade regime questionable. Amsden
in her recent work (1989) even argues that the success of Korean textile
exports in the 1960s was due to the effective subsidies, not because their
relative prices were 'market-correct'.

One must note in passing that calculations of effective protection involve
econometrically intractable problems of what to include and exclude and, in
particular, of how to quantify non-tariff barriers. The problem is serious,
since the Korean government resorted to export targeting, quantitative restrictions, non-market incentives and sanctions that defy quantification. More
importantly, the comparison becomes more complex since a free trade regime
would possibly reduce the rent-seeking activities in the economy.

On the conceptual plane, if market rationality implies that economic deci-
sion-makers are not only efficient selectors of alternative courses of action, but
also optimal estimators (Stein, 1978), many of the state actions in the 1960s
and 1970s would not fit into this framework. It is difficult to reconcile such
practices as picking the winners and the losers for infant industry development,
credit allocation favouring big businesses, and output targeting at the firm
level, with 'market-conforming' or 'market-friendly' activities. More importantly, even if the empirical claim for neutrality of Korean trade policy proved
correct, it still is questionable as to whether or not a bias in favour of both
export- and import-substituting activities would have the same effects as a free
trade regime. The answer must be sought beyond the neoclassical bounds of
allocative efficiency. There are other issues, such as scale economies, X-effi-
ciency or inter-industrial linkages, that must be taken into account in the
comparison. The concept of neoclassical rationality ignores other factors. Therefore, it is not a useful concept in describing the behaviour of the Korean state.
The state's actions, in particular during the export-led phase, can be viewed as
rational by other standards. One can argue that the state's behaviour is rational
by the standard of the national objective for rapid industrialization. Viewed in
this context, the market-conforming activities of the state, when necessary,
only facilitate the attainment of its other prioritized goals.

THE INDIAN EXPERIENCE

After India achieved independence from British rule in 1947, the government embarked on a programme of planned economic development. The Five-Year Plans were put into operation from 1951, and with the exception of a few 'Plan holidays' (due to adverse exogenous shocks), Indian development has been guided by state planning (see Chakravarty, 1987). The general goal of planning was to increase growth with equity and self-reliance in the context of a mixed economy consistent with the socialist orientation of the leadership. The predominant agricultural sector was left in private hands, although land reforms to improve the pattern of land tenure were attempted. In the industrial sector the state intervened more strongly, by directly engaging in production and through industrial licensing and tariff policies, with the goals of increasing production and productivity (especially in key sectors such as heavy industries, following the Mahalanobis strategy of the Second Five-Year Plan) encouraging small-scale industries (especially for employment generation), ensuring regionally balanced growth, preventing the concentration of monopoly power, and controlling foreign investment in domestic industry. With failed harvests in the mid-1960s and generally poor agricultural performance, the government decided to change its agricultural policy to spread the 'green revolution' by promoting the use of scientific inputs and de-emphasizing land reform. In response to growing concern with the growing problem of poverty, from the mid-1970s the redistributive aspects of the development strategy were emphasized, and the earlier policy of emphasis on heavy industries was altered to provide more resources for the agricultural sector. In the 1980s there were various attempts at liberalizing the economy by reducing the scope of government regulation and control, and these efforts have been speeded up in recent months.

Though the development performance of the economy was generally better than when under colonial rule (and important strides were undoubtedly made in developing a heavy industries base), it can hardly be called impressive. It was poor compared to that of many other less developed economies and, as we have seen, embarrassingly so compared to Korea's; India's position in the world economy gradually regressed. There have been some variations in growth performance, especially in that of the industrial sector, with comparatively higher growth before 1965 and after 1975 (especially in the 1980s), and with low growth in between (Sandesara, 1992) .

In this section we first note some aspects of India's experience prior to planning. We next turn to some explanations of stagnation, first briefly discussing the role of religious values, and then examining more narrowly-economic obstacles to development. Finally, we consider the nature of the state and its relationship to civil society, to develop a political-economy analysis of India's development problems.[28]

Historical Background

By way of background we begin with four brief comments on India's historical experiences.

First, we note the 'overarching significance of rulership' (Rudolph and Rudolph, 1987, p. 65). Until the advent of British rule and its technologically sophisticated military power, Indian history can be thought of as the history of the rise and decline of centralized states, the ambition of every chieftain being to establish a subcontinental empire tapping the revenue extractable from a relatively productive agricultural system. While the large size of the country and frequent inter-ruler rivalry made the establishment of centralized rule somewhat episodic, the central ruler has been seen as an object of awe and wonder. A good ruler must dispense justice with a strong hand, be Guardian and Protector to their subjects, and keep potential rivals at bay. This notion of the state continued through the period of British rule and even thereafter.

Secondly, despite this macrocosmic turbulence, the microcosm of the Indian village community has remained virtually unchanged through the millennia. Central rulers typically found it expedient not to interfere with the structure of local law-enforcement and tax collection systems as long the revenue kept flowing in. The division of labour and occupational hierarchy provided by the caste system maintained this structure and generally provided local stability (see Lal, 1988a, pp. 3, 24–6).

Thirdly, the fortunes of manufacturing industry have changed over the years. Prior to British rule there developed large pockets of industrial development catering to the needs of royal courts and producing handicrafts for local as well as foreign (including European) markets (Dutt, 1992a). There is considerable evidence that within a few years of the establishment of British rule, and in large part due to tariff policies and the 'drain' of financial wealth to Britain, the situation was radically altered, and the Indian economy was transformed from being an exporter of manufactured goods (such as cotton textiles) to an exporter of primary products and an importer of manufactured goods (see Dutt, 1992a). A cumulative process of deindustrialization with specialization in primary production arguably set in, with adverse consequences far outweighing the possible favourable effects of colonial rule on 'good government' (see Dutt, 1992a).

Finally, while it is true that initial specialization in primary production does not preclude economic growth, and there may in fact be some benefits in late industrialization, in the absence of any systematic industrial policy on the part of India's foreign government (see Bagchi, 1972; Charlesworth, 1982), such benefits largely escaped India. Though there was respectable growth in modern factory industry after 1850, especially in cotton textiles (India was in 1914 the world's fourth greatest cotton manufacturing country), jute textiles and iron and steel, as late as 1931 workers in factory industry numbered just over 1.5 million out of a population of 353 million. India lacked the major 'new' industries such as chemicals and heavy electricals which played a vital role in late industrialization in Europe, and industrial growth was unstable and regionally concentrated. The agricultural sector also performed poorly under colonial rule. Except for an expansion of irrigation in the more easily irrigable north, there was hardly any technological change. Though the land tenure system, especially the *zamindari* system of the east, with its propensity to increase subinfeudation, increased the growth of 'cash crops', there was a stagnation in per capita agricultural production, and some decline over most of the first half of the 20th century (Charlesworth, 1982).

As noted above, the experience with planning did imply some gains, especially in developing an industrial base, and it changed the situation compared to that described in the last two comments of the previous paragraph. However, planning could not increase the rate of growth substantially, nor could it make a dent in the problems of inequality and poverty. We turn to alternative explanations for these before developing a political economy perspective.

Role of Religious Values

Religious values have been argued to have an important effect on economic development, at least since Weber's seminal work on the protestant ethic. In fact, Weber (1958) argued that Hinduism (and other Indian religions engulfed by it) had an essentially negative effect on economic development, and several writers (see Nair, 1962; Kapp, 1963; Lal, 1988a, 1988b) have followed his lead. While current debates on the constraints on Indian growth do not typically stress these factors, the currency of such phrases as 'Hindu equilibrium' and the 'Hindu rate of growth',[29] and the resurgence of interest in religious values in explaining Japanese and Asian NIC growth (see Morishima, 1982; Vogel, 1991), do not allow us to neglect them altogether. Our remarks are confined to three brief comments.

First, while the argument that the general Hindu system involving the belief in the doctrine of *karma* (that is, the belief that one's actions in the present life determine one's status in the next) causes one fatalistically to accept one's material conditions and lead an ascetic life, seems plausible enough, it is by no means clear to what extent such beliefs block development. One can raise questions regarding the existence of a monolithic ideology for India; the degree to which formal religious thought affects actual behaviour given the fact that such ideas are confined to a small élite; and why the pursuit of duty must have poor economic results (for instance, it could help investment by strengthening animal spirits). Most importantly, it is possible to provide examples which suggest that religious values actually did not block development in many instances (see Morris, 1967, pp. 596–602; Charlesworth, 1982, pp. 39–43).

Secondly, while it has been argued that the caste system played an anti-developmental role by reducing socio-economic mobility and dampening economic aspirations among the lower castes, promoting speculative mentality among trading castes (even when they moved into industry), and reducing the supply of labour, much empirical work suggests that these effects can easily be exaggerated (Morris, 1967, pp. 605–7).

Thirdly, if religious values – especially those emanating from the caste system – do in fact constrain India's economic development, it is much more likely that this works through its influence on the nature of the state and the relationship between the state and civil society. This could be due, for instance, to the social relationships between politicians and bureaucrats on the one hand, and industrialists on the other, as stressed by Lal (1988a); to the caste background of politicians and bureaucrats and their élitist tendencies, as stressed by Sen (1990); and to the role of caste divisions in affecting the relative power of different groups in India's civil society, as stressed by Rudolph and Rudolph (1987). These issues are better postponed until we turn to political economy issues below.

Economic Constraints on Development

Turning next to more narrowly-economic constraints on India's economic development, we consider in turn constraints on agricultural growth, industrial growth, and distributional and social development.

Regarding low agricultural growth, there seem to be three explanations. First, the failure of land reforms relating to land ceilings and tenancy conditions (the abolition of *zamindari* intermediary rights, though successful, also did not reduce the economic power of the former *zamindars* substantially) due to delayed and faulty enactment, along with half-hearted enforcement by state governments, arguably limited agricultural growth to larger farms in some parts of the country, and made it slower than it could have been (in view of findings on the inverse size–productivity relationship of farms and tenurial disincentives).[30] Secondly, Bardhan (1984, pp. 13–15) stresses the low level and misuse of government provision of irrigation facilities, which imply low levels of land utilization in the presence of externalities in irrigation use. Thirdly, it is argued (see Lipton, 1977; Mitra, 1977; Chakravarty,

1979) that the government has followed policies which have resulted in unfavourable output and input prices for the agricultural sector. If one accepts arguments of this type, one is led to ask questions such as: why did the land reforms not succeed? Why did the government not invest more in irrigation?

On industrial growth, several competing explanations were offered during the stagnation in industrial growth from the mid-1960s (see Bardhan, 1984; Ahluwalia, 1985). First, low industrial growth was blamed on low agricultural growth, through the supply side (by squeezing industrial profits through upward pressure on the product wage generally, and by raising input prices in agro-based industries), and from the demand side (due to a slow growth in purchasing power of the agricultural population). Secondly, it is argued that increased income inequality narrowed the home market for industrial goods in India. In a one-sector setting, it has been shown that a shift in income distribution favouring workers (perhaps due to a reduction in the degree of monopoly in industry) who have a higher propensity to consume will, through accelerator effects on investment, increase the growth rate of the economy (Dutt, 1984). When this analysis is extended to consider two sectors, distinguishing between luxury and basic goods (Taylor, 1983, 1991) and between agricultural and industrial goods (Taylor, 1983; Dutt, 1991), this positive relationship between growth and distribution may – though not necessarily – hold. Thirdly, it is argued that a decline in public industrial investment – which crowds in private investment due to demand effects and the complementarity between government infrastructural and other investment – reduced industrial capital formation, and this lowered industrial growth (Bardhan, 1984; Ahluwalia, 1985) .

Finally, it is pointed out that excessive government control and production activity resulted in various types of inefficiencies in industry, slowing down growth. In trying to achieve the diverse goals of its industrial policy, the government introduced: a system of industrial regulations and licensing to control entry and expansion in large-scale industries; import restrictions through tariffs, quotas and bans; price controls in specific industries producing 'essential inputs'; regulations on import of foreign technology and capital; and a large public sector by nationalizing some industries and establishing public sector firms in 'commanding heights' industries, infrastructure and in banking and finance. These policies have been argued (see Bhagwati and Desai, 1970; Bhagwati and Srinivasan, 1975; Ahluwalia, 1985; Lal, 1988a, 1988b) to result in: an inter-sectoral misallocation of resources; inefficiencies within industries due to reduced competition, creation of excess capacity as a result of the allocation of licences for imports, and due to soft budget constraints in public sector firms; reduction in investment incentives by increasing uncertainty due to changes in policy; rent-seeking and other directly unproductive profit-seeking activities; bureaucratic delays; and outmoded technology due to the reduced flow of foreign technology. All this arguably slowed down the rate of technological change caused high capital–output ratios and further slowed down the growth of exports, with adverse consequences for industrial growth (due to demand or foreign exchange problems).

While supporters of different explanations of industrial stagnation in the mid-1960s have argued why their preferred explanation is better than the others (see Bardhan, 1984; Ahluwalia, 1985, for instance), it is plausible that all of these constraints can explain why the industrial sector has grown slowly in India, since the parameters stressed by each one of these explanations may in fact affect the rate of industrial growth. The relevant question is, then, why have these parameters not been changed to increase the rate of industrial growth? For instance: why is income distribution not more even? Why is government investment not higher? Why are government policies not successfully changed – for instance, by liberalization of imports – to increase the rate of growth of exports? The fact that we have not been too choosy about these alternative explanations does not, of course, imply that all of them are equally important in the Indian context. For instance, the low share of foreign trade and luxury demand in national income in India suggests that Korean and Brazilian development strategies may not be 'successful' in India, and the high share of agriculture suggests that growth and equity in India cannot be substantially improved without changing agricultural conditions.

Regarding income distribution, poverty and social indicators, it is sometimes argued – based on a trickle-down view – that improvements in these categories did not occur because growth was so slow. However, the cases of China and Sri Lanka show that performance in these areas is not necessarily correlated with per capita income, and India's own relatively poor state, Kerala, has done remarkably well (Franke and Chasin, 1991). These examples suggest that suitable government policies may improve these indicators at a given level of per capita income. Given India's overall poor performance in these respects, the question again arises: why were appropriate government policies not adopted?

A Political Economy Analysis

The argument presented in this subsection is that the Indian state is highly constrained in making policy changes and in implementing its policy, because of the lack of autonomy in relation to society. These constraints can be traced to the strengths and weaknesses of each of the dominant classes in India, the interests of these classes, and the relationship of each class to the others and to the state.[31] These constraints operate at different levels: at the level of policy formulation by the central and state governments, and at the grass-roots level of policy implementation, and imply that the state must accommodate the dominant and other classes in certain ways and respond to their multiple veto powers. This means that the state is generally incapable of promoting economic development by changing the conditions laid out in the preceding discussion. In what follows we examine first some aspects of the state, then the dominant and other classes, then the relationship between the different classes in society to each other and to the state, and finally the implications of these power relationships and interests for Indian development.

The state

We take the state as a relatively autonomous actor in society, on the methodological ground that this allows an analysis of the degree to which the state is autonomous, and to reflect the fact that the state in India is all-pervasive, and has a major effect on economic activity.

We have already seen that throughout India's history the state has been a major actor. This was so in pre-colonial times, and the tendency was intensified during colonial rule, given the exigencies of political control and domination. As we have seen, after independence, the state came to play an even larger role in India's economy. The share of the public sector in GDP has gone up from 9.2 per cent in 1960–61 to 27 per cent in 1984–85. Its share in gross domestic capital formation has increased from about 40 per cent in 1961–62 to over 48 per cent in 1984–85. The presence of the public sector in heavy industries, and in insurance and banking, is ubiquitous. The government owned more than 60 per cent of all productive capital in the industrial sector in 1978–9; in 1990 it ran seven of the ten largest industrial units (and 16 of the top 25) in the country. In 1988 India's public sector employed 71.1 per cent of all workers employed in the organized sector. State agencies have also become plurality holders of equity capital in most large companies; the state has thus been able to control and direct the management and personnel of private firms to some degree.

Given this relative autonomy, we can ask where the state's interests lie. First, as stressed in the public choice approach, individuals within the state may be interested in maximizing their private incomes; while the importance of this cannot be denied, it would be a mistake to focus only on it. Secondly, there is the interest of remaining in power; given India's system of parliamentary democracy, this translates into wanting votes and money to conduct elections. Thirdly, the state has its own ideology, based on the historical experience of the country and the ideas of influential leaders. Given India's colonial background and struggle for independence, the state's ideology has been development-oriented and nationalist. Moreover, Mahatma Gandhi's views on the importance of cottage-industry sectors, and on non-violence and the absence of class conflict, are important influences, as are Nehru's Fabian socialist views, democratic ideals and admiration of Soviet-style industrialization. Finally, one could expect the state to represent the class interests of those who comprise it, especially if such classes are fairly homogeneous. Having already mentioned rent-seeking behaviour, and postponing issues raised in the second and fourth points about the relationship of the state to society, we consider briefly the state's ability to implement developmental goals consistent with its ideology. Evans (1992) has argued that this ability depends on 'embedded autonomy', where 'autonomy' refers to the capacity to operate without being constrained by society, and 'embeddedness' allows it to respond in a sophisticated manner to changes in economic reality. For this Evans emphasizes: first, a Weberian bureaucracy with highly selective meritocratic recruitment and long-term career paths, within a system providing insulation as well as commitment; secondly, informal networks within the bureaucracy providing it with internal coherence; and thirdly, dense institutional networks between public officials and social actors.

On the first issue the Indian bureaucracy has strong foundations, and its Indian Administrative Service (IAS) (which grew out of its colonial administration's Indian Civil Service) is described as a 'highly professional, technically expert, and well organized bureaucracy' (Rudolph and Rudolph, 1987, p. 2), virtually unparalleled in the Third World. However, particularly due to the political style of Indira Gandhi and subsequent changes in government, the atmosphere has become highly politicized: appointments and transfers in the IAS have recently been made largely by politicians to reward loyal supporters rather than on the basis of merit. This has destroyed insulation (the decision-making power of the bureaucrats has also been reduced by political interference), and morale has fallen (see Rudolph and Rudolph, 1987, pp. 74–83). On the second issue, all members of the bureaucracy are not from the same élite university but from several (given the large size of the country), and this means that the 'old-boy network' is not strong; this situation is exacerbated by political corruption and rivalry, and the opening up of jobs to lower castes (which, though good in itself, has created further disunity). In the absence of an effective bureaucracy, the government's political party can be expected to play an important role, especially at the grass-roots level (as was the case for the Kuomintang party in Taiwan). However, India's Congress Party, despite its many strengths, has not filled this need: the needs of the independence movement led the party to increase its numbers too rapidly to maintain a unified purpose and party discipline, and its organizational basis was further weakened by Mrs Gandhi's circumvention of party channels. On the third issue, the cultural (and caste) distance between the bureaucrat and the private capitalist has been emphasized: while links between individual business houses and the state are not uncommon, and have indeed been used by private industrialists to further their own ends in a highly regulated system, this is not the same thing as a shared vision and a social contract between the state and private industry, with the latter providing information to the state and the state providing appropriate carrots and sticks. The issue of autonomy, however, cannot be taken up independently of looking at the nature of classes in society and their relation to the state and to each other, and to these issues we now turn.

Classes and other groups

Following Bardhan (1984) we can identify India's dominant classes as the industrial capitalists, rich farmers, and white-collar workers and managerial classes. We will argue that each class is strong, but none hegemonic.

The industrial capitalists were, at the time of independence, reasonably strong, but given the small size of factory industry, not an important force. Since then they have been strengthened by state support, but also weakened by state regulation. Their strength is evident from their concentrated structure which increases the possibility of cohesion,[32] and the relative insignificance of foreign ownership and control in the sector.[33] However, their weaknesses are revealed by: the pervasive presence of the state, as noted above, in ownership of industrial firms, in the financing of the private sector, and in regulating it; clear divisions within the industrial capitalist class between new and old industrial houses (with the former wanting to attract more state patronage and to dislodge the latter), and between houses more linked to foreign companies and those with weaker links of this type; the rapid growth of small-scale industry relatively unshackled by government regulation and often in competition with large-scale industry; and the absence of open political voice through a political party.

The power of the class of rich farmers (mostly belonging to middle castes) grew after independence, with the transfer of land to them through early land reforms from non-cultivating landlords. This was consolidated by their economic gains from the green revolution and their political gains due to the rise of the Lok Dal in its different incarnations. Although their exact identification is somewhat arbitrary,[34] their strengths are derived from their large size (given the large size of the agricultural sector); from the high degree of concentration in asset holding;[35] from their clientelist relationship with poor agriculturalists (who are employees and debtors, and whom they have been able to mobilize for their political agitations for lower taxes, higher subsidies and higher prices); and from the support of the intermediate class of family farmers who also benefit (although disproportionately less) from these same demands.[36] An internal weakness of this group comes from the fact that the rich farmers are often fragmented along caste lines, even within a localized area, but such divisions are mitigated by their common opposition to land ceiling legislation and desire for higher farm prices. Caste can also divide and disunite other agriculturalists and create bonds between sections of rich farmers and some of their less fortunate caste-mates.

The proprietary status of the third class of 'professionals (civil and military), including white collar workers' (Bardhan, 1984, p. 51), comes from their ownership of human capital – education, skills and status (as a job filter). Having its historical origins in the centralized empires of pre-colonial India and the civil service tradition of the British raj, this class is largely drawn from 'middle class' groups usually unlinked to trade and industry, and generally averse to such activities. Its power comes from its élite status based on its domination of the education system, and its disproportionate share in the bureaucracy.[37] This, in turn, is related to the economic control imposed by the state over the economy, through its regulatory mechanisms and direct controls – which partly blurs the distinction between the state itself and this proprietary class.

The absence of hegemonic power of any one of the dominant classes implies that they (or their constituents) have had to form uneasy alliances with each other and with the non-dominant classes – industrial workers, small farmers and rural landless workers. While industrial workers are weakened by their small size given the small relative size of the industrial sector, the relatively small size of its organized segment,[38] the large reserve army of the unemployed caused by slow industrial growth, the segmented nature of the industrial labour force, the low proportion (about 30 or 40 per cent (six to ten million) of organized sector workers) unionized, the divisions within the union movements (there are 11 national trade union federations which can co-exist in a firm), the high share of organized labour (over 70 per cent) in the (socialist and Guardian-like) state sector, and the officially mediated system of conciliation and arbitration in industrial relations which diverts attention to manipulating procedures, politicians and labour courts (Rao, 1990), industrial workers cannot be dismissed as powerless. In the organized sector, labour appears to be virtually a fixed factor, with retrenchment and firm closing, and even lay-offs, impossible or expensive. While such security can be explained in terms of party partisanship, state paternalism (as Protector) or socialist ideology, it is certainly partly a spillover from patronage to white collar workers in the public sector to obtain their votes (though given their relatively small size this cannot be terribly important) and to weaken industrial capitalists (especially since labour laws can be enforced selectively). Small farmers and agricultural workers are far more numerous; the former often share the economic interests of large farmers, the latter are often locked into patron–client relationships with large and middle farmers. Despite their lack of organization, these agricultural groups (because of their numbers) are important for votes, and dominant classes and politicians have sought to mobilize these groups with populist slogans (an easy task, given their economic plight). Mobilization has led to what Rudolph and Rudolph (1987) call the growth of demand politics (rather than politics through organized channels) of 'taking to the roads', and sometimes violent rebellions, but overall it seems unlikely that poor peasants and the landless can become an independent voice which can shape their own destinies (Rudolph and Rudolph, 1987, pp. 376–92).

To these class distinctions we must add non-class ones based on caste, religion, linguistic and ethnic factors. Political parties representing such divisions have sprung up and increased their popularity, and religious and linguistic groups, especially as minorities, have mattered in elections (see Rudolph and Rudolph, 1987, pp. 193–5). Moreover, as mentioned above, caste also plays a decisive role as a natural building block for political parties and groups, and for splitting the solidarity of the poor (see Frankel, 1986, pp. 163–4). The incidence of divisions along these non-class lines seems to have intensified in recent times.

The state and classes: their interrelationships
We now turn to an examination of the relationships between the three dominant classes, and to the relationships between the state and different classes.

On the first issue, while dominant classes clearly have their common goal of staying dominant, they are also deeply divided. The most important divisions are those between rich farmers and the urban (industrial and professional) dominant classes, and between industrial capitalists and the managerial classes (Bardhan, 1984). The urban–rural divide, though usually focused on the issue of the agricultural terms of trade, is more generally the political conflict between town and country, of India versus Bharat. The conflict between professional classes in the public sector and private capitalists stems from the fact that the latter are against the licence-giving powers of the state and its professional classes – although through legal (lobbying) and illegal (bribery) means they can often circumvent them, while the professionals – for caste reasons, for Indian ideas of statism, and for their personal pockets no doubt – lend legitimacy to the controls. Moreover, as the state has taken over more units and nationalized them, the job prospects of the professionals have grown. It is in the interests of these groups to keep in place these regulations, and they are unlikely to allow a thoroughgoing liberalization of the economy.

On the second issue, let us first consider the relationship between the state and industrial capitalists. The state helps the latter by providing finance (such loans being the major source of industrial finance), by providing infrastructure, by sheltering them from foreign and domestic competition, by allowing them (selectively) to violate industrial and labour regulations, and by taking over their 'sick units' making large losses. For their part, industrial capitalists help (legally and illegally) by financing political parties to run their elections, and through bribes to politicians and bureaucrats. The class also provides support for the state's policies of industrial growth and the replacement of imports by domestic products.

Turning next to rich (and other) farmers the state helps with support prices on food, subsidies for inputs, institutional credit and through tax breaks – there is little taxation of agricultural income or wealth. They, in turn, help the state through vote banks (given their command over rural votes) and possibly with funds. Finally, on the relationship between the state and non-dominant classes, the state helps by keeping inflation within reasonable bounds, by supplying cheap food, and sometimes through its redistributive efforts, and the latter in turn can help the party in power by providing votes during elections, and supplying political legitimacy, and by supporting the implementation of government policies (such as land reforms and labour laws) at village and firm level.

Implications for development

Given the conflicting and complementary interests of the different dominant classes, given that none of them have political hegemony and thus often have to woo elements of non-dominant classes, and given the role of caste, ethnic, regional and linguistic forces, the Indian political arena is a stage for the dominant class of shifting alliances and mutual concessions among themselves, and for concessions to the non-dominant classes. Two implications regarding policy formulation and implementation follow. First, this causes widespread effort by the state and dominant groups to placate each other and members of non-dominant groups, acquiescing to their demands by providing positive 'favours' such as subsidies and other economic opportunities. Secondly, not wishing to displease different groups, the state gives them multiple veto powers on policy adoption and implementation: this binds it *not* to do some things, that is, provide negative 'favours'. These tendencies, which are present at central and state government level and at lower firm and village level, affect Indian economic development by working through the 'economic' constraints discussed above. We briefly consider four illustrative examples.

1. *Proliferation of subsidies and fiscal crisis.* Subsidies and other financial concessions to various groups in the form of support prices for farm products, low food prices for consumers, low input prices for industrial capitalists and farmers, subsidized credit, and subsidies to exporters have proliferated (Bardhan, 1984, pp. 61–9); their total has been calculated to

be about 15 per cent of GNP (Mundle and Rao, 1991). In addition, other government budgetary expenses, including salaries of public sector white-collar workers, have increased. Public sector firms have run at large losses, and the public sector has also had to take over 'sick' private firms.[39] Subsidies are in part garnered by 'power brokers' and thugs who take cuts for supplying political brokerage and violence during elections. These payments, often made with 'black money' provided by industrial capitalists and large farmers, represent a further leakage from tax revenues. As more and more groups increase their share of the loot, expenditure on police and paramilitary forces to contain their pressure grows, further reducing the government's financial resources. Given (until recent years) conservative monetary policies, explicable in terms of fears of inflation which can erode the government's political support among large groups whose incomes are not indexed to inflation (see Patnaik, 1988, pp. 21–4; Bardhan, 1991, pp. 242–6), the state has often cut its investment expenditure in both the industrial and the agricultural sectors, leading to their slower growth.

2. *Inefficiency in the public sector.* By providing jobs for the purpose of political patronage, particularly at senior managerial level, the state has promoted inefficient management and low morale. By buying off white-collar workers in the public sector with tenure rights, it encourages mass absenteeism and low productivity. The general level of demoralization and parasitism of managerial and technical personnel and workers feeds on itself, further increasing inefficiency; in this climate theft and looting add to the losses. In addition to poor economic performance and high capital–output ratios in public sector firms, this causes low profits which exacerbate fiscal problems (Bardhan, 1984, pp. 69–72).

3. *The failure of land reforms.* Lack of interest in land reforms may have sprung from the élitist character of most political parties and their leaders (and is therefore not unrelated to the caste system), but must be interpreted primarily as a concession to rich farmers, who have attempted to block implementation at state and bloc level. Moreover, the state did not need land reform to obtain votes if the rich could use their patron–client relationships to get them the votes from the poor. Problems of legislation and implementation could have been overcome, and India's age-old practice of allowing the village to govern itself (in the interests of the more privileged) altered, with a stronger Congress Party organization more committed to reform. However, given the domination of the party by landed élites, this was not to be (Kohli, 1987, pp. 59–60). Other parties have lacked village-level party organizations; only leftist parties have thus far been relatively successful, as the case of West Bengal and its subsequent good agricultural performance, suggests.

4. *Problems of industrial and labour policy*. Given their clientelist relation-
    ship, the state is unable to twist the arms of industrial capitalists to
    enforce performance standards, to ensure selectivity in interventions,
    and to meet the rigours of internal and external markets. Moreover, given
    this relationship, the state finds it extremely difficult to reduce concen-
    tration in domestic industry, and to improve income distribution in this
    manner. Regarding labour policy, the various concessions to labour im-
    ply low levels of productivity (see Lal, 1988b); government policy on
    unions and arbitration leads to industrial unrest which also reduces pro-
    ductivity, and labour laws also militate disproportionately against large
    firms, leading to fragmentation and loss of scale economies.

All this is not to imply that the state is completely powerless in India in all
situations, or that the Indian economy is incapable of achieving higher rates
of growth. On the first issue, even given the relationships between the state
and civil society discussed here, the relative autonomy of the state can
change due to such factors as the 'newness' of governments (the Indian state
after independence under Nehru has more relative autonomy in this sense);
(somewhat paradoxically) the 'weakness' of governments (when governments, with little hope of staying in power, may not fear societal pressures);
great strength in legislatures (which occurred under Nehru and Indira Gandhi, reducing the need to make concessions); during wars and other emergen-
cies, and external pressures (say, from the IMF). However, our discussion
highlights the importance of paying careful attention to the socio-economic
nexus of power relationships. On the second issue, we have already referred
to the increase in India's rate of industrial growth after 1975. Some analysts
have argued (see Ahluwalia, 1991, pp. 85–97) that this turnaround was caused
by industrial and trade policy liberalization and improvements in the level
and utilization of government infrastructural investment. While the growth-
inducing effects of the rationalization of industrial and trade regulations
cannot be denied, these developments do not undermine our argument regarding political constraints. An examination of the recent developments (see
Jalan, 1992; Mundle and Rao, 1992) reveals that higher growth has been
accompanied by alarming increases in the government debt–GNP and external debt–GNP ratios, and the economy has teetered on the brink of fiscal and
foreign exchange crises. This suggests that the higher growth cannot be
sustained if the political economy constraints are not overcome, but only
sidestepped by internal and external borrowing which appear to be
unsustainable in the long run. Moreover, higher growth was accompanied by
extremely low employment growth which, in addition to its undesirable
distributional implications, explains why industrial growth has not been constrained by agriculture.

KOREA AND INDIA COMPARED

While there are other important differences between the experiences of the two countries – for instance, those having to do with differences in colonial history, religious values and the concept of statism[40] – we confine our comparison to four issues: state intervention versus markets, the nature of government intervention, the narrowly-economic causes of growth and stagnation (especially export growth) and the role of the state and its relationship to civil society.

The State Versus Markets

Regarding the claim that Korea was more successful because it was more market-oriented, and Indian stagnation was largely due to state intervention, two points may be noted.

First, while the Indian state was highly interventionist, the Korean state was hardly less so. The share of the public sector in the Korean and Indian economies was comparable – in 1972 state-owned enterprises in India contributed to 15 per cent compared to Korea's 13 per cent in non-agricultural GDP, and the industries in which the state operated in the two countries were similar (Encarnation, 1989, p. 205). The state dominated the financial sector in both countries: in India the state nationalized much of banking and insurance, and in Korea the government depended on the mechanisms of selective command and administrative discretion and discipline of the private sector through its near-monopoly of domestic credit (as well as underwriting of foreign borrowing). The Korean state provided price support and fertilizer subsidies to agriculture, as did India's. The Korean state was as restrictive (in terms of its policies) of multinational firms as India was, both states trying to link concessions to multinationals to their export performance (see Encarnation, 1989). Moreover, the Korean state forced prices far from what would have prevailed in free markets (Amsden, 1992); in this regard it was no different from the Indian state. It should also be noted that the liberalization and privatization that has occurred in Korea recently was *after* the spurt in economic growth had already taken place. In the face of all this evidence it would be rather fanciful to argue that on balance the Korean interventions cancelled themselves out, with the result that the system was very similar to a relatively 'undistorted' economy (Wade, 1990).

Secondly, there are neither empirical nor theoretical reasons to expect that government intervention is necessarily bad for less developed countries. The experience of countries other than Korea, such as Japan and Taiwan, would back up the case that state intervention can be extremely useful for growth. Even for India, there is some evidence that state intervention had some desirable outcomes. The successful promotion of cottage textile industries through state policies of disseminating new techniques, imposing quality controls and providing sales outlets in major cities, is a case in point (Datta-Chaudhuri, 1990). More generally, India's successes in developing its heavy industries, and even in exporting technology to other Third World countries (Singh and Ghosh, 1988) shows that import substitution has had the effect of reducing import dependence and the possibilities of import compression, and in making India's industrial base technologically sophisticated. Returning to the experience of Japan and the East Asian NICs, as Amsden (1992) points out, the notion that cheap labour costs achieve export success (with or without multinational corporations) is a myth in an age in which the state must play a leading role in helping to adapt new types of technology and to break into foreign markets.

Theoretical considerations along standard neoclassical lines support these arguments in terms of traditional market failures, and new neoclassical economists such as Stiglitz (1988) particularly emphasize informational problems related to technology and markets. Neoclassical economists also argue, of course, that government intervention may not help just because, due to market failures, free markets may not perform in a (constrained) Pareto-optimal manner. Aside from governmental information and incentives problems, neoclassical critics of government intervention have stressed the problem of directly unproductive profit-seeking activities such as rent seeking, and used this problem to support attempts at liberalization. Against this view one may ask, following Evans (1992): if office holders are all rent-seekers, why do they not all free-lance? Indeed, pushed to its limit, since the state has a monopoly on the legal use of force in society, what prevents it from using it for directly unproductive profit-seeking activities even when it acts only as 'night-watchman'? Not only does this suggest that this approach ignores the fact that the state may have other motives or objectives of a developmental and collective kind, but it also shows that privatization and deregulation in a rent-seeking environment may not stop or even reduce rent-seeking by private and state agents. More generally, markets do not operate in a vacuum: 'non-contractual elements of contract' are required to make them work smoothly. If such elements have not developed historically, the state may be in a position to provide them, and reducing the role of the state may in fact make markets operate less smoothly.

The Nature of State Intervention

Even if it is argued that state intervention is not necessarily a bad thing, it is not possible to dismiss all the evidence that there is widespread inefficiency in Indian industry caused by government intervention. The question arises if the differences in the effects of Korean and Indian state intervention can be attributed to the differences in the nature of intervention in each country. We examine the merits of some hypotheses on this issue.

1. *Korea has been more outward-oriented and has relied more on export promotion, while India has been more inward-looking and has relied more on import substitution.* This argument certainly has some merit (and can be explained by the fact that Korea, given a smaller domestic market, had to look abroad, while India, given a larger domestic market, did not). A more careful examination presents a more complex picture. First, it can be argued that the essential foundations of successful Korean export promotion were laid through successful import substitution. Secondly, Korea continued to protect domestic industries through tariff barriers after embarking on aggressive export promotion. Thirdly, India has tried out many methods of promoting exports – including providing subsidies, import replenishment licences to exporters and export incentives to multinationals – without Korea's success.

2. *Korean state intervention was more market-friendly than India's in the sense that Korea has made greater use of market (price) rather than quantity interventions, or that Korean firms have been more exposed to the rigours of the market.* The first interpretation posits that although market imperfections do exist, they can be overcome with tax/subsidy policies following neoclassical normative theory (see Lal, 1983). The nature of government intervention in Korea (which frequently targeted exports and imposed quantitative restrictions and sanctions), however, does not allow us to accept this interpretation of Korea's experience. The second interpretation, however, has considerable validity.

3. *In Korea, as compared to India, private industry and public sector units are generally more accountable for their actions, and performance standards are clearer. This has contained (although not eliminated) rent-seeking activities and other inefficiencies.* This claim seems valid.

4. *In Korea intervention was far more selective than it was in India.* In India, state regulation and control has been all-pervasive, and based on no clear criteria or long-term economic considerations. Korea, on the other hand, has selected specific areas – such as shipbuilding, petrochemicals and automobiles – for government attention, identified on grounds of home demand and long-term possibilities of penetrating foreign markets, rather than on grounds of static comparative advantage. The lack of selectivity dilutes the effectiveness of the interventions in key sectors, especially given the limited administrative capacities of the government.

5. *Whereas Korea had an unwavering loyalty to the objective of growth, India, in trying to achieve various goals simultaneously, has not focused*

sufficiently on any one, and in fact has pursued contradictory policies (for instance, attempts to develop small scale industries by restricting entry arguably strengthened monopoly power). While some of these goals (such as balanced regional growth) may have been more necessary given India's larger size, it does appear that the Korean government has been less concerned about sacrificing some goals at the altar of growth, as suggested by the earlier neglect of issues such as poverty and balanced regional growth, and tolerance of greater industrial concentration. Neglect of social dimensions, of course, is not necessarily a good thing, and Korea's record on distributive equity has not been excellent; but neither, it may be argued, has India's.

In sum, in points (2) to (5) we find some plausible reasons for Korea's more successful record. However, they lead us to ask why Korean state intervention was different from India's in the ways that made Korea more successful.

The Role of Export Growth

Korea's economic success, at the level of purely economic analysis, is undoubtedly due to its success in accelerating growth in exports. This does not imply, however, that India should follow Korea's export-led path to development, or that the rapid growth of exports is necessary and sufficient for India to grow rapidly.

On the sufficiency argument, we have pointed out in the previous section that higher export growth could have increased the rate of industrial growth in India, perhaps by increasing the demand for industrial goods, or by relaxing foreign exchange constraints at crucial junctures. However, there are reasons to believe that such a strategy, which ignores other economic constraints on growth discussed above, may fail to generate rapid economic growth in India's case. First, since foreign trade as a proportion of national income is very low in India, Indian exports would have to grow more rapidly than Korea's to raise India's growth rate to Korea's level. Secondly, as Cline (1982) has argued, it is far more difficult for large countries such as India to expand exports without inciting protectionist moves in advanced countries, than it is for smaller economies such as Korea's. While this argument cannot dismiss the claim that India can, with suitable policies, expand her exports substantially, it does reveal the limits of policies of export-led growth for countries such as India.

On the necessity argument, it has already been pointed out that other parameters which determine Indian growth rates can be changed to raise the rate of growth – for instance, the rate of agricultural growth, or the distribution of income. This is not to imply that with these policies it would not be necessary to increase exports; on the contrary, in the absence of significant changes in technology (reducing its import intensity), an expansion in exports would be required to increase the availability of foreign exchange required by faster growth.

The State and Civil Society

The main difference between Korean and Indian development seems to lie in the fact that the Korean state has been far more capable of responding, through appropriate policies, to the emergence of problems and new opportunities than has the Indian state. As we have seen before, the Korean state was able to conduct efficient import substitution, and then aggressive export promotion with continued import protection, by controlling both industrial capitalists and workers, while the Indian state was unable to prevent inefficiencies and rent-seeking behaviour in the conduct of its trade, industrial policies, and labour policies, unable to conduct land reforms, unable to provide industrial and agricultural infrastructure on a sustained basis, and generally unable to make a dent in the problem of income distribution. To explain this we draw on our previous discussion and compare the nature of the Korean and Indian states, their bureaucracies and the relationship of the state to civil society.

On the nature of the state, both the Korean and the Indian states, emerging with mass poverty from colonial backgrounds, had strong developmental goals. However, there are some important differences: while the Indian state was committed to a socialist ideology based on Nehru's political views, the Korean state was pushed away from socialism due to US influence and a desire to differentiate itself from North Korea. This difference did not imply, as we have seen, less state presence or intervention in the economy in the case of Korea than in the case of India, but may explain the Korean government's more pragmatic attitude and single-minded pursuit of the objective of growth, as well as its greater propensity to expose firms – public and private – to the discipline of markets.

More important than goals are differences in the nature of the bureaucracy. Although both Korea and India have long bureaucratic traditions, there are important differences. Korea's bureaucracy under Japanese rule received more experience with direct economic intervention than did India's, which was more involved with legal and general administration given Britain's *laissez-faire* economic policies in India. Moreover, though the Rhee regime bypassed civil service examinations and made political appointments, the Park regime reinstituted the traditional civil service examinations, thereby building up a strong Weberian bureaucracy; in India, on the other hand, there is a growing tendency towards politicization of the bureaucracy. Further, unlike India's case, there is coherence and loyalty within the bureaucracy in Korea, based on shared background at its élite university. Finally, while in Korea the bureaucracy is strongly embedded – albeit in a top-down manner of command and control – in the industrial sector, in India the industrial and bureaucratic classes are separated because of the lingering effects of caste and British influence, and because of their growing economic rivalry.

With regard to the relationship between the state and civil society, we consider in turn industrial capitalists, state personnel, industrial labour and landed interests. Regarding industrial capitalists, the Korean state under the Park regime initially totally dominated industry by means such as criminal trials (even parading leaders of industry through the streets as corrupt parasites). However, this changed over time and the links between the state and the large *jaebol* became stronger, and the state even allowed these *jaebols* to increase their dominance in the industrial sector as part of a corporatist system with the government as senior partner in 'Korea, Inc.'. While this was helped by Korea's small size and cultural homogeneity, these factors militated against the establishment of a similar relationship in India, where the caste system, the Indian conception of state as Protector and Guardian, and the patron–client relationships on more personal lines made for a more rivalrous relationship between the state and industry. Turning next to state personnel, while the Korean bureaucracy, with common long-term goals and the relatively low incidence of rent-seeking, reduced the principal–agent distinction between the state and the state personnel, the very different condition in India made the bureaucracy and government white-collar classes act more like a third dominant class. Regarding labour, although compared to India a larger proportion of the non-agricultural labour force is unionized in Korea, the unions take the shape of corporatist organizations over which state control has increased over time. This type of arrangement has, at least until the mid-1970s, allowed wage increases to fall short of productivity growth, raising both profits and exports. In India, on the other hand, despite the weaknesses of unions, it has been difficult to raise worker productivity because of the government's labour policies; organized labour has not been able to achieve much for itself, but has held back efficiency and technological change. Finally, while landed interests in India play a very important role (for instance) in blocking land reforms, in Korea (as in Taiwan and Japan) land reforms were conducted under military occupation after World War II, and this rendered rich farmers powerless.

CONCLUSION

This chapter has argued that the great difference between Korean and Indian development experience cannot be adequately understood in terms of such simple dichotomies as the market and the state, or outward and inward orientation, but requires a deeper analysis which emphasizes the role of history, religious values, strictly economic constraints and, most importantly, the nature of the state and its relationship to civil society. Our main conclusions are as follows.

1. To argue that Korean strategies were market-oriented and Indian policies more *dirigiste* is incorrect and misleading. The Korean state was highly interventionist, and in fact Korean success was largely due to this interventionist stance. In India's case, however, the success of state intervention was more limited, and indeed resulted in gross inefficiencies and rent-seeking. Explanations in terms of greater exposure to markets in Korea may contain a germ of truth, but raise the question as to why this was not the case in India.

2. Korean success was largely due to successful export promotion and rapid export growth. This does not imply that India's failure was due to the fact that it was unsuccessful in pushing up exports at such a rapid rate. We have argued that such policies may be neither sufficient for Indian development, nor indeed, necessary. A proper understanding of India's lacklustre development performance requires a thorough analysis of the economic constraints on Indian development, and we have examined a variety of such constraints, including those arising from agricultural stagnation, unequal income distribution, low level of government investment, and inefficiencies due to excessive government control.

3. In the Korean case a strong state and an autonomous and embedded bureaucracy were able to overcome societal obstacles to direct Korea along a path of rapid development through export growth. In the Indian case the state was heavily constrained by social pressures, and thus unable to do what is necessary to promote development. We have tried to locate what these social constraints were in India's case, and why Korea was able to escape them, in terms of a political economy analysis of the state and its relationship to civil society.[41]

NOTES

1. Many recent studies do acknowledge that Korea did in fact follow an interventionist approach. However, it appears to us that this debate has by no means been resolved: while

some extreme claims on the role of markets in Korean development have been revised, there is still the strong view that Korean intervention was not 'very' distortionary, and in fact much more 'market friendly' as compared to the Indian case (see World Bank, 1991, p. 7). Some even argue that Korea was successful *despite* the fact that the state was interventionist. See Little (1988, p. 98), Lal (1988b) and the discussion in Wade (1990).

2.   Although we have found no book – or even paper-length treatment – solely concerned with a comparison of the development experience of South Korea and India, there has been some discussion of this issue, especially in works concerned with Indian economic development. See, for example, Ahluwalia (1985, pp. 163–4), Bardhan (1984, pp. 71–4, 1991), Chakravarty (1987, pp. 70–74), Datta-Chaudhuri (1990), Encarnation (1989, pp. 204–15), Evans (1991) and Lal (1988b). Lal's study comes closest to a direct comparison, but he compares India to all four East Asian NICs, and concentrates mostly on the Indian case.

3.   There is also the issue of authoritarianism versus democracy, which we do not directly address in this chapter.

4.   Since 1962 the real income of the poorest groups has risen at about the same rate as GNP with actual declines registered in their relative share in the total population: the proportion of the population considered poor fell from 40.9 per cent in 1965 to 9.8 per cent in 1981 and to 5.1 per cent by 1987. The land reform in 1949 actually provided a foundation for equitable development in Korea. For instance, between 1947 and 1964 tenant farmers fell from 42 per cent of the total farm households to a mere 5 per cent, while tiller-owners increased from 16.5 to 72 per cent. However, although the incidence of absolute poverty has diminished, there is some evidence to indicate that inequalities in the relative sense have failed to improve in recent years (Kim, 1991, pp. 6–9) .

5.   In terms of value added, the share of manufacturing rose from 2 per cent in the early 1910s to around 13 to 15 per cent of GNP by 1940, while the share of primary activities declined from about two-thirds of GNP to about a half.

6.   The interest rates on time and savings deposits and loans (except export credits) almost doubled in 1965, and as a result the share of time and savings deposits in the rapidly expanding total loan funds of the deposit money banks increased from less than 20 per cent before 1965 to nearly half in 1971.

7.   For instance, the Electronics Promotion Law in 1969 recognized electronics as a 'strategic export industry'.

8.   In passing, it must be noted that, beginning with the fifth five-year plan during the 1980s, the practice of sector targeting has been gradually phased out as the economy becomes increasingly sophisticated and complicated to manage. Except for the high-tech sector, which continues to receive government support, measures that can benefit all indiscriminately are now being implemented.

9.   During the 1963–73 period, export expansion in relation to import substitution made a more than three-fold contribution. However, prior import substitution in the 1960s had already created possibilities of improved utilization of capital for export expansion in subsequent periods.

10. General Park was concerned with the possibility of losing rural votes in the 1971 presidential re-election.

11. South Korea is still considered to be a reasonably egalitarian society by international standards. Two factors, cultural and historical, have contributed to this: (1) the universal spread of education, and (2) even-assets ownership in rural areas. Successful land reforms prior to industrialization eliminated land-tenancy. Although the average farm size is insufficient to provide adequate income, state subsidies have largely enabled peasants to escape impoverishment. The high literacy rate in Korea is attributed to the wide spread of education among the populace, which reflects culturally rooted enthusiasm for education.

12. Although Korea's rapid growth was achieved under a fairly equitable income distribution by developing country standards, the distribution worsened markedly during the period of rapid growth in the mid-1970s (See Choo and Kim, 1978).

13. In 1983 Japan promised some $4 billion worth of packages of loans and aids.

14. Government expenditure now amounts to about 0.5 per cent of GNP in 1990. In the 1960s it was a trivial amount.
15. The Korean state has often been compared to the authoritarian state described by O'Donnell (1973).
16. An example of this was the 1971 Special Emergency Law enacted under the umbrella of a series of national security provisions: In a situation of emergency threatening national security, the settlement of labour disputes would automatically fall under the jurisdiction of the government-controlled Labour Tribunals; open walk-outs would then be illegal; other forms of restriction would be imposed on collective bargaining.
17. After 1977 real wages gained some ground over productivity increases. These gains reflect the impact of structural adjustment in labour markets, which was instituted in response to increasingly militant labour movements.
18. Note that the rate of change in labour's share of GDP reflects the difference between the rates of change in real wages and productivity.
19. Another important benefit from supporting big businesses was the political funds the president could count on from them.
20. The largest four conglomerates are Hyundai, Dae Woo, Samsung and Gumsung, which together recently accounted for close to 10 per cent of total exports. Furthermore, ten Korean conglomerates were recently listed among the top 500 corporations in the world, excluding the United States, in *Fortune* magazine.
21. In the earlier days of industrialization, the business environment was conducive to opportunities for forward or backward integration in industry. A broad spectrum of sectors opened up for entrepreneurs to participate in, as export demand suddenly rose in diversified areas. Access to financing was made easy, as the government provided easy credit in efforts to promote exports. Once the government was convinced the entrepreneur could succeed, this would usually have a snow-balling effect, success breeding success, since government credit was largely based on past achievements. This type of credit policy made it possible for successful entrepreneurs to launch several ventures at the same time, which eventually led to a race for empire-building in business.
22. In terms of output, the largest group of firms employing more than 500 persons grew at an annual rate of 27.6 per cent between 1967 and 1979, compared to 11.1 per cent for the smallest units employing fewer than nine persons. In Korea, any establishments employing less than 500 persons are considered as small and medium units.
23. In 1981 real wages fell 5 per cent while labour productivity rose 16 per cent.
24. Although Roh was able to organize a coalition with two of the opposition parties, creating the Democratic Liberal Party, his regime continued to face dissensions within the party and sharp criticism from the largest remaining opposition party, led by Kim Dae Jung.
25. For a fuller account of the Confucian influence on business in Korea, see Kim (1988) and Steinberg (1988).
26. Calculated from Economic Planning Board annual reports.
27. See a review by S. Younger of G.M. Meier's *Emerging from Poverty* (New York: Oxford University Press, 1984) in the *Journal of Economic Literature*, December 1985, p. 1793.
28. This section draws heavily on Dutt (1992b).
29. The phrase 'Hindu equilibrium' is from the title of Lal's (1988a) volume and the phrase 'Hindu rate of growth', referring to a low 3.5 per cent annual increase in national income, is reportedly due to Raj Krishna (see Rudolph and Rudolph, 1987, p. xvi).
30. On the economic necessity and effects of land reform, see Frankel (1978) and Datta (1986); on the failure of such reform, see Ladejinsky (1977) and Kohli (1987).
31. This approach is by no means a novel one: at most it can claim to weave together the political economy approaches of a group of scholars, including Myrdal (1968), Lipton (1977), Mitra (1977), Frankel (1978, 1986), Bardhan (1984), Rudolph and Rudolph (1987), and Kohli (1987, 1990), although they are not in agreement on every point, and we do not endorse all their views.
32. It is estimated that in 1976 the top 20 business houses controlled nearly two-thirds of the total productive capital in the private sector.

33. In 1981–82 only about 10 per cent of total value-added in the factory sector, mining and manufacturing was accounted for by foreign firms, although their share and importance in a few industries is quite high (see Bardhan, 1984, p. 44). New foreign private direct investment has been low, although there have been many instances of foreign collaborative ventures not involving foreign participation in equity capital (see Encarnation, 1989).
34. Bardhan (1984, pp. 46–7) identifies them with the group of 'large and very large farm households, cultivating holdings above 4 hectares' (4 hectares is 9.9 acres; 100 hectares is 1 sq. kilometre, which is 0.3861 sq. miles), and finds that in 1975 they constituted 19 per cent of the rural agricultural population, accounted for 60 per cent of the cultivated area and 53 per cent of the crop output.
35. In 1971 about 20 per cent of all households owned 63 per cent of rural assets (which included, in addition to land, livestock, buildings and so on).
36. This discussion shows that there is no necessary contradiction between Bardhan's focus on rich farmers and Rudolph and Rudolph's (1987, pp. 52–5) on bullock capitalists, who have, on average, smaller farms than Bardhan's rich farmers.
37. The root of its strength is underscored by the frequent demand of underprivileged groups for reservations of seats in the bureaucracy and in educational institutions.
38. The absolute number of workers in the organized sector is large – about 23 million – and in size comparable to the number in several larger OECD countries; only 10 per cent of all workers are in the organized sectors (figures relate to the early 1980s).
39. These enormous subsidies and other expenses, often meted out as political favours, are unlikely to have caused much social benefit to offset their negative effects on government finances.
40. As noted previously, Confucian ideology inculcates the virtue of authority and legitimizes state intervention. For India, Hindu value systems can at best be argued *not* to play a negative role. The Indian concept of statism is also as Protector and Guardian, or as a Taxer, rather than as an agent of change. The colonial experience was also very different, given that India was clearly on the periphery as a producer of raw materials, while Japan tried to incorporate Korea as a part of the metropolis.
41. While it is beyond the scope of this chapter to discuss the economic and policy implications of our analysis, it is *not* to advocate either thoroughgoing liberalization or authoritarianism in stagnating Third World countries such as India. Regarding liberalization, our analysis suggests that this may be unfeasible in India, and if successful would weaken the state further, making it less able to develop markets and remove market failures. Moreover, external liberalization will make foreign exchange constraints more binding over time, retarding growth in a Latin American way. Regarding authoritarianism, as Bardhan (1984) argues, it is an option unlikely to be wanted by the dominant classes for whom democracy provides a workable forum to 'fight it out', and it is unlikely to insulate the state from rent-seeking or to improve its performance if it meets with opposition from the masses, who have got used to having their voices heard, if not their stomachs filled.

BIBLIOGRAPHY

Ahluwalia, I.J. (1985), *Industrial Growth in India. Stagnation since the Mid-Sixties*, Delhi: Oxford University Press.

Ahluwalia, I.J. (1991), *Productivity and Growth in Indian Manufacturing*, Delhi: Oxford University Press.

Amsden, A.H. (1989), *Asia's Next Giant: South Korea and Late Industrialization*, Oxford: Oxford University Press.

Amsden, A.H. (1992), 'A Theory of Government Intervention in Late Industrialization', in L. Putterman and D. Rueschemeyer (eds), *The State and Market in Development*, Boulder, Colorado: Lynn Reiner.

Anstey, V. (1929), *The Economic Development of India,* London: Longmans, Green and Co., 3rd (revised and enlarged) edn, 1942.

Bagchi, A.K. (1972), *Private Investment in India. 1890–1939,* Cambridge: Cambridge University Press.

Balassa, B. (1982) (ed.), *Development Strategies in Semi-industrial Economies,* Baltimore: Johns Hopkins University Press.

Bardhan, P.K. (1984), *The Political Economy of Development in India,* Oxford: Oxford University Press.

Bardhan, P.K. (1988), 'Dominant Proprietary Classes and India's Democracy', in A. Kohli (ed.), *India's Democracy. An Analysis of Changing State–Society Relations,* Princeton: Princeton University Press, 114–24.

Bardhan, P.K. (1991), 'India's Macroeconomic Performance in a Comparative Political Economy Perspective', in D. Banerjee (ed.), *Essays in Economic Analysis and Policy,* Delhi: Oxford University Press, 241–60.

Bardhan, P.K. (1992), 'A Political-Economy Perspective on Development', in B. Jalan (ed.), *The Indian Economy: Problems and Prospects,* New Delhi: Viking.

Bhagwati, J.N. and Desai, P. (1970), *India: Planning for Industrialization. Industrialization and Trade Policies Since 1951,* Oxford: Oxford University Press, for the OECD Development Centre, Paris.

Bhagwati, J.N. and Srinivasan, T.N. (1975), *Foreign Trade Regimes and Economic Development: India,* New York and London: Columbia University Press, for the NBER.

Chakravarty, S. (1987), *Development Planning. The Indian Experience,* Oxford: Clarendon Press.

Charlesworth, N. (1982), *British Rule and the Indian Economy. 1800–1914,* London: Macmillan.

Choo, H. C. and Kim, D. M. (1978), *Probable Size Distribution of Income in Korea: Over Time and By Sectors,* Seoul: Korea Development Institute.

Cline, W.R. (1982), 'Can the East Asian Model of Development Be Generalized?', *World Development,* **10**(2), February, 81–90.

Datta, A. (1986), *Growth and Equity. A Critique of the Lewis–Kuznets Tradition,* Calcutta: Oxford University Press.

Datta-Chaudhuri, M.K. (1990), 'Market Failure and Government Failure', *Journal of Economic Perspectives,* **4**(3), Summer, 25–39.

Dutt, A.K. (1984), 'Stagnation, Income Distribution and Monopoly Power', *Cambridge Journal of Economics,* March, 25–40.

Dutt, A.K. (1991), 'Stagnation, Income Distribution and the Agrarian Constraint: A Note', *Cambridge Journal of Economics,* **15**(3), September, 343–51.

Dutt, A.K. (1992a), 'The Origins of Uneven Development: The case of the Indian Subcontinent', *American Economic Review,* **82**(2), May, 146–50.

Dutt, A.K. (1992b), 'Constraints on India's Economic Development: A Political Economy Approach', unpublished, University of Notre Dame, April.

Encarnation, D.J. (1989), *Dislodging Multinationals. India's Strategy in Comparative Perspective,* Ithaca and London: Cornell University Press.

Evans, P. (1992), 'The State as Problem and Solution: Predation, Embedded Autonomy and Structural Change', in S. Haggard and R. Kaufman (eds.), *The Politics of Adjustment: International Constraints, State Structures and Distributive Conflicts,* Princeton: Princeton University Press.

Frank, C.R. *et al.* (1975), *Foreign Trade Regimes and Economic Development: South Korea,* NBER, New York: Columbia University Press.

Franke, R.W. and Chasin, B.H. (1991), 'Kerala State, India: Radical Reform as Development', *Monthly Review,* 42(8), January, 1–23.

Frankel, F. (1978), *India's Political Economy, 1947–1977. The Gradual Revolution,* Princeton: Princeton University Press.

Frankel, F. (1986), 'Compulsion and Social Change: Is Authoritarianism the Solution to India's Economic Development Problems?', in A. Kohli (ed.), *The State and Development in the Third World,* Princeton: Princeton University Press.

Henderson, G. (1988), 'Constitutional Change from the First to the Fifth Republics: 1948–1987', in I.J. Kim and Y.W. Kihl (eds), *Political Changes in South Korea,* New York: Paragon House, 22–43.

Hofstede, G. (1980), *Culture's Consequences: International Differences in Work-Related Values,* New York: Sage Publications.

Jalan, B. (1992), 'Balance of Payments, 1956–1991', in B. Jalan (ed.), *The Indian Economy: Problems and Prospects,* New Delhi: Viking.

Jones, L.P. and Sakong, I. (1980), *Government, Business, and Entrepreneurship in Economic Development: The Korea Case,* Cambridge, Mass.: Harvard University Press.

Kapp, K.W. (1963), *Hindu Culture, Economic Development and Economic Planning in India,* New York: Asia Publishing House.

Kim, K.S. (1973), 'An Analysis of Economic Changes in Korea under Japanese Colonial Rule', in A. Nahm (ed.), *Korea under Japanese Colonial Rule. Studies of the Policy and Technique of Japanese Colonialism,* Kalamazoo, Mich.: Western Michigan University Press.

Kim, K.S. (1988), 'The Korean Case: Culturally Dominated Interactions', in L. Tavis (ed.), *Multinational Management and Host Government Interactions,* Notre Dame, In.: University of Notre Dame Press.

Kim, K.S. (1991), 'The Korean Miracle Revisited (1962–1980) – Myths and Realities in Strategy and Development', Kellogg Institute Working Paper 166, University of Notre Dame.

Kohli, A. (1987), *The State and Poverty in India. The Politics of Reform,* Cambridge: Cambridge University Press.

Kohli, A. (1990), *Democracy and Discontent. India's Growing Crisis of Governability,* Cambridge: Cambridge University Press.

Krueger, A.O. (1978), *Liberalization Attempts and Consequences,* New York: National Bureau of Applied Research.

Krueger, A.O. (1979), *The Developmental Role of the Foreign Sector and Aid,* Cambridge, Mass.: Harvard University Press.

Ladejinsky, W. (1977), 'Agrarian Reform in India', in L. J. Walinsky (ed.), *The Selected Papers of Wolf Ladejinsky. Agrarian Reform as Unfinished Business,* New York and Oxford: Oxford University Press.

Lal, D. (1983), *The Poverty of Development Economics,* London: Institute of Economic Affairs, Cambridge, Mass.: Harvard University Press, 1985.

Lal, D. (1988a), *The Hindu Equilibrium, I. Cultural Stability and Economic Stagnation – India c1500 BC – AD 1980,* Oxford: Clarendon Press.

Lal, D. (1988b), 'Ideology and Industrialization in India and East Asia', in H. Hughes (ed.), *Achieving Industrialization in East Asia,* Oxford: Oxford University Press.

Landes, D.S. (1965), 'Japan and Europe: Contrasts in Industrialization', in W. W. Lockwood (ed.), *The State and Economic Enterprise in Japan,* Princeton: Princeton University Press.

Lipton, M. (1977), *Why the Poor Stay Poor,* London: Maurice Temple Smith.

Little, I.M.D. (1982), *Economic Development. Theory, Policy and Industrial Relations*, New York: Basic Books.

Little, I.M.D. (1988), 'Comments on "Trade, Development and the State"', in G. Ranis and T.P. Schultz (eds.), *The State of Development Economics. Progress and Perspectives*, Oxford: Blackwell, 96–9.

Little, I.M.D., Scitovsky, T. and Scott, F.M.G. (1970), *Industry and Trade in Some Developing Countries*, Oxford: Oxford University Press, for OECD Development Centre, Paris.

Luedde-Neurath, R. (1988), 'State Intervention in South Korea', in G. White (ed.), *Development States in East Asia*, New York: St Martin's Press.

Mitra, A. (1977), *Terms of Trade and Class Relations*, London: Frank Cass.

Morishima, M. (1982), *Why Has Japan 'Succeeded'?*, Cambridge: Cambridge University Press.

Morris, M.D. (1967), 'Values as an Obstacle to Economic Growth in South Asia: An Historical Survey', *Journal of Economic History*, 27(4), 588–607.

Mundle, S. and Rao, G.M. (1991), 'Volume and Composition of Government Subsidies in India, 1987–88', *Economic and Political Weekly*, 26(18), 4 May, 1157–72.

Mundle, S. and Rao, G.M. (1992), 'Issues in Fiscal Policy', in B. Jalan (ed.), *The Indian Economy: Problems and Prospects*, New Delhi: Viking.

Myrdal, G. (1968), *Asian Drama. An Inquiry into the Poverty of Nations*, 3 Volumes, New York: Pantheon.

Nair, K. (1962), *Blossoms in the Dust*, New York: Praeger.

Nam, C.-H. (1981), 'Trade and Industrial Policies, and the Structure of Production in Korea', in W. Hong and L. B. Krause (eds.), *Trade and Growth of the Advanced Developing Countries in the Pacific Basin*, Seoul: Korea Development Institute.

O'Donnell, G.A. (1973), *Modernization and Bureaucratic-Authoritarianism in South American Politics*, Berkeley: University of California Institute for International Studies.

Park, Y.-C. (1988), 'Korea', in R. Dornbusch and F.L.C.H. Helmers (eds), *The Open Economy: Tools for Policy Makers in Developing Countries*, New York: Oxford University Press.

Patnaik, P. (1988), *Time, Inflation and Growth: Some Macroeconomic Themes in an Indian Perspective*, Calcutta: Orient Longman.

Rao, J.M. (1990), 'Capital, Labor and the Indian State', unpublished, University of Massachusetts, Amherst.

Robinson, T.W. (1990) (ed.), *Democracy and Development in East Asia – Taiwan. South Korea and the Phillipines*, Washington, D. C.: AEI Press.

Rudolph, L.I. and Rudolph, S.H. (1987), *In Pursuit of Lakshmi. The Political Economy of the Indian State*, Chicago: University of Chicago Press.

Sandesara, J.C. (1992), *Industrial Policy and Planning, 1947–91. Tendencies, Interpretations and Issues*, New Delhi: Sage.

Sen, A.K. (1990), 'How is India Doing?' in R.A. Choudhary, S. Gamkar and A. Bose (eds), *The Indian Economy and its Performance Since Independence*, Delhi: Oxford University Press.

Shafer, D.M. (1990), 'Sectors, State and Social Forces: Korea and Zambia Confront Economic Restructuring', *Comparative Politics*, 22(2), January, 127–50.

Singh, A. and Ghosh, J. (1988), 'Import Liberalization and the New Industrial Strategy: An Analysis of their Impact on Output and Employment', *Economic and Political Weekly*, 23 (45–7), Special Number, November, 2313–42.

Stein, J. (1978), 'Can Decision Makers Be Rational and Should They Be? Evaluating the Quality of Decisions', *Jerusalem Journal of International Relations*, 3(2–3), Winter–Spring, 316–39.

Steinberg, D. (1988), 'The Confucian Backdrop: Setting the Stage for Economic Development', in L. Tavis (ed.), *Multinational Management and Host Government Interactions*, Notre Dame, In.: University of Notre Dame Press.

Stiglitz, J.E. (1988), 'Economic Organization, Information and Development', in H. Chenery and T.N. Srinivasan (eds), *Handbook of Development Economics*, Vol. 1, Amsterdam: North-Holland.

Taylor, L. (1983), *Structuralist Macroeconomics*, New York: Basic Books.

Taylor, L. (1990), 'Macro Constraints on India's Economic Growth', in L. Taylor (ed.), *Socially Relevant Policy Analysis*, Cambridge, Mass.: The MIT Press.

Taylor, L. (1991), *Income Distribution, Inflation and Growth. Lectures on Structuralist Macroeconomic Theory*, Cambridge, Mass.: MIT Press.

UNDP (1991), 'Poverty Alleviation in Asia and the Pacific', report of a Regional Workshop, Kuala Lumpur, May.

Vogel, E.F. (1991), *The Four Little Dragons. The Spread of Industrialization in East Asia*, Cambridge, Mass.: Harvard University Press.

Wade, R. (1990), *Governing the Market. Economic Theory and the Role of Government in East Asian Industrialization*, Princeton: Princeton University Press.

Weber, M. (1958), *The Religion of India*, translated and edited by H. H. Gerth and D. Martindale, Glencoe, Ill.: The Free Press.

Westphal, L.E. (1978), 'The Republic of Korea's Experience with Export-Led Industrial Development', *World Development*, 6(3), 347–82.

Westphal, L.E. (1990), 'Industrial Policy in an Export-Propelled Economy: Lessons from South Korea's Experience', *Journal of Economic Perspectives*, Summer, 41–59.

Westphal, L. *et al.* (1981), 'Korean Industrial Competence: Where it Came From', Staff Working Paper, No. 469, Washington, D.C., World Bank.

World Bank (1991), *World Development Report 1991. The Challenge of Development*. Oxford: Oxford University Press.

Index